MW01119840

Volunteer Tourism

Just a generation ago the notion that holidays should be invested with ethical and political significance would have sounded odd. Today it is part of the lifestyle political landscape.

Volunteer tourism is indicative of the growth of lifestyle strategies intended to exhibit care and responsibility towards others less fortunate, strategies aligned closely with developing one's ethical identity and sense of global responsibility. It sits alongside telethons, pay-per-click, Fair Trade and ethical consumption generally as a way to "make a difference".

Volunteer tourism involves a personal mission to address the political question of development. It draws upon the private virtues of care and responsibility and disavows political narratives beyond this. Critics argue that this leaves the volunteers as unwitting carriers of damaging neoliberal or postcolonial assumptions, whilst advocates see it as offering creative and practical ways to build a new ethical politics. By contrast, this volume analyses volunteer tourism as indicative of a retreat from public politics into the realm of private experience, and as an expression of diminished political and moral agency.

This thought provoking book draws on development, political and sociological theory and is essential reading for students, researchers and academics interested in the phenomenon of volunteer tourism and the politics of lifestyle that it represents.

Jim Butcher teaches at Canterbury Christ Church University, UK. His research interests lie in the sociology and politics of tourism.

Peter Smith teaches at St Mary's University, UK. His main areas of interest lie in the sociology of volunteer and ecotourism.

'Butcher and Smith have provided the definitive unpacking and critical analysis of the mainstreaming of volunteer tourism. Reading this book may change your life more than doing a gap year and will make you think about volunteer tourism differently and with insight.'

Professor Kevin Hannam, Leeds Beckett University, UK

'Butcher and Smith's fascinating study goes beyond the existing debates on volunteer tourism to consider the changing nature of contemporary politics and international development. They explore how volunteer tourism involves the search for social meaning against the shrinking of the public political imagination. Volunteer tourism assumes significance because of how politics and development have become re-orientated around projects of therapeutic self-realisation as opposed to national material transformation. Indeed they suggest that volunteer tourism outsources the responsibilities of cultivating global citizenship onto the South. The book raises important questions for those of us seeking to understand North-South relations and politics today.'

Dr Vanessa Pupavac, Politics and International Relations,
University of Nottingham, UK

Contemporary Geographies of Leisure, Tourism and Mobility
Series Editor: C. Michael Hall
Professor at the Department of Management, College of Business and Economics, University of Canterbury, Christchurch, New Zealand

The aim of this series is to explore and communicate the intersections and relationships between leisure, tourism and human mobility within the social sciences.

It will incorporate both traditional and new perspectives on leisure and tourism from contemporary geography, e.g. notions of identity, representation and culture, while also providing for perspectives from cognate areas such as anthropology, cultural studies, gastronomy and food studies, marketing, policy studies and political economy, regional and urban planning, and sociology, within the development of an integrated field of leisure and tourism studies.

Also, increasingly, tourism and leisure are regarded as steps in a continuum of human mobility. Inclusion of mobility in the series offers the prospect to examine the relationship between tourism and migration, the sojourner, educational travel, and second home and retirement travel phenomena.

The series comprises two strands:

Contemporary Geographies of Leisure, Tourism and Mobility aims to address the needs of students and academics, and the titles will be published in hardback and paperback. Titles include:

The Moralisation of Tourism
Sun, sand... and saving the world?
Jim Butcher

The Ethics of Tourism Development
Mick Smith and Rosaleen Duffy

Tourism in the Caribbean
Trends, development, prospects
Edited by David Timothy Duval

Qualitative Research in Tourism
Ontologies, epistemologies and methodologies
Edited by Jenny Phillimore and Lisa Goodson

The Media and the Tourist Imagination
Converging cultures
Edited by David Crouch, Rhona Jackson and Felix Thompson

Tourism and Global Environmental Change
Ecological, social, economic and political interrelationships
Edited by Stefan Gössling and C. Michael Hall

Cultural Heritage of Tourism in the Developing World
Edited by Dallen J. Timothy and Gyan Nyaupane

Understanding and Managing Tourism Impacts
An integrated approach
C. Michael Hall and Alan Lew

An Introduction to Visual Research Methods in Tourism
Edited by Tijana Rakic and Donna Chambers

Tourism and Climate Change
Impacts, adaptation and mitigation
C. Michael Hall, Stefan Gössling and Daniel Scott

Tourism and Citizenship
Raoul V. Bianchi and Marcus L. Stephenson

Routledge Studies in Contemporary Geographies of Leisure, Tourism and Mobility is a forum for innovative new research intended for research students and academics, and the titles will be available in hardback only. Titles include:

Living with Tourism
Negotiating identities in a Turkish village
Hazel Tucker

Tourism, Diasporas and Space
Edited by Tim Coles and Dallen J. Timothy

Tourism and Postcolonialism
Contested discourses, identities and representations
Edited by C. Michael Hall and Hazel Tucker

Tourism, Religion and Spiritual Journeys
Edited by Dallen J. Timothy and Daniel H. Olsen

China's Outbound Tourism
Wolfgang Georg Arlt

Tourism, Power and Space
Edited by Andrew Church and Tim Coles

Volunteer Tourism
Theoretical frameworks and practical applications
Edited by Angela Benson

The Study of Tourism
Past trends and future directions
Richard Sharpley

Children's and Families' Holiday Experience
Neil Carr

Tourism and National Identity
An international perspective
Edited by Elspeth Frew and Leanne White

Tourism and Agriculture
New geographies of consumption, production and rural restructuring
Edited by Rebecca Torres and Janet Momsen

Tourism in China
Policy and development since 1949
David Airey and King Chong

Real Tourism
Practice, care, and politics in contemporary travel culture
Edited by Claudio Minca and Tim Oakes

Last Chance Tourism
Adapting tourism opportunities in a changing world
Edited by Raynald Harvey Lemelin, Jackie Dawson and Emma Stewart

Tourism and Animal Ethics
David A. Fennell

Actor Network Theory and Tourism
Ontologies, methodologies and performances
Edited by René van der Duim, Gunnar Thór Jóhannesson and Carina Ren

Liminal Landscapes
Travel, experience and spaces in-between
Edited by Hazel Andrews and Les Roberts

Tourism in Brazil
Environment, management and segments
Edited by Gui Lohmann and Dianne Dredge

Slum Tourism
Edited by Fabian Frenzel, Malte Steinbrink and Ko Koens

Volunteer Tourism

The lifestyle politics of
international development

Jim Butcher and Peter Smith

Routledge
Taylor & Francis Group

LONDON AND NEW YORK

First published 2015
by Routledge
2 Park Square, Milton Park, Abingdon, Oxon OX14 4RN

and by Routledge
711 Third Avenue, New York, NY 10017

Routledge is an imprint of the Taylor & Francis Group, an informa business

British Library Cataloguing in Publication Data
A catalogue record for this book is available from the British Library

Library of Congress Cataloging in Publication Data
A catalog record for this book has been requested

ISBN: 978-0-415-74901-5 (hbk)
ISBN: 978-1-315-79637-6 (ebk)

Typeset in Times
by Saxon Graphics Ltd, Derby

Contents

Acknowledgements

We would like to thank the people who have discussed the ideas with us over the last few years, including: Kevin Hannam, Heather Hindman, Cori Jakubiak, Vanessa Pupavac, Alex Standish, Duleep Allirajah, Neil Davenport, Derek Walton, Bruno Waterfield, Angus Kennedy and Joanna Williams.

We have been able to present the ideas and refine them at conferences organised by the American Association of Geographers, Royal Geographical Society and the New York Salon. Thanks to all those involved, including our respective institutions for providing funding. Thanks also to Pippa Mullins and the production team at Taylor & Francis, and our copy-editor, Julene Knox.

The following people and organisations kindly agreed to the use of extracts from their writing: Pippa Biddle, Lattitude Global Volunteering, World Activity Philippines and Viv Regan at spiked-online.

Jim: To my brother Mick, much loved and missed.

Peter: Thanks to Rachel, who has been a continued source of support – all my love. In memory of my father, George Edward Smith, a true autodidact.

1 Introducing the lifestyle politics of volunteer tourism

An influential study defines volunteer tourists as those who 'undertake holidays that might involve aiding or alleviating the material poverty of some groups in society, the restoration of certain environments or research into aspects of society or environment' (Wearing, 2001: 1). Another defines it as 'utilizing discretionary time and income to travel out of the sphere of regular activity to assist others in need' (McGehee and Santos, 2005: 760). Volunteer tourism can be characterised as a form of moral consumption, the aim of which is to assist development and conservation in the global South.

It is doubtful whether anyone saw their holidays as a chance to address the social and political problems of the day up until recently. The relationship of holidays to interventions into social and political issues was simply as a respite from the rigours of working life and perhaps community volunteering or political campaigning, a chance to recharge batteries or get inspired through visiting iconic cultural sites. Yet today volunteer tourism is part of a pervasive trend towards imbuing lifestyle choices themselves with social and political meaning.

Prior to the last two decades it is doubtful many international development volunteers saw their efforts as part of their holidays. Volunteers with organisations such as the United States Peace Corps and Voluntary Service Overseas (VSO) in the UK would have baulked at the suggestion that their efforts were in any respect leisure pursuits. Today volunteering to help others abroad is readily linked to tourism. Fun, tailor-made itineraries and character-building experiences are prominent in the marketing of a growing number of commercial and charitable volunteer tour operators.

The association of conspicuous lifestyles with social and even political endeavours is novel and very much of our times. To talk of volunteer tourism a generation ago would have seemed odd. Today it is part of the culture in many societies. This book seeks to make sense of that.

Ethical fun and life-changing travel

'Does the idea of travel to far off destinations appeal to you? How about the adventure of joining an expedition into the world's greatest mountain ranges? And I expect you'd like to help a disadvantaged community and acquire new skills while working on an aid project ... At the same time you're probably thinking about how your gap year will fit into the broader picture, will it be something to impress future employers and how will it look on your CV?'

(Excerpt from Venture Co publicity cited in Simpson, 2004: 684)

'Want to be more than a tourist? Have you got a taste for adventure? Do you want to make a real difference to the places you visit rather than just passing by? If so, why not combine adventure travel with important volunteer projects. Imagine ... spotting a herd of wild elephants in South Africa before teaching some English lessons to local children ... or hurtling through the Costa Rican jungle on a zip wire after helping to save endangered leatherback turtles. Your adventure starts here.'

(Excerpt from I-to-I Travel publicity, ibid.: 419)

A growing trend

Volunteer tourism has a profile in tourism marketing in media commentaries on the burgeoning ethical tourism sector and in education too. In the majority of this, the worthy gap year project or volunteer tourism scheme seamlessly merges fun-packed adventures with the acquisition of global citizenship and the chance to 'make a difference' in the world (an aspiration previously associated with politics).

According to the influential web site VolunTourism.org the first ever use of the term 'voluntourism' (synonymous with volunteer tourism) was by the Nevada Board of Tourism in 1988, who coined it to encourage volunteers to help in rural tourism projects (voluntourism.org, undated). David Clemmons, volunteer tourism entrepreneur and founder of Voluntourism.org, points out that Google had no search hits for 'voluntourism' in 2000, but by 2010 the term yielded over 300,000 hits, and that for something Clemmons argues is still in its infancy (cited in Vasquez, 2010). Commercial volunteer tourism companies and ethical gap year organisers have boomed. Some non-governmental organisations have also adapted to the trend, offering visitor-friendly trips to their development projects (Wearing and McGehee, 2013).

Today volunteer tourism projects operate in many countries and are organised by a range of operators including private companies, conservation and educational organisations, as well as non-governmental organisations (Broad, 2003; Söderman and Snead, 2008; Raymond and Hall, 2008). A 2008 survey of over 300 volunteer tourism organisations worldwide concluded that the market caters to 1.6 million volunteer tourists a year, with a monetary value of between

£832 million and £1.3 billion ($1.7 billion and $2.6 billion) (ATLAS/TRAM, 2008). Growth in the sector has been most marked since the late 1990s (ibid.; Smith and Holmes, 2009). There is a focus on gap year volunteers, normally in the 18–25 age range, who make up the primary market (ATLAS/TRAM, 2008: 5; Jones, 2011: 535). Volunteer tourism is now mainstream, with gap years a significant part of pre- and post-university life in the USA, Canada, Australia, New Zealand, UK and a number of other European countries (Tomazos and Cooper, 2012; Lyons *et al.*, 2012).

According to a UK government commissioned report on gap year provision (defined in the report as 'a period of time between three and twenty four months taken out of education or a work career', hence a wider category than volunteer tourism), internationally there are over 800 organisations offering overseas volunteer placements in 200 countries (Jones, 2004). In total these organisations offer around 350,000 placement opportunities annually (ibid.). A 2007 Mintel study calculated that people undertaking volunteer projects abroad account for 10 per cent of the UK's outbound tourism expenditure amounting to £960 million annually (Travel Weekly, 2007). In 2010 a further UK study estimated that up to 500,000 gap year students volunteered abroad. Their main activities included teaching English, animal conservation and building homes in poor rural communities (Neeves and Birgnall, 2010).

The activities undertaken by volunteers are diverse. The range includes community work such as building a school or clinic (Raleigh International, 2009), teaching English (Jakubiak, 2012) and conservation-based projects that involve scientific research or ecological restoration such as reforestation and habitat protection (Wearing, 2004). Typically volunteer projects involve linking community wellbeing and conservation in countries in the global South (Butcher and Smith, 2010).

The focus of the gap year and volunteer-sending organisations resonates with significant numbers of young people seeking to act upon their world outside of traditional political channels through the ethical consumption of holidays. It is in this spirit that gap year projects are encouraged by governments (Jones, 2004, 2011; Heath, 2007). Volunteering is seen as a way of developing a sense of global citizenship, the latter now a well-established part of the remit and curriculum of schools and universities (Advisory Group on Citizenship, 1998; Bednarz, 2003; Standish, 2008; Baillie Smith and Laurie, 2011). It is also endorsed by commercial companies seeking professional employees with international experience and an appreciation of global issues (Heath, 2007). Volunteer tourism has become a rite of passage taken by increasing numbers of internationally mobile young people, to do good, to be good and to make good.

Since Jost Krippendorf's call for tourists to reflect, learn and moderate their behaviour in his book *The Holiday Makers: Understanding the Impact of Leisure and Travel* (1987), ethical tourism has grown and become a rhetorical orthodoxy amongst campaigners and concerned travellers. There are many variations on the theme: ecotourism, philanthropic travel, green tourism, community tourism, justice tourism and others. Volunteer tourism is just one, albeit prominent, focus of calls to make holidays morally virtuous – the volunteers are at the committed end of the ethical tourism spectrum (Coghlan, 2006). All the various ethical prefixes share a desire to distance their clientele from the mass consumption of tourism and the tourists who partake. All seek to reform the industry along 'ethical' lines (Butcher, 2003). Volunteer tourism is a case study that can reveal much about this wider advocacy of ethical tourism.

Adventures in humanitarian travel

In her 2011 *New York Times* account journalist Heidi Mitchell describes how tasks were determined largely by the volunteer organisations rather than by the locals. She sees it as dangerously close to poverty tourism. She cites the following volunteer tourism organisations and projects:

Project Brazil: favela Rocinha in Rio, day care for under 6-year-olds.

Community Development Peru: building traditional efficient cooking stoves and work in a women's weaving co-op.

Elevate Destinations: to Haiti to rebuild orphanages in Port au Prince and Jacmel area.

Tribewanted: in what is described as a sustainable community experiment, 'tribe members' commit to one month average sleeping in basic accommodation and helping locals with microfinancing, tree clearing and building. One project is in Vorovorom, Fiji, where volunteers tend gardens, feed animals and plant trees.

Global Vision International: in Madagascar travellers can work alongside villagers to conserve, plant trees, promote fuel efficient stoves and educate residents on the environment.

Habitat for Humanity's Global Village: house building in poor communities.

Global Volunteer Network: has placed more than 14,000 in twenty-two countries in the last nine years. Travellers sign up for a week or longer to orphanages, schools, refugee camps and animal shelters. On their organic farming project in Uganda, they help teach raised bed and double-dug farming as ways to maximise the soil's potential. They also explain techniques of water conservation, composting and recycling. Also teachers.

African Conservation Experiences: focus on the long-term sustainability of wildlife, and this includes helping locals understand the importance of wildlife to their economies.

(Mitchell, 2011)

Volunteer tourism as politics?

Volunteer tourism has generated a significant field of study in human geography, tourism studies and sociology. Much of the literature seeks to ensure that the sector becomes 'ethical', and that it realises its potential as an innovative way to intervene to help others (e.g. Wearing, 2001; Broad, 2003; McGehee, 2002; Wearing and Deane, 2003; Zahra and McIntosh, 2007; Söderman and Snead, 2008; Pearce and Coghlan, 2008). This is effectively critical advocacy. This literature, like much of the advocacy of the 'new moral tourism' more broadly, tends to focus on small-scale, community-oriented tourism that explicitly aims to promote both conservation and community wellbeing (Mowforth and Munt, 1998; Butcher, 2003, 2007).

Other writing on volunteer tourism considers it in the context of either the rise of neoliberalism, the market-oriented focus of all aspects of life (e.g. Wearing and Wearing, 1999; Conran, 2011; Jones, 2011; Baillie Smith and Laurie, 2011; Tomazos and Cooper, 2012); or alternatively the legacy of colonialism (e.g. Caton and Santos, 2009; Guttentag, 2009; Palacios, 2010).

On both counts volunteer tourism is criticised as negative and lauded as positive in fairly equal measure. Sometimes the tourists are portrayed as perpetuating a neocolonial legacy (Simpson, 2005; Lyons *et al.*, 2012), and at other times as a potential counter to this (Higgins-Desboilles and Mundine, 2008). Sometimes they are presented as unwittingly caught up in a neoliberal project (Vrasti, 2012; Mostafanezhad, 2013), yet for others volunteer tourism has the potential to challenge the spread of market values into intercultural relationships (Wearing *et al.*, 2005; Wearing and Ponting, 2009; Wearing and Darcy, 2011; Wickens, 2010).

We focus on what the conflation of consuming holidays with the hitherto political issue of development tells us about social and political agency today – how some young (and not so young) people frame the issues of the day and how they see their ability to act on them, principally through lifestyle.

The association of lifestyle with politics may seem tenuous but many assert the link. Barnett *et al.* (2011) see responsible lifestyles connected to buying Fairtrade goods as a spur to a wider political focus for progressive change. Campaigner Higgins-Desboilles argues that volunteer tourism itself can 'challenge the very foundations of contemporary tourism and capitalist globalisation' (cited in Zavitz and Butz, 2011: 412). Wearing has argued that volunteer tourism has the potential to generate more authentic human contact and be part of a wider project of challenging neoliberal orthodoxies (Wearing 2001; Wearing and Ponting, 2009; Wearing and Darcy, 2011).

Such bold statements make sense when we consider the recent trajectory of politics itself – tourism has not had to move too far to become 'political'. Ideology and the erstwhile political outlooks of Right and Left have vacated the public realm of political deliberation over the last three decades, a situation described by some as postpolitical (Zizek, 1999). The politics of consumption and lifestyle has become prominent in their place. A prominent example is Fairtrade, regarded in one survey as the principal way in which the public relate to the issues of development in the global South (Darnton and Kirk, 2011). The growth of new 'ethical' tourisms such as volunteer tourism is another.

Our emphasis is to ask why people look to tourism to realise their social or political ambitions, a notion that would have seemed decidedly unusual just a generation ago. To begin to answer this we look at the changed character of what constitutes politics. The discussions of neoliberalism and postcolonialism and their relationship to volunteer tourism are relevant here, as are the attempts to make the tourism industry 'ethical'. However, we argue that volunteer tourism is part of a contemporary lifestyle politics of development, which reflects and reinforces a diminished political subject and an attenuated political scene. Therefore to talk down volunteer tourism as neoliberal or neocolonial practice, or to talk it up as an ethical counter to this, is to miss an important point. Both sides in such a debate share a focus on the politics of lifestyle with an attendant emphasis on consumption and personal behaviour.

In contrast to this lifestyle politics we refer throughout the book to what Arendt (1958) champions as an 'agonistic' politics. This is a politics premised on vigorous public discussion and debate of competing interests, perspectives and ideologies. Such a politics does not deny the importance of human attributes associated with volunteer tourism such as affect, care and the taking of personal responsibility for social problems. However, it emphasises politics as a public and contested realm in which the individual, alongside others, can act in shaping society.

These attributes of a truly public politics are conspicuous by their absence today. One aim of the book is to emphasise the pressing need for a genuinely political discussion of development options that aspires to much more than the well-meaning lifestyle initiatives, such as volunteer tourism, that often characterise the public face of development.

The public face of development

The public face of development refers to the ways that development issues are presented to the public through the media and in culture generally (Smith and Yanacopulos, 2004). We argue that there has been a very significant shift away from a political framing of development issues through campaigns, political parties and political philosophies, towards an emphasis on affective responses mediated through lifestyle.

Prior to the 1980s, the focus for people's aspirations to challenge poverty abroad was to a considerably greater extent mediated through politics: the politics of nationhood and sovereignty; support for free markets as the best option for growth; or, opposition to capitalism and skewed, structurally unequal markets. A distinctive lifestyle politics of development came to prominence in the 1980s. In 1984 Bob Geldof's Live Aid initiative captured the imagination of many and was a watershed in the public profile of development issues. Since then new, innovative ways of 'making a difference' that avoid ideological narratives and structural questions have become established (Richey and Ponte, 2008).

The year 1984 was also notable in Geldof's own country, the UK, for the year-long miners' strike against pit closures, which ended in March 1985 (Milne, 1994). The strike's defeat and the high-profile Live Aid concert provide a telling contrast. The end of the bitter, militant dispute to defend miners' jobs and communities from the results of the market is often seen as a watershed in the demise of the politics of class, a politics that through calls for reform, or even revolution, contested the basis on which society is organised. Live Aid sought help for individuals through an emotional appeal to care, not to challenge society's basis. The images of the starving Ethiopian children in desperate need of help, and the celebrity exhortations to care and give, were indicative of important changes in the constitution of politics. The trends in political consciousness illustrated by Live Aid and the miners' strike in 1984/5 are indicative of wider changes across the world.

Telethons have become a focus for charitable giving. In the UK they typically feature celebrities travelling to city slums and impoverished rural villages, witnessing poor people's lives and imploring television audiences to donate to make a difference to the lives they have glimpsed on their television sets. Similar televised events exist throughout Europe and North America. Telethons do not involve 'being there' (apart from the celebrities sent to reveal the plight of the poor). However, as with volunteer tourism, there is usually an attempt to humanise the relationship between (relative) western affluence and poverty in the global South by focusing on individuals and their day-to-day lives. We can see the people we are aiding and the conditions they live in. We can know their names and see the expressions on their faces, as well as those of the celebrities, understandably moved by their experiences. This personalisation of the public face of development is sometimes considered to break down barriers of distance and to facilitate an ethic of care through an emotional connection (Smith, 2000; Barnett *et al.*, 2005). Volunteer tourism takes this personalisation to its logical conclusion as personal encounters replace media representations and distant acts of charity.

One descendant of Live Aid was the 2005 Live 8 rock concert, which alongside the Love 8 Summit was part of a concerted attempt to pressure the creditor nations to cancel some of their debt with the global South. Whilst arguably having a wider political focus that the original Live Aid, this awareness-raising rock concert involved little if any political engagement (Darnton and Kirk, 2011). It acted as a large public show of sympathy for the debtors, and moral castigation of the creditor states and banks (ibid.). The moral pressure the rock fans sought to express was hardly accompanied by political argument or, in most cases, any commitment (ibid.). We will argue that the sentiments of volunteer tourists express a similar moral stance. Political engagement is eschewed in favour of conspicuous lifestyle identification with the cause.

In the last few decades Fairtrade has become a widespread and mainstream expression of the desire to act upon a perceived lack of fairness in international trade and development (Raynolds *et al.*, 2007). According to Darnton and Kirk's influential study *Finding Frames: New Ways to Engage the UK Public in Global*

Poverty it became the principal way the public relate to development issues from around 1997. It has a clear lifestyle orientation, and is an expression of the politics of consumption – the notion that people can bring about what they perceive to be progressive outcomes through what they buy at the shops, cafés and travel agents. Volunteer tourism is a consumption-oriented personal strategy for social action. It suggests that through buying the right kind of holiday we can meet our own needs and desires, whilst at the same time addressing the deleterious effect of the market generally on other societies. It is very much a part of a pervasive consumer-oriented politics of lifestyle (Kim, 2012).

Another example of today's public face of development are television programmes such as Channel 4's (UK) *Millionaires Mission*, an initiative backed by the charity WorldVision (Ingram, 2008). Here, wealthy self-made entrepreneurs from the UK were taken to poor communities in the developing world to see how they live and for the former to try to use their personal, entrepreneurial attributes to effect change. The programme is typical of a number of media initiatives to make poverty in poorer countries personal and in a sense relevant to the lives of western audiences. One of the projects featured was the 'Teach In Hotel', which was designed to attract volunteer tourists (ibid.). The desire to relate personally to the object of one's concern is key to such media representations, and whilst this could be read as a progressive humanisation of development, we argue that in fact it reflects a very limited individualism, incapable of articulating the attendant issues much beyond personal feelings.

What is characteristic of all of these examples is a drawing together of the project of development with actions that an individual can undertake in order to, directly and personally, 'make a difference'. They do not all involve actually experiencing first hand the people and places concerned. However, they all link the everyday and the intimate with the hitherto macroeconomic project of development. There is no need to subscribe to a political outlook, to vote a particular way, to take sides or argue for a brand of politics. Rather, personal qualities such as care, awareness and responsibility are constantly invoked in this lifestyle politics of development.

Volunteer tourism is a good case study through which to consider how people are invited to make sense of the world and to act upon it. It combines a number of features that are characteristic of discussions of the public face of development today: the focus on consumption and lifestyle; the sense that action is intimately associated with the construction of one's personal ethical identity; the localism and postdevelopment-influenced outlook influential in alternative development thinking; and, finally, the projection of personal qualities such as care and responsibility into the space previously occupied by political ideologies.

WorldActivity Philippines

'You've finally decided you'd like to take a different type of holiday. Your friends are off to spend a week partying and relaxing by the beach. But that's not enough for you. You've done that many times before and realize how boring and unfulfilling it is. You want more than that. You need more than that.

You feel the time is right in your life and now you're ready to make positive and meaningful contribution out there in the world ...'

Testimonials:

Rachel, Haarlem: 'Spending this month in the Philippines was a great experience. The combination of volunteering and getting the chance to see this beautiful country was a great opportunity for me. It is very nice to be able to make yourself useful for the people here who do not "have it all". Despite this fact, they are always smiling! I guess that is something we could definitely learn from.'

Renske, of Amsterdam, went to work at St Martin in Bustos in Philippines: 'This place, founded by Father Boyet with the purpose of providing former street children of Manila a safe and healthy environment, took a little piece from me. In the very short time of two weeks that I was there, St Martin managed to attach me to itself, hence I know I will return to that place over and over again once I get the chance. The site is situated in a gorgeous and peaceful valley surrounded by green rice fields, the staff working there is very passionate about their mission, and the children are so brave, cheerful and very very sweet ... As one of the trainers said during my preparation training given by the staff of WorldActivity Philippines "you will learn more from being there in person that from watching 1,000 hours of documentaries, or reading 100 books about the society."'

Madeleine, Amsterdam, worked with sexually abused girls: 'My presence inspired the girls and gave some fun and hope in their tough lives. In turn, the girls inspired me with their enormous courage and perseverance.'

Clemens, Frankfurt, home for street children: 'The smiling children let the sunshine into my heart!'

Ingrid, Amsterdam: 'It's easy to look at the country and its people through your own eyes, since that is all we have. But you have to change your reference frame and take everything from such a different angle.'

(Excerpt from publicity WorldActivity Philippines, undated)

Why 'development'?

Volunteer tourism projects focus on development (broadly defined) and conservation. In this book we use the term 'development' throughout. However, trends in development thinking and conservation, especially in the last three decades, mean that it is not really possible to separate them. In general, the aims of non-governmental organisations and institutions focused on development and conservation respectively have tended to converge. Conservationists, criticised for a 'fortress conservation' or 'fences and fines' approach in the 1970s, have long since adopted 'people-centred' conservation as an orthodoxy (Wells and Brandon, 1992). For example, Coral Cay Conservation, a sizeable conservation non-governmental organisation catering for volunteer tourists, state on their publicity that the mission of any Coral Cay Conservation Volunteer is 'to help sustain livelihoods and alleviate poverty' (Coral Cay, undated). Conservation work is combined with 'capacity building and alternative livelihood programmes in the community' (Coral Cay, undated a).

Development initiatives, roundly criticised in the past for failing to factor in conservation, have, following the 1992 UN Rio Conference on Environment and Development and the establishment of sustainability as orthodoxy, moved towards factoring in conservation in the name of sustainable development (Adams, 2008). The two trends met in the middle, and led to the growth of integrated conservation and development projects from the 1980s (Wells and Brandon, 1992; Ghimire and Pimbert, 1997). Ecotourism was adopted by a number of high-profile conservation and rural aid agencies in the 1990s on the basis of this philosophy (Butcher, 2007). Volunteer tourism projects draw heavily on that legacy.

Volunteer tourists want to help in resolving social problems as they see them. The projects they engage in are small-scale development projects, albeit with a local and very limited focus. Volunteers aspire to make a difference, often to individuals rather than to a society more broadly. Probably the category of 'wellbeing' better describes their focus (Butcher and Smith, 2010). A generation ago this would probably not have been seen as development at all. However, the aspirations of volunteer tourists are significantly aligned with neopopulist and postdevelopment strands of development thinking that have become mainstream and even orthodoxies in alternative development circles over the last thirty years. Indeed, the category wellbeing itself is influential in alternative development (McGregor and Gough, 2010).

Volunteer holidays in context

We aim to develop some historical and political perspective on volunteer tourism in order to emphasise what is novel and distinct about it. This is important as some authors accentuate supposed neocolonial continuities with organisations such as the US Peace Corps and Voluntary Service Overseas (UK), and their equivalents in many other countries. These organisations established a means through which skilled volunteers could play a part in assisting poorer countries to develop. Development here was understood in a distinctly modernist fashion, associated with achieving increases in wealth, improved infrastructure and better access to modern technology. Yet today a host of volunteer tourism oriented and gap year companies offer ubiquitous holidaying opportunities combined with varied development-related activities to a wide range of people, premised upon their aspiration to adopt an ethical lifestyle rather than upon distinctive skills they may have. Development as economic transformation is not a feature of volunteer tourism.

The interest in development and conservation volunteering, and in gap year projects abroad, is not surprising when we consider that such activities are today linked with a sense of mission for young people in a world in which more traditional avenues for their political aspirations appear uninspiring or discredited. The decline of grand narratives associated with development, and the growth of 'life politics' (Giddens, 1994), are the backdrop for volunteer tourism. Development thinking has been transformed too, from modernist-inspired models such as Rostow's (1960) stages of economic growth and structural schemas of the dependency school in the 1970s, through to postdevelopment ideas that deny development as a universal progressive phenomenon (Peet and Hartwick, 2009). We place an emphasis on this wider context – how the realm of the political is understood, and how people see their role as political and social agents.

We seek to develop an analysis of the *lifestyle politics of development*. Whereas in the 1950s development volunteering was just that, volunteering (tourism was something very different), today tourism has been 'lifestyle politicised' (after Giddens) – it is a realm of people's everyday life and experience within which they are encouraged to act ethically, to make a difference in the world. These life political acts are affirmed in education and in culture generally as a route to ethical, global citizenship.

Volunteer tourism seems to personalise development in an age when political parties and macro agendas stand discredited. Cynicism, disillusionment and disorientation are characteristic of the response to the narrow managerialist politics that predominate in our postpolitical times. By contrast, personal projects to help others and, equally importantly, develop one's own sense of self and ethical identity, seem to offer a creative, fun and 'doable' (albeit problematic) way to act in pursuit of a better world. Through volunteer tourism, along with other lifestyle and consumption-based ethical projects such as Fairtrade, the public face of development has been redefined away from a macroeconomic, transformative project, premised upon substantial change. It replaces this with a personal mission to aid wellbeing, or simply help or contribute, often through projects that are premised on a highly circumspect view of transformative macroeconomic development.

Synopsis

The chapters comprise a series of linked essays. They look at volunteer tourism from a number of perspectives, but they share some common themes. Principally, they all consider the sense in which volunteer tourism reflects a diminished political landscape in which the public face of development revolves around personal lifestyle interventions in major social and political issues.

Chapter 2 focuses on volunteer tourism in historical perspective. The narrative runs from the small number of volunteering organisations set up, usually by governments, in the 1950s and 1960s (we focus on Voluntary Service Overseas (UK) and the US Peace Corps), up to the present day in which there is a veritable industry selling volunteering opportunities. Whilst we make allusions to politics pre-1945, we do this primarily to justify the focus on post-1945 period, and that of decolonisation in particular. This period has distinctive characteristics – the concept of the third world, the Cold War (up until the 1980s), the growth of international travel opportunities – and these characteristics frame the sort of volunteering we are interested in here.

We consider the view that development volunteering of VSO, the Peace Corps and similar bodies established in most other developed countries was a form of Cold War politicking (it is often argued that the big power blocs, East and West, played out the Cold War in the third world, and claiming common cause with its inhabitants was undoubtedly a factor here).

The aim of the chapter is to contrast this type of volunteering with the more contemporary volunteer tourism and gap year industry of recent decades, decades in which so many of the assumptions people held about politics and their place within it have changed. In particular, the end of the Cold War has had a profound impact on ideologies and politics. Whilst some see strong elements of continuity between the two volunteering traditions – damaging postcolonial assumptions about other societies being one strong theme – we see at least as much change. Volunteer tourism is short term, unskilled and generally focuses on the care and responsibility exercised by tourists rather than any wider political or moral agenda. Indeed, some studies have illustrated that far from seeking to impose 'development' upon those being assisted, many modern gap year participants, and the projects in which they volunteer, exhibit a distinctive relativism and a rhetorical deference to the culture of the society in which they are operating (see interviews with volunteer tourists in Vrasti, 2012 and Mostafanezhad 2013, 2014).

Chapter 3 situates volunteer tourism within wider trends in development thinking. As referred to above, the origins of VSO and the Peace Corps are often associated with modern development – principally economic in character, measureable in monetary terms and (although volunteering itself did not address this) with an inclination towards infrastructure development, modern technology and urbanisation. Today's volunteer tour operators adopt a very different outlook, orienting their endeavours around local culture, indigenous resources and maintaining the viability of rural life. Such themes draw on now well-established strands of thinking in development, such as postdevelopment, green development and alternative development (Escobar, 1995; Rahnema and Bawtree, 1997; Willis, 2011). Trends in development volunteering are indicative of these trends in development.

To illustrate how volunteer tourism's view of development draws upon development thinking, we consider the writings of Robert Chambers. Chambers, considered the guru of rural development projects, pioneered a school of thought that saw development work both as an aid to rural communities but also as something profoundly important from the perspective of the consciousness of the development worker or volunteer themselves (Chambers, 1983, 1997). He also endorsed a suspicion of 'western' technology and championed localism, both influential in alternative development thinking. We argue that this shift from development as a macro phenomenon towards a promotion of localism, cultural sensitivity in the form of relativism and the development of self-awareness is significant in informing the contemporary rationale for volunteer tourism projects.

In Chapter 4 we consider volunteer tourism as the expression of private emotion and experience coming to occupy the place in political and social consciousness previously held by ideology. The advocacy of volunteer tourism and many accounts of the tourists themselves are articulated through a language heavy on personal qualities and attributes such as care, awareness and responsibility and light on political ideology and context. To develop this critique we draw on the dual notion of the private and public sphere, developed by, amongst others, Habermas (1989), Sennett (1986) and Arendt (1958). It is the decline of an agonistic public sphere, able to mediate individual experience and interests through political debate, that elevates care and responsibility – commendable personal qualities as they are – to the status of a lifestyle politics of development. Put simply, the decline of politics has led to hitherto political issues such as development being interpreted through private emotion, private interests and personal morality, cut adrift from a political framing.

In Chapter 5 we establish that volunteer tourism is illustrative of a politics of ethical lifestyle. Tourism lifestyle has long been invoked in cultural politics, from the Grand Tour of the eighteenth century to the hippie trail of the 1960s and 1970s. We consider how tourism lifestyles have featured in political identity over the last sixty years.

There is much that is new and distinctive about volunteer tourism compared to previous lifestyle expressions of social and political agency. Sociologists have theorised around a modern politics of lifestyle. Giddens coined the term 'life politics' – a new configuration of individual experience and the realm of politics, but one that connects the latter to intimate aspects of daily life, such as consumption. We see life politics as an accurate description of what volunteer tourism represents, but not as a positive model.

In this chapter we also intend to consider the sense in which lifestyle politics is indicative of 'the culture of narcissism' (Lasch, 1979). This is a rejoinder to the view that emphasises the salience of and potential in ethical identity making, or 'ethical selving' (Barnett *et al.*, 2011), for a reconfigured, progressive politics. Eminent geographers have recently made the latter claim in relation to ethical consumption in general (ibid.), and in relation to volunteer tourism in particular (Wearing, 2001).

Chapter 6 focuses on global citizenship. In this chapter we broach the argument that development volunteering's value is not and need not be in remarkable development outcomes, but that it resides in the creation of global citizens. We ask whether global citizenship through volunteer tourism leads to greater understanding of the political issue of development, especially given that the principal institutions through which political power and authority are exercised and contested are nation states. Is not citizenship best conceived of at the national level, which itself hardly precludes active interest in global politics?

One distinctive point that we want to develop in this chapter is the sense in which the project of citizenship is being outsourced to the global South. It has been argued that post-Cold War political disorientation has contributed to states seeking moral meaning and status abroad through ethical foreign policies (Chandler, 2007). We argue that an emptying of national citizenship has generated a parallel search for meaning, or moral citizenship, abroad. Just as the world becomes an arena for insecure powers to try to establish moral credentials, so it becomes a stage for individuals to seek out a sense of self expressed through 'global citizenship'. The issue of global poverty becomes a backdrop for western identity making.

Chapter 7 considers the question of agency in volunteer tourism. Volunteer tourists' attempts to act on the issues they hold dear are sometimes criticised as perpetuating colonial assumptions of inferior or less capable societies. Other critiques see it in the context of neoliberalism. They argue that in a world dominated by market forces, volunteer tourism shows that even the desire to challenge this is packaged up and sold as part of an 'ethical' market, thus strengthening the grip of neoliberal ideology across all aspects of life (Mostafanezhad, 2014; Vrasti, 2012).

Yet on both the above counts volunteer tourism is also advocated, either as an antidote to neoliberalism or as having the potential to challenge neocolonial assumptions about other societies. Notably some of volunteer tourism's advocates and sometimes the tourists themselves articulate a critique of colonialism and of the market, so it is ironic that volunteers' efforts are reproached for supporting these very same things.

We argue that it is not useful to see volunteer tourists as either postcolonial or neoliberal subjects. We introduce a third view, that of the diminished subject. The limited development outlook explicit in volunteer tourism, alongside the personalisation of development, are indicative of a retreat from the politics of development into lifestyle. A pervasive disorientation towards politics and disillusionment with modern society fuels the sense that transformative development may be neither possible nor desirable. We situate the diminished subject in these broad trends in politics.

In the conclusion, Chapter 8, we simply want to draw together the principal lines of argument of the book and suggest some ways to take the issues forward. In the spirit of the book, we are not looking to say whether volunteer tourism is good or bad or answer the question 'how can we make gap years more ethical?' Rather we want to comment on what the advent of volunteer tourism as an ethical lifestyle strategy of aspirant, socially conscious people tells us about the politics of our day.

We conclude that it is very important to focus on the politics that inform volunteer tourism, sometimes explicitly and sometimes implicitly, and to separate this out from the act of volunteering. Altruism, charity and basic human solidarity are invaluable human impulses, and can be expressed through volunteering. Yet imbuing such important, pre-political characteristics of our humanity with political meaning in the sphere of development conflates private charity with political strategy and individual initiative with political action. Lifestyle is not politics and volunteer tourism is not development.

Overall we take the line that trends in tourism reflect wider social and political trends. The book is a critique of the ethical claims made for this niche market, but at the same time questions the wider retreat from politics bound up in the search for ethical consumption and lifestyles.

References

Adams, W.M. (2008) *Green Development: Environment and Sustainability in a Developing World*, Routledge, London.

Advisory Group on Citizenship. (1998) *Education for Citizenship and the Teaching of Democracy in Schools: Final Report of the Advisory Group on Citizenship*, Qualifications and Curriculum Authority, London.

Arendt, H. (1958) *The Human Condition*, University of Chicago Press, Chicago.

Association for Tourism and Leisure Education/Tourism Research and Marketing (ATLAS/ TRAM) (2008) *Volunteer Tourism: a Global Analysis*, Association for Tourism and Leisure Education, Arnhem.

Baillie Smith, M. and Laurie, N. (2011) International volunteering and development: global citizenship and neo-liberal professionalisation today, *Transactions of the Institute of British Geographers*, 36, 545–59.

Barnett, C., Cloke, P., Clarke, N. and Malpass, A. (2005) Consuming ethics: articulating the subjects and spaces of ethical consumption, *Antipode*, 37 (1), 23–45.

Barnett, C., Clarke, N., Cloke, P. and Malpass, A. (2011) *Globalising Responsibility: the Political Rationalities of Ethical Consumption*, Wiley-Blackwell, London.

Bednarz, S. (2003) Citizenship in the post-9/11 United States: a role for geography education?, *International Research in Geographical and Educational Education*, 12 (1), 72–80.

Broad, S. (2003) Living the Thai life – a case study of volunteer tourism at the Gibbon Rehabilitation Project, Thailand, *Tourism Recreation Research*, 28 (3), 63–72.

Butcher, J. (2003) *The Moralization of Tourism*, Routledge, London.

Butcher, J. (2007) *Ecotourism, NGOs and Development: a Critical Analysis*, Routledge, London.

Butcher, J. and Smith, P. (2010) Making a difference: volunteer tourism and development, *Tourism Recreation Research*, 35 (1), 27–36.

Caton, K. and Santos, C. (2009) Images of the other: selling study abroad in a postcolonial world, *Annals of Tourism Research*, 48 (2), 191–204.

Chambers, R. (1983) *Rural Development: Putting the Last First*, Longman, London.

Chambers, R. (1997) *Whose Reality Counts? Putting the First Last*, Intermediate Technology Publications, London.

Chandler, D. (2007) Hollow hegemony: theorising the shift from interest-based to value-based international policy-making. *Millennium, Journal of International Studies*, 35 (3), 703–23.

Coghlan, A. (2006) Volunteer tourism as an emerging trend or an expansion of ecotourism? A look at potential clients' perceptions of volunteer tourism organisations, *International Journal of Nonprofit and Voluntary Sector Marketing*, 11 (3), 225–37.

Conran, M. (2011) They really love me! Intimacy in volunteer tourism, *Annals of Tourism Research*, 38 (4), 1454–73.

Coral Cay Conservation Expeditions (undated), Welcome, *Coral Cay Conservation Expeditions*. Available at http://www.coralcay.org/ (accessed 17 March 2014).

Coral Cay (undated a). Community conservation project. Available at http://www.coralcay.org/capacity-building-community-education/ (accessed 10 December 2014).

Darnton, A. and Kirk, M. (2011) *Finding Frames: New Ways to Engage the UK Public in Global Poverty*, Oxfam/DFID, London.

Escobar, A. (1995) *Encountering Development – the Making and Unmaking of the Third World*, Princeton University Press, Chichester.

Ghimire, K.B. and Pimbert, M.P. (eds) (1997) *Social Change and Conservation: Environmental Politics and Impacts of National Parks and Protected Areas*, Earthscan, London.

Giddens, A. (1994) *Beyond Left and Right: the Future of Radical Politics*, Polity, Oxford.

Guttentag, D.A. (2009) The possible negative impacts of volunteer tourism, *International Journal of Tourism Research*, 11 (6), 537–51.

Habermas, J. (1989) *The Structural Transformation of the Public Sphere: an Inquiry into a Category of Bourgeois Society*, Polity Press, Cambridge.

Heath, S. (2007) Widening the gap: pre-university gap years and the 'economy of experience', *British Journal of Sociology of Education*, 28 (1), 89–103.

Higgins-Desboilles, F. and Russell-Mundine, G. (2008) Absences in the volunteer tourism phenomenon: the right to travel, solidarity tours and transformation beyond the one-way, in *Journeys of Discovery in Volunteer Tourism: International Case Study Perspectives*, (eds) K.D. Lyons, and S. Wearing, Wallingford, CABI Publishing, pp.182–94.

Ingram, J.M. (2008) Volunteer tourism: does it have a place in development? Hons thesis, University of Tasmania.

Jakubiak, C. (2012) 'English for the globe': discourses in/of English language voluntourism, *International Journal of Qualitative Studies in Education*, 25 (4), 435–51.

Jones, A. (2004) *Review of Gap Year Provision*, Department for Education and Skills (DfES), University of London. Available at www.dfes.gov.uk/research/ (accessed 17 October 2014).

Jones, A. (2011) Theorising international youth volunteering: training for global (corporate) work?, *Transactions of the Institute of British Geographers*, 36, 530–44.

Kim, Y.M. (2012) The shifting sands of citizenship toward a model of the citizenry in life politics, *Annals of American Academy of Political and Social Science*, 644 (1), 147–58.

Krippendorf, J. (1987) *The Holiday Makers: Understanding the Impact of Leisure and Travel*, Butterworth-Heinemann, London.

Lasch, C. (1979) *The Culture of Narcissism: American Life in an Age of Diminishing Expectations*, Norton, New York.

Lyons, K., Hanley, J., Wearing, S. and Neil, J. (2012) Gap year volunteer tourism: myths of global citizenship?, *Annals of Tourism Research*, 39 (1), 361–78.

McGehee, N. (2002) Alternative tourism and social movements, *Annals of Tourism Research*, 29, 124–43.

McGehee, N. and Santos, C. (2005) Social change, discourse, and volunteer tourism, *Annals of Tourism Research*, 32 (3), 760–76.

McGregor, J.A. and Gough, I. (2010) *Development as the Pursuit of Human Wellbeing*, Institute of Development Studies, Brighton.

Milne, S. (1994) *The Enemy Within: The Secret War Against the Miners*, Verso, London.

Mitchell, H. (25 March 2011) Adventures in Humanitarian Travel. *New York Times (Travel)*.

Mostafanezhad, M. (2013) The politics of aesthetics in volunteer tourism, *Annals of Tourism Research*, 43, 150–69.

Mostafanezhad, M. (2014) *Volunteer Tourism: Popular Humanitarianism in Neoliberal Times*. Ashgate, Farnham.

Mowforth, M. and Munt, I. (1998) *Tourism and Sustainability: New Tourism in the Third World*, Routledge, London.

Neeves, J. and Birgnall, M. (2010) Paying the price for a gap year of adventure, *The Guardian*, 26 June. Available at http://www.guardian.co.uk/money/2010/jun/26/paying-price-gap-year-adventure (accessed 17 October 2014).

Palacios, C. (2010) Volunteer tourism, development, and education in a postcolonial world: conceiving global connections beyond aid, *Journal of Sustainable Tourism*, 18 (7), 861–78.

Pearce, P.L. and Coghlan, A. (2008) The dynamics behind volunteer tourism, in *Journeys of Discovery in Volunteer Tourism: International Case Study Perspectives*, (eds) K.D. Lyons and S. Wearing, CABI, London, pp.130–43.

Peet, R. and Hartwick, E. (2009) *Theories of Development: Contentions, Arguments, Alternatives, second edition*, Guilford Press, New York.

Rahnema, M. and Bawtree, V. (eds) (1997) *The Postdevelopment Reader*, Zed Books, London.

Raleigh International (30 July 2009) *Raleigh and Department for Business, Innovation and Skills Launch Bursary Award for Recent Graduates.* Available at www.raleighinternational.org/.../Raleigh%20Graduate%20Bursary%20Award%20official%20release (accessed 17 October 2014).

Raymond, E. and Hall, X. (2008) The development of cross-cultural (mis)understanding through volunteer tourism, *Journal of Sustainable Tourism*, 16 (5), 530–43.

Raynolds, L.T., Murray, D. and Wilkinson, J. (2007) *Fair Trade: The Challenges of Transforming Globalization*, Routledge, London.

Richey, L.A. and Ponte, S. (2008) Better Red™ than Dead? Celebrities, consumption and international aid, *Third World Quarterly*, 29 (4), 711–29.

Rostow, W.W. (1960) *The Stages of Economic Growth: a Non-communist Manifesto*, Cambridge University Press, Cambridge.

Sennett , R. (1986) *The Fall of Public Man*, Penguin, London. Original 1977.

Simpson, K. (2004) Broad horizons: geographies and pedagogies of the gap year, unpublished PhD thesis, University of Newcastle.

Simpson, K. (2005) Dropping out or signing up? The professionalisation of youth travel, *Antipode*, 37 (3), 447–69.

Smith, D.M. (2000) *Moral Geographies: Ethics in a World of Difference*, Edinburgh University Press, Edinburgh.

Smith, K. and Homes, K. (2009) Researching volunteers in tourism: going beyond, *Annals of Leisure Research*, 12 (3/4), 403–420.

Smith, M. and Yanacopulos, H. (2004) The public faces of development: an introduction, *Journal of International Development, Special Issue: The Public Faces of Development*, 16 (5), 657–64.

Söderman, N. and Snead, S. (2008) Opening the gap: the motivation of gap year travellers to volunteer in Latin America, in *Journeys of Discovery in Volunteer Tourism: International Case Study Perspectives*, (eds) K.D. Lyons and S. Wearing, CABI, London, pp.118–29.

Standish, A. (2008) *Global Perspectives in the Geography Curriculum: Reviewing the Moral Case for Geography*, Routledge, London.

Tomazos, K. and Cooper, W. (2012) Volunteer tourism: at the crossroads of commercialisation and service? *Current Issues in Tourism*, 15 (2), 405–23.

Travel Weekly (30 August 2007) Volunteer tourism: is it really helping? Available at http://www.travelweekly.co.uk/Articles/2007/08/30/25031/volunteer-tourism-is-it-really-helping-30-aug-2007.html (accessed 17 January 2014).

Vasquez, E. (10 August 2010) Do celebs like Jolie inspire voluntourism? CNN. Available at http://edition.cnn.com/2010/TRAVEL/08/10/celebrity.humanitarian.travel/index.html (accessed 17 October 2014).

Voluntourism.org, (undated) Available at http://www.voluntourism.org/ (accessed 17 October 2014).

Vrasti, W. (2012) *Volunteer Tourism in the Global South: Giving Back in Neoliberal Times*, Routledge, Abingdon.

Wearing, S. (2001) *Volunteer Tourism: Experiences that Make a Difference*, CABI Publishing, Wallingford.

Wearing, S. (2004) Examining best practice in volunteer tourism, in *Volunteering as Leisure/Leisure as Volunteering: An International Assessment*, (eds) R.A. Stebbins and M. Graham, CABI, Wallingford, pp.209–24.

Wearing, S. and Darcy, S. (2011) Inclusion of the 'othered' in tourism, *Cosmopolitan Civil Societies Journal*, 3 (2), 18–34.

Wearing, S. and Deane, B. (2003) Seeking self: leisure and tourism on common ground, *World Leisure Journal*, 45 (1), 4–12.

Wearing, S. and McGehee, G. (2013) Volunteer tourism: a review, *Tourism Management*, 38, 120–30.

Wearing, S. and Ponting, J. (2009). Breaking down the system: how volunteer tourism contributes to new ways of viewing commodified tourism, in *The Sage Handbook of Tourism Studies*, (eds) T. Jamal and M. Robinson, Sage, London, pp.254–69.

Wearing, S. and Wearing, M. (1999) Decommodifying ecotourism: Rethinking global–local interactions with host communities, *Society and Leisure*, 22 (1), 39–70.

Wearing, S., McDonald, M. and Ponting, J. (2005) Building a decommodified research paradigm in tourism: the contribution of NGOs, *Journal of Sustainable Tourism*, 13 (5), 424–39.

Wells, M. and Brandon, K. (1992) *People and Parks: Linking Protected Area Management*, World Bank, Washington DC.

Wickens, E. (2010) Journeys of the self: volunteer tourists in Nepal, in *Volunteer Tourism: Theory Framework to Practical Applications*, in A. Benson (ed.), Routledge, Oxon. pp.42–52.

Willis, K. (2011) *Theories and Practices of Development* (Routledge Perspectives on Development), Routledge, London.

WorldActivity Philippines (undated) Testimonials. Available at: http://www.worldactivity.ph/ (accessed 17 October 2014).

Zahra, A. and McIntosh, A.J. (2007) Volunteer tourism: evidence of cathartic tourist experiences, *Tourism Recreation Research*, 32 (1) 115–19.

Zavitz, K. and Butz, D. (2011) Not that alternative: short-term volunteer tourism at an organic farming project in Costa Rica, *ACME: An International E-Journal for Critical Geographies*, 10 (3), 412–41.

Zizek, S. (1999) *The Ticklish Subject: the Absent Centre of Political Ontology*, Verso, London.

2 From Peace Corps to volunteer holidays

Volunteer tourism is a novel and distinct aspect of contemporary leisure culture. However, comparisons, implicit and explicit, are often made with a tradition of state-sponsored volunteering that started in the 1950s and 1960s. Notably, Voluntary Service Overseas (VSO) was founded in 1958 in the UK and the United States Peace Corps in 1961. Further examples of state involvement in promoting international development volunteering at this time include: Australian Volunteers Abroad founded in 1963, the Dutch SNV founded in 1965, the Japan Overseas Corporation volunteers (JOVC) founded in 1965 and the Canadian Executive Service Organisation (CESO) founded in 1967.

There was an emphasis in these organisations on practical, technical skills and education to help newly sovereign states in the global South on their path to modern development, a path favoured not just by western governments, but also by many of the local elites in recently decolonised countries (Hobsbawm, 1995; Preston, 1996). The technical assistance on offer from the volunteers fitted with the view that the global South could and should seek capitalist development as a better route to development than the communist alternative. The organisations involved were established or supported directly by government initiative and their establishment was linked to clear narratives of transformative economic development and national interest, narratives not at all evident in volunteer tourism today.

Critics have argued that these organisations were far from simply representing state-sponsored altruism. The charge that they reflected distinctive western interests in the context of decolonisation and the Cold War has often been made. Radical critics have accused the US Peace Corps in particular of neocolonialism.

In a number of studies volunteer tourism is held to share important characteristics with these organisations (Simpson, 2004; McGehee, 2002; McGehee and Santos, 2005; Palacios, 2010; McGehee, 2012; Tomazos and Cooper, 2012). Notably, the charge of colonialism or neocolonialism has been levelled against both traditions on the grounds that they share a portrayal of formerly colonised peoples as in need of western benevolence in order to progress (Simpson, 2005; Brown and Hall, 2008; McGehee and Andereck, 2008; Guttentag, 2009; Sin, 2009; Baillie-Smith and Laurie, 2011; Mostafanezhad, 2014).

Yet there is far more change than continuity from 1960s Peace Corps and VSO volunteers to today's volunteer tourists. The practice of volunteer tourism is novel and distinct. Just as the Peace Corps, VSO and similar organisations reflected the politics of the time, so the emergence of volunteer tourism is indicative of a very different political world.

An overview of the origins of the Peace Corps and VSO respectively reveals their relationship to the politics of the day, and facilitates a comparison with contemporary volunteer tourism. Latterly we highlight the distinctiveness of volunteer tourism and identify some key themes to be pursued throughout the book.

The Peace Corps

The US Peace Corps is a development-focused volunteer organisation and its establishment in the early 1960s was the spur for other countries to develop their own organisations along similar lines and principles (Cobbs-Hoffman, 1996; Tomazos and Cooper, 2012). It became a reality almost by accident when the concept was first raised by the then Senator John F. Kennedy on the American Presidential campaign trail in the Autumn of 1960. In the area of foreign policy Kennedy was keen to both assert American values and appeal to nationalist sentiment in developing countries, many of which had recently achieved independence. It was hoped that a corps of young development volunteers would act to counter the appeal of communism (Dockrill and Hopkins, 2006).

Decolonisation should be seen in an international context where Soviet–American rivalry dominated (Hobsbawm, 1995; Painter, 2003). The fear that the Soviet Union would be the main beneficiary of the anticolonial struggles in Africa and Asia became the dominant theme in US policy at the time (Rees, 1967; Furedi, 1994a).

President Khrushchev had set out a policy of 'peaceful co-existence' with the West at the 1956 Twentieth Congress of the Communist Party of the Soviet Union (Rees, 1967: 65–70; Painter, 2003: 37–39). Khrushchev subsequently embarked on well-publicised visits to India, Burma and Afghanistan (Kennedy-Pipe, 1998) and Soviet officials toured Egypt, Indonesia and India: all newly independent states (Cobbs-Hoffman, 1996). The Soviet Union crucially played the role of offering newly decolonised states an alternative model of development to that of the USA (Harrison, 1988; Hobsbawm, 1995). The American leadership recognised that newly independent and highly nationalistic nations were more susceptible to influence from the Soviet Union than more prosperous and developed nations (Hall, 2007). The desire to counter Soviet influence gave the vague idea of a youth corps momentum.

On 14 October 1960 at the University of Michigan, Presidential candidate Kennedy addressed a crowd of 10,000 students and asked how many were prepared to contribute two years of their lives to be doctors, technicians or engineers as overseas volunteers (Redmond, 1986; Meisler, 2011). Meisler notes that Kennedy's call for international volunteers tapped into a new decade's 'mood for enlisting in a cause' (ibid.: 7), or 'youthful enthusiasm and noble purpose' in the words of the Peace Corps' first director R. Sargent Shriver (1963: 695).

This bold assertion of the American values of voluntarism and optimism appealed to Americans of all political persuasions (Cobbs-Hoffman, 1998). Following

Kennedy's speech there began a campaign to lobby the Democratic Party to establish a youth international volunteer organisation, and a committee was formed to drum up support. Soon hundreds of college students had signed a pledge to volunteer. Democratic Party officials were astounded by the students' response. Hall notes that there was a desire on the part of the USA's leaders to promote American ideals at this time, and the Peace Corps reflected that (2007). It was held to reflect America's 'altruistic values' as well as 'universal values and progress' tied to economic and technological modernisation (Cobbs-Hoffman, 1998: 26).

Sensing the mood of the times, Senator Kennedy's speech writers Sorenson, Goodwin and Archibald-Cox wrote the draft for what became Kennedy's 'peace speech', which was delivered on 2 November 1960, six days before the election. In front of 20,000 supporters at the Cow Palace in San Francisco, Kennedy made more explicit reference to the establishment of 'a peace corps of talented young men and women, willing and able to serve their country in this fashion for three years as an alternative or as a supplement to peacetime selective service' (Kennedy, 1960). Thirty thousand Americans wrote immediately to support this idea and thousands volunteered (Shriver, 1963: 694).

Following President Kennedy's inauguration in 1961, the job of developing the Peace Corps as a reality was given to his brother-in-law R. Sargent Shriver (Sorenson, 1965; Lowther and Lucas, 1978). By this stage Kennedy had received 30,000 letters offering to volunteer for the Peace Corps and Gallup polls showed 71 per cent of Americans approved of the creation of the Peace Corps (Cobbs-Hoffman, 1997: 505). Indeed more people wrote to the President-elect volunteering for the Peace Corps than for all existing government agencies combined (ibid.).

The establishment of the Corps progressed swiftly. The task force assembled by Shriver completed its report within two weeks. The following Wednesday, 1 March 1961, President Kennedy signed Executive Order 10924, creating the temporary agency of the Peace Corps and assigning $1.5 million to fund the agency's establishment (Sorensen, 1965: 347; Cobbs-Hoffman, 1998: 47). Whilst Congress did not make this permanent for six months with the Peace Corps Act, Meisler notes that this is regarded as the organisation's official birthday (2011: 7). Executive Order 10924 included the aspiration to have 500 or more volunteers in the field by the end of the year.

Whilst Executive Order 10924 was committed to 'the cause of world peace and human progress', and stressed that the Peace Corps 'is not designed as an instrument of diplomacy or propaganda or ideological conflict', the initiative was part of a wider reorientation of American foreign policy by the new Democratic administration (Kennedy, 1961).

The Peace Corps was certainly motivated by the desire, as Shriver put it, to 'help in the world wide assault against poverty, hunger, ignorance and disease' (Shriver, 1961 cited in Roberts, 2004) and formally, at least, it was proposed as a distinct initiative separate from and independent of other foreign policy strategies at the time. Shriver specifically warned against using the Peace Corps as another Cold War policy, stressing that it was important that it be developed 'not as an arm of the Cold War but as a contribution to the world community' (Shriver, 1961: 16).

However, as is now widely acknowledged the proposal and subsequent launch of the organisation was part of a wider strategic national policy goal of promoting an image of American altruism as well as helping the newly decolonised states to modernise along free market lines. The aim was to reduce the threat to western interests from the influence of communism (Lowther and Lucas, 1978; Cobbs-Hoffman, 1996, 1998; Amin 1999; Hall, 2007; Meisler, 2011). According to Sorensen, Kennedy desired stable international relations made up of a stable community of 'free and independent nations, free from the unrest on which communism fed' (1965: 529).

Kennedy's well-known 'peace speech' on 2 November 1960 itself is peppered with allusions to the need for the US to counter the rising challenge from the eastern bloc countries. In urging Americans to do better in promoting freedom and peace, Kennedy noted that, 'out of Moscow and Peiping [sic] and Czechoslovakia and Eastern Germany are hundreds of men and women, scientists, physicists, teachers, engineers, doctors, nurses, studying in those institutes, prepared to spend their lives abroad in the service of world communism' (Kennedy, 1960). Kennedy went on to make particular reference to young Russians studying Swahili and African customs at the Moscow Institute of Languages alongside their primary role as engineers and nurses. He suggested these volunteers were preparing to act in Africa as 'missionaries for world communism' (Kennedy, 1960). Pointedly, foreign language tuition was central to the training of the early Peace Corps volunteers (Shriver, 1961: 16).

Kennedy was increasingly sensitive to the perceived threat from eastern bloc countries, suggesting it could be countered by 'the skill and dedication of Americans who are willing to spend their lives serving the cause of freedom' (Kennedy, 1960). Kennedy's speech was as much a scathing attack on the existing foreign service's lack of preparedness and skills in acting as ambassadors for the free world as it was about laying down an alternative, which at this early stage was only taking shape (Meisler, 2011). Elsewhere Hubert H. Humphrey, then Democratic Senator and future Vice-President, said in 1961 that the Peace Corps was to be seen as part of the foreign policy of the United States, 'to combat the virus of communist totalitarianism' (Hapgood and Bennett, 1968: 37).

Whilst the Peace Corps was formally independent of the State Department, the US wanted to use it to influence attitudes towards America in the newly independent, non-aligned countries of Asia and sub-Saharan Africa, and counter any potential appeal of the Soviet model of development (Cobbs-Hoffman, 1997, 1998; Waldorf, 2001). Crucial to the success of the Peace Corps was the requesting of volunteers by these states. To this end, soon after signing Executive Order 10924, Shriver left the US for a 26-day tour of eight crucial countries: Ghana, Nigeria, India, Pakistan, Burma, Malaysia, Thailand and the Philippines (Cobbs-Hoffman, 1998). Shriver's first destination was Ghana, seen as important because it was the first black African country to achieve independence and because of its status in the wider national liberation struggles in the region (Cobbs-Hoffman, 1997). Ghanaian President Kwame Nkrumah, keen to exploit the Cold War tensions between the US and USSR, played one off against the other, first sending

Ghanaians to Russia for military training and visiting Moscow himself in 1962 (ibid.), then despite much internal discussion and disagreement (and at various times denunciations of western countries) eventually agreed to request Peace Corps volunteers to work in education (Lowther and Lucas, 1978).

Shriver then went on to visit India. Cobbs-Hoffman records that his meeting with Indian Prime Minister Jawaharlal Nehru was somewhat 'lukewarm' (1998: 74). However, a commitment to request Peace Corps volunteers was secured. Whilst the request was for only twenty-five or so volunteers for the state of Punjab, the agreement with Nehru had symbolic importance. India was crucially important as it was considered to be the leading light of the non-aligned movement, which had been established in Belgrade in 1961 with the aim of representing the interests of countries that aligned themselves with neither the US nor USSR in world affairs (Hobsbawm, 1995; Painter, 2003).

In securing Ghana's and India's support, albeit for limited numbers of volunteers, the Peace Corps now had the approval of two of the leading non-aligned countries in Asia and Africa (Cobbs-Hoffman, 1998). With both Nkrumah and Nehru requesting Peace Corps volunteers few of the other third world countries were likely to reject them (Meisler, 2011). Indeed, soon after Shriver's eight-country tour in spring 1961, the Peace Corps received requests for volunteers from over twenty third world countries (Cobbs-Hoffman, 1996: 85).

The first group of fifty-one Peace Corps volunteers arrived in Accra on 30 August 1961, following a farewell ceremony hosted by President Kennedy at the White House. In Accra the volunteer teachers were met at the airport by the Minister of Education and other dignitaries (Cobbs-Hoffman, 1998).

From this humble yet symbolically significant beginning the Corps grew rapidly in influence and numbers. The programme in Ghana was deemed successful, and by December 1961 over 500 volunteers were serving in nine host countries: Chile, Colombia, Ghana, India, Nigeria, the Philippines, St Lucia, Tanzania and Pakistan. Then there was a rapid escalation of programmes over the following six months involving twenty-eight host countries: Afghanistan, Belize, Bolivia, Brazil, Cameroon, Côte d'Ivoire, Cyprus, Dominican Republic, Ecuador, El Salvador, Ethiopia, Honduras, Iran, Jamaica, Liberia, Malaysia, Nepal, Niger, Peru, Sierra Leone, Somalia, Sri Lanka, Senegal, Thailand, Togo, Tunisia, Turkey and Venezuela. By 30 June 1962, 2,816 volunteers were in the field (Peace Corps, 2011). Shriver notes that by December 1962, the non-aligned states were 'lining up behind the Peace Corps' (Cobbs-Hoffman, 1998: 107) and thirty countries had requested volunteers in numbers far exceeding the agency's ability to recruit and train them (Lowther and Lucas, 1978: 27). Within two years of the initial departure of volunteers to Ghana, Peace Corps programmes were operating in forty-six countries and by June 1966 more than 15,000 trainees and volunteers were serving in the field (Lowther and Lucas, 1978: 29; Hall, 2007: 55).

The Peace Corps itself also acted as a spur to other western countries to develop their own international volunteer organisations. In Britain VSO had already been established in 1958 by Alec and Mora Dickenson, who had also sent their first volunteers to Ghana (Dickenson, 1964). Small volunteer programmes had also been established by Canada and Australia, and these were carrying out pioneering volunteer work in newly independent states. The US was keen for other western countries to develop their own versions of the Peace Corps and in October 1962 in Puerto Rico Peace Corps staff organised the International Conference on Middle Level Manpower to that end. In 1963, the Netherlands, Germany, Denmark, France and Norway started new international volunteer programmes.

Whilst a number of studies question the effectiveness of many of the Peace Corps projects on the ground, participation and idealism are seen as important (Cobbs-Hoffman, 1998). Generally, the assessment of the Peace Corps ideal is positive and the initiative is seen as one of Kennedy's lasting legacies. Cobbs-Hoffman (1997, 1998) argues that the Peace Corps largely fulfilled its role. It could be argued to have served the needs of other nations, to promote a better local understanding of America and to have fostered Americans' understanding of other societies. It also served the larger goal of US foreign policy: to counter the influence of the Soviet Union through peaceful, cultural means, utilising educated international volunteers drawn to a cause and inspired by Kennedy's vision of American altruism.

Voluntary Service Overseas

The mid to late 1950s presented distinct difficulties for Britain. Recovery from the Second World War, a new post-war balance of power favouring the US and ascendant anticolonial movements made colonialism morally and politically unfeasible. As the pre-eminent colonial power, the demise of colonialism was especially problematic for the UK. At the same time the newly dominant world power, the US, was attempting to forge an orientation to the global South, utilising a language critical of colonial domination and racial superiority. The need to manage the process of decolonisation and the continued threat of the Soviet Union form the political and international context within which to view the emergence of VSO.

A fledgling overseas volunteer organisation had been founded in Britain prior to the US Peace Corps in 1956 by Alec Dickenson, following his experience of assisting refugees on the border of Hungary fleeing the suppression of the 1956 uprising (Bird, 1998). Dickenson claims that the early British volunteers provided the example and inspiration for America to follow suit (Dickenson, 1964). Coming from a colonial background, Dickenson believed in the special place of Britain on the world stage and its responsibilities to its former colonies (Cobbs-Hoffman, 1998). He thought that British volunteers could influence the emerging national outlook of newly independent states (Dickenson, 1964). Later, with the accelerating development of the Peace Corps in the US, he feared Britain was, 'getting hopelessly left behind in comparison' (Cobbs-Hoffman, 1996: 85).

The threat of Soviet influence in Britain's ex-colonies prompted Dickenson to lobby the Colonial Office to show them 'how much more adept communist countries were at winning friends through overseas youth work than the West' (Bird, 1998: 38). In a study of the first ten years of VSO, Adams notes that abroad Britain was at this time 'constantly on the retreat' (1968: 30), and it was in this context that Dickenson thought a voluntary overseas organisation could contribute to promoting a better image of the UK in the third world.

Dickenson first approached the Colonial Office in 1956 requesting funding for a voluntary scheme for young people (Bird, 1998) but it was not until 1958 that VSO was formally established as a non-governmental voluntary agency – funded by commercial companies – with eighteen volunteers, growing to sixty the following year (Adams, 1968: 65). In January 1960 VSO was more formally established with its first office donated by the Royal Commonwealth Society (ibid.). In 1959 the service obtained Colonial Office funding of £9,000 (Bird, 1998: 18). The organisation grew rapidly, sending 86 volunteers to 25 countries in 1960–61 and 176 volunteers to 38 countries in 1961–62 (ibid.).

At first VSO recruited school leavers and young apprentices (aged 18–19) aiming to utilise their 'youth and enthusiasm' for social development (Dickenson, 1964: 12–13). By the early 1960s it was recognised that there was a need for volunteers with particular knowledge and skills, so Graduate VSO was established (Bird, 1998).

Whilst the number of volunteers in the early years of VSO is modest, by 1961 the British government had begun to recognise its importance and the Foreign Office actively sought out possible openings for volunteers. The call was met with an enthusiastic response and the British government gave a grant of £17,500 to the organisation. This was one of the first acts of the new Department of Technical Co-Operation. Soon afterwards Prince Philip became patron of the organisation, which remained non-governmental and therefore formally independent of government policy (which it remains today) (ibid.).

Unlike the Peace Corps, the emergence and establishment of VSO were formally independent from government, and in an important sense therefore more voluntary. However, VSO had its roots in the establishment world of the colonial office, public schools and the church (ibid.). The changing international political environment was the key influence on the organisation's founding, as much as it was for the Peace Corps. Anti-communist rhetoric was less obvious in the early discussions of VSO than in the United States, but Dickenson believed that young British volunteers could play their part in retaining British influence in often newly independent British ex-colonies (ibid.).

The Peace Corps and VSO in context

From the accounts of Peace Corps and VSO it is clear that these organisations are shaped by political imperatives of the time. Peace Corps volunteers were not simply altruistic individuals, but part of a post-Second World War American identity. The American state plays a central role in projecting that identity through the founding and sponsorship of the organisation. Also, whilst the individuals involved were not generally motivated directly by geopolitical concerns, there is a clear recognition that the Peace Corps was there to play a role in protecting American interests. The Cold War was played out, and often fought out, in the third world undergoing decolonisation. Gaining influence was a key policy goal.

In the UK, the fraught process of decolonisation also necessitated the establishment of good relations with and continued influence in the former colonies. VSO was not originated by the British government, but reflected a shared concern with managing the geopolitics of the day in the UK's interests. Its founders were well aware of what was at stake.

VSO and the Peace Corps both played a role in countering the appeal of the Soviet Union in the third world during the Cold War. Voluntary friendship and assistance towards a prospective prosperity countered the Soviet's claim to offer similar. Both sides in the Cold War proposed transformative economic development, epitomised by US economist Walt Rostow's (1960) notion of stages of economic development and the eastern bloc's plans to drastically raise the 'forces of production' through its five-year plans respectively. Rostow's view was part economic theory, part Cold War ideology. He argued that all countries could – with the right policies and conditions – progress through similar stages to reach the promised land of consumer capitalism. The desire for growth was shared by newly liberated third world states. Volunteers in the Peace Corps and VSO generally brought with them the desire to play a small but important part in this.

Altruism contested

It is important to note, however, that the narratives of altruism and allusions to universal values of freedom, friendship and development were contested both at home and abroad. In the USA, the persistence of racial segregation through the 1960s and beyond undermined claims to moral authority in international affairs in the eyes of critics (Zimmerman, 2001; Cobbs-Hoffman, 1998). Demands for racial equality were, after all, explicit in the colonial revolts and claims for independence in the South (Furedi, 1998; Arsenault, 2006).

In the USA this questioning of altruistic intent existed in spite of a courting of anticolonial movements by US politicians. For example, in 1957 Kennedy, then as Congressman and a member of the Foreign Relations Committee, famously spoke out in favour of Algerian independence during its anticolonial war with France (Sorensen, 1965) and he later supported Angolan nationalists against Portugal (ibid.). The US sided with Egypt against Britain and France in the Suez Canal crisis in 1956 and Vice-President Nixon attended ceremonies marking Ghana's independence from Britain in 1957 (Cobbs-Hoffman, 1998).

The US was keen to tap into the widely held anticolonial sentiments to influence newly independent nations. As the major ex-colonial power the UK's situation was different, but in managing the process of decolonising they similarly wished to retain an influence in their former colonies (Furedi, 1994b). In the specific British context this was accomplished by the shift from ruling an 'Empire' to leading a 'commonwealth' of nations (Hyam, 2007; Darwin, 2009).

The receivers of aid were not universally grateful for the assistance offered and anticolonial sentiment called western altruism into question. Perhaps most notably Kwame Nkrumah, then Ghanaian president, did a volte-face and caused uproar in the US State Department in 1965 when he labelled Peace Corps and US policy in general as neocolonialist in his book *Neocolonialism: The Last Stage of Imperialism* (1965). The State Department responded by cutting aid to the newly independent Ghanaian government.

One much publicised incident indicative of the salience of postcolonial tensions involved Margery Jane Michelmore, volunteering in Nigeria with the Peace Corps. She described her situation there as 'primitive' and painted an unflattering picture of her posting in a postcard to a friend back home. A Nigerian student saw the card, took offence and showed it to other students. Consequently rallies passed resolutions denouncing the volunteers as 'America's international spies' and called the Peace Corps a 'scheme designed to foster neocolonialism'. Volunteers were denounced as agents of imperialism (Meisler, 2011: 38–44).

The reaction to the Vietnam War is indicative of the inability of the USA to project itself as a champion of freedom and democracy. For considerable numbers of Americans, the war contradicted claims to be championing self-determination. Many decided that they wanted to express opposition to what American stood for.

The Peace Corps featured in the debates about the war in a number of ways. Defenders of America's foreign policy accused Peace Corps joiners of doing so in order to dodge the draft. Radical critics of America's role labelled the organisation a part of the state's imperialist mission. Many Peace Corps volunteers themselves were unhappy about America's involvement in Vietnam. In 1965 an article by future novelist Paul Theroux opposing the war was published in a volunteer newspaper in Malawi and in 1968 ninety-two volunteers publically opposed the war, going against the organisation's instructions not to make public statements on political issues (Meisler, 2011: 98–99). Further private and sometimes public protest against the war by volunteers was common in this period (Meisler, 2011). This was not an isolated sentiment. In fact from the first Peace Corps recruits onwards volunteers had expressed doubts about their role in exporting American values (Zimmerman, 2001).

The outlook of the critics and doubters of the Peace Corps, just as much as its advocates, was shaped by the political assumptions of the time. Colonialism and imperialism loomed large in the consciousness of people in newly independent states and of domestic critics and doubters of the West's role. Those who questioned America's aims invoked national sovereignty, anticolonialism and even revolution. The Cold War framed the political contestation of what it was to be American (indeed, to be critical of America's foreign policy was to risk the charge of being 'unAmerican').

Volunteer tourism

Political context

Volunteer tourism is a symptom of a wholly new political scene. In contrast to the 1960s, today ideological commitments are conspicuous by their absence. The context of the Cold War no longer exists. Its end brought into relief an exhaustion of erstwhile political identities of the Left or the Right, linked to nation, the West, capitalism or class.

Arguably ideologies of liberalism and communism had lacked the capacity to inspire throughout the post-Second World War period. A half century of major wars and crises, and the degeneration of the Russian Revolution into a Stalinist bureaucracy, led Daniel Bell to declare *The End of Ideology* in his seminal analysis of 1960. For Bell capitalist society, as well as its Stalinist rival, had lost the capacity to project a positive and inspiring vision of their respective societies already by this time. However, relative post-Second World War prosperity in the West, an alternative political system in the East and liberation movements in the former colonies meant that ideology – narratives beyond the individual relating to how society could and should be organised – remained prominent, albeit increasingly expressed in a cultural form (Furedi, 2014).

Moral meaning

The post-Cold War collapse of political ideologies thus constituted has created a crisis of political identity that has yet to be resolved. Disorientation towards, and a high degree of disillusionment with, politics shapes contemporary culture. The absence of ideology is the key characteristic of this culture. Volunteer tourism expresses a journey towards selfhood, a quest for moral meaning that in the absence of ideology or transcendental belief finds expression through lifestyle.

Joiners and critics of the Peace Corps in the 1960s were also engaged in a search for moral meaning. Accounts of early volunteers exude a sense of looking for a way to be moral, and to be a part of a USA with a moral role in world politics (Shriver, 1963; Cobbs-Hoffman, 1998). The search for moral identity was problematic for idealistic young volunteers, many of whom were influenced by a more relativistic view of culture and of the USA's role in the world (Zimmerman, 2001). The relative faith and confidence in American values that is argued to have characterised the 1940s and 1950s (see for example Arthur Miller's autobiography, *Timebends* (2012)), and that Kennedy appealed to in founding the Peace Corps, had already ebbed by its inception (see Bell, 1960; and as explored in the television series *Mad Men*). The growth of the countercultural rejection of American values influenced radical thinking. For Lasch this rejection of America's claim to universal values was accompanied by a retreat from social change into psychology and the self, a process he labelled *The Culture of Narcissism* (1979).

Yet this search for meaning is contrasting. Lasch's critique of the rise of identity politics in the 1960s and 1970s should be seen differently today. The search for identity may be a shared feature from development volunteers of the 1960s to volunteer tourists today, but today the absence of ideology means that the attempts to forge ethical lifestyles on the part of volunteer tourists shun rather than invoke political ideologies. Social change is neither on the agenda nor advocated – it barely features in the expressed sentiment of volunteer tourists. Instead, social identities are forged around private virtues such as care, awareness and responsibility, with political change eschewed. The identity politics of the 1970s are today shorn of politics, and personal identity forged around private virtue is what is left. Volunteer tourism is indicative of that.

Altruism

If the role of political ideology (or lack of it) today contrasts strongly with the earlier period, it is equally important not to overlook what both types of volunteers share: a commendable altruism, an impulse to help others and make a difference. Radical critics labelled Peace Corps volunteers as neocolonial patsies and today the altruism of volunteer tourists attracts cynicism and the charge of naivety. Altruism as a private impulse has been tainted through its association with politics. Yet the inclination to do something to help others remains a positive human impulse. It is important to separate out this positive human spirit from the political context of today, a context which distorts simple charity and care by insisting it occupies the public sphere, that it 'takes sides' in political questions such as development. We broach the consequences of trying to make care political in this way in Chapter 4.

Notwithstanding this, the Peace Corps/VSO narrative of altruism is very different to that of volunteer tourism today. Identification of volunteer tourists with the mission of their own government or society is conspicuous by its complete absence. Today's narrative is a personal one, with no illusions in or allegiance to government or 'the West'. Volunteer holidays are purchased to enable the individuals to bring to bear their own personal altruism in pursuit of their own development and 'journey of the self' (Wickens, 2010: 42). As Wearing describes it, volunteer tourism provides 'an opportunity for an individual to engage in an altruistic attempt to explore "self"' (2001: 3). He argues this in the spirit of exploring the possibilities for forging new political and social identities.

However, Lasch regarded similar as part of the 'culture of narcissism' with the emphasis firmly on 'self-realisation *rather than* social change' (1979: 28; italics added). For Lasch, exploring self through politics marked a retreat of the subject from the social world into the psychological. The focus on the self is also suggestive of Chouliaraki's 'posthumanitarianism': a humanitarian impulse that can only find expression through narcissistic projects of the self in a world lacking any political or transcendental basis for human commonality (2013).

Development

A clear contrast between the two traditions of volunteering is the orientation towards economic transformation, or development of any scale. The assumption in the heyday of the Peace Corps and similar organisations was that they were contributing to social and economic progress in the societies in which they operated, and further aimed to act as 'change agents' who would lead by example and endear the decolonised world to western values (Hapgood and Bennett, 1968;

Adams, 1968). But whilst that desire is mediated through a narrative of progress, growth and technology in the case of the former, with the latter it largely translates as 'care', 'help' or 'giving back' with little reference to development beyond local wellbeing and small-scale projects that are extremely limited as development goals. Where development is invoked directly it is very much influenced by postdevelopment. Wearing is explicit that volunteer tourism should be part of the promotion of an ecocentric outlook rather than economic growth:

> [The] underlying ideology of volunteer tourism represents a transition in society from an anthropocentric view, where the world is interpreted in terms of people and their values, to an ecocentric view, where the world fosters the symbiotic relationship between humans and nature.
>
> (Wearing, 2001: 157)

We look at volunteer tourism in the context of important changes in development thinking in Chapter 3.

Neocolonialism

As the summaries reveal, the Peace Corps and VSO are implicated in postcolonial politics, and arguably can be charged with neocolonialism in that they were part of a process to secure influence in former colonies. The notion of benevolent West and incapable South has long been connected with justifications for colonialism by radical critics, and could arguably be seen as implicit in the Peace Corps and similar volunteer organisations.

Volunteer tourism, too, is associated with the image of the benevolent volunteer and the vulnerable third world. As a result, contemporary analysis seems quick to regard volunteer tourism through the prism of postcolonialism and as a form of neocolonialism (Simpson, 2005; Barkham, 2006; Brodie and Griffiths, 2006; Frean, 2006; Womack, 2007; Brown and Hall, 2008).

Yet despite the postcolonial imagery used by volunteer tourist and gap year organisations (Caton and Santos, 2009) it is wrong to argue that today's tourist fantasies mimic those of colonial times (Tickell, 2001), or even that volunteer tourism presumes westernisation and modernisation as a part of the development process (Simpson, 2004). Rather, the dim view of agency of the voluntoured that may be implicit in many images advertising volunteer tourism has more to do with postpolitics than postcolonialism (see Chapter 7).

There are no assumptions of western superiority, or even too many of western agency, in volunteer tourism. Volunteers are not trying to impose an ideology or assert moral or any other kind of superiority. They are not trying to develop the societies they visit, but to help the individuals they encounter and in the process engage in a form of self-help for themselves: 'a journey of discovery' (Lyons and Wearing, 2008a). As we show elsewhere, the sentiment of volunteer tourists would seem at times to invert colonial assumptions (see for example contributions to Apale and Stam, 2011).

Conclusion

In the past the individual and selfhood were considered very differently than today. Identity was linked to class interest, national mission, religion and political ideology (Sennett, 1986; Bauman, 2000). Today the narrative of the 'self' replaces these transcendental narratives. Formerly the social and economic transformation of the global South was the shared goal of competing political theories that assumed growth and modernisation as progress (Harrison, 1988; Ben-Ami, 2010; Chang, 2010). Contemporary volunteering on the other hand tends to reject such transformative models of development in favour of modest 'sustainable' projects focusing on localism and community wellbeing, adopting Schumacher's antidevelopment maxim 'small is beautiful' and rejecting materialism (Brown, 2005).

But whilst a relationship between the volunteering organisations of the 1950s and 1960s and western interests in the post-Second World War period is clear, modern volunteer tourism's relationship to national or other interests is far less so. What characterises the sentiments of volunteer tourists today is a rejection of any national mission or interest, a rejection of any agenda to aid the transformation of poor societies fundamentally and a distancing from the legacy of modern development. In all three respects, contemporary volunteer tourism contrasts with Peace Corps/VSO-type organisations, and hence it is difficult to sustain the idea that the former shares any postcolonial traits with the latter.

Both the Peace Corps in America and VSO in Britain harnessed the desires of able, idealistic young people to play a role in economic and social modernisation in the global South. It would have been strange in the 1950s and 1960s to talk of international volunteers as 'tourists', or of 'volunteer tourism'. What characterises the advocacy of international volunteering in the 1960s, exemplified by the foundation of the Peace Corps and VSO, was a belief in economic and political development on a transformative scale, and the role of the market in bringing that about.

Today by contrast, volunteer tourists are more likely to reject any free market or state-led philosophy connected with macroeconomic transformation, replacing it with: 'sustainable living' (Wearing, 2001); a 'decommodified' approach to community development (Wearing *et al.*, 2005); a politics of 'care' (Popke, 2006); or, an 'ethics of care for nature' (Wearing *et al.*, 2005: 426). Narratives of personal growth and self-development through the gaining of cultural understanding dominate (Raymond and Hall, 2008; Lepp, 2008; Matthews, 2008; Wearing *et al.*, 2008; Palacios, 2010; Sin, 2010). Rather than seeking to impose 'western' standards upon ex-colonies, volunteer opportunities and gap years today are sold on the basis that the volunteer has as much if not more to learn from the society visited than vice versa (Raymond and Hall, 2008).

These latter themes are explored in more depth in the following chapters where we discuss how contemporary volunteer tourism is indicative of a personalised conception of development, an individual lifestyle approach to politics and the normative goal of global citizenship. This chapter has also contrasted the shift from the modernisation as development approach that characterised the Peace Corps and VSO to the small scale and wellbeing emphasised by volunteer tourists today. The following chapter looks at volunteer tourism in the context of development thinking.

References

Adams, M. (1968) *Voluntary Service Overseas: the Story of the First Ten Years*, Faber and Faber, London.

Amin, J. (1999) The perils of missionary diplomacy in the United States: Peace Corps volunteers in the Republic of Ghana, *The Western Journal of Black Studies*, 23 (1), 35–48.

Apale, A. and Stam, V. (eds) (2011), *Generation NGO*, Between the Lines Books, Toronto.

Arsenault, R. (2006) *Freedom Riders: 1961 and the Struggle for Racial Justice*, Oxford University Press, Oxford.

Baillie Smith, M. and Laurie, N. (2011) International volunteering and development: global citizenship and neo-liberal professionalisation today, *Transactions of the Institute of British Geographers*, 36, 545–59.

Barkham, P. (2006) Are these the new colonialists? *The Guardian*. Available at http://www.theguardian.com/society/2006/aug/18/internationalaidanddevelopment.education (accessed 17 October 2014).

Bauman, Z. (2000) *Liquid Modernity*, Polity, Oxford.

Bell, D. (1960) *The End of Ideology*, Free Press, Glencoe, IL.

Ben-Ami, D. (2010) *Ferraris for All: in Defense of Economic Progress*, Policy Press, Bristol.

Bird, D. (1998) *Never the Same Again: a History of VSO*, Lutterworth Press, Cambridge.

Brodie, J. and Griffiths, T. (26 August 2006) Are gappers really the new colonialists? *The Guardian*. Available at http://www.theguardian.com/travel/2006/aug/26/gapyeartravel.guardiansaturdaytravelsection

Brown, F. and Hall, D. (2008) Tourism and development in the global south: the issues, *Third World Quarterly*, 29 (5), 839–49.

Brown, S. (2005) Travelling with a purpose: understanding the motives and benefits of volunteer vacationers, *Current Issues in Tourism*, 8 (6), 479–96.

Caton, K. and Santos, C. (2009) Images of the other: selling study abroad in a postcolonial world, *Annals of Tourism Research*, 48 (2), 191–204.

Chang, H. (2010). Hamlet without the Prince of Denmark: how development has disappeared from today's 'development' discourse, in *Towards New Developmentalism: Market as Means Rather than Master*, (eds) S. Khan and J. Christiansen, Routledge, Abingdon.

Chouliaraki, L. (2013) *The Ironic Spectator: Solidarity in the Age of Post Humanitarianism*, Polity, London.

Cobbs-Hoffman, E. (1996) Decolonization, the Cold War, and the foreign policy of the Peace Corps, *Diplomatic History*, 20 (1), 79–105.

Cobbs-Hoffman, E. (1997) Diplomatic history and the meaning of life: towards a global American history, *Diplomatic History*, 21 (4), 499–518.

Cobbs-Hoffman, E. (1998) *All You Need Is Love: the Peace Corps and the Spirit of the 1960s*, Harvard University Press, Cambridge, MA.

Darwin, J. (2009) *The Empire Project: the Rise and Fall of the British World System 1830–1970*, Cambridge University Press, Cambridge.

Dickenson, M. (1964) *A World Elsewhere: Voluntary Service Overseas,* Dennis Dobson, London.

Dockrill, M.L. and Hopkins, M.F. (2006) *The Cold War 1945–1991*, Palgrave-Macmillan, Basingstoke.

Frean, A. (15 August 2006). Gap years create 'New Colonialists'. *The Times* (London).

Furedi, F. (1994a) *The New Ideology of Imperialism: Renewing the Moral Imperative*, Pluto, London.

Furedi, F. (1994b) *Colonial Wars and the Politics of Third World Nationalism*, I.B. Tauris, London.

Furedi, F. (1998) *The Silent War: Imperialism and the Changing Perception of Race*, Pluto, London.

Furedi, F. (2014) *The First World War: Still No End in Sight*, Bloomsbury, London.

Guttentag, D.A. (2009) The possible negative impacts of volunteer tourism, *International Journal of Tourism Research*, 11 (6), 537–51.

Hall, M.R. (2007) The impact of the US Peace Corps at home and abroad, *Journal of Third World Studies*, 24 (1), 53–57.

Hapgood, D. and Bennett, M. (1968) *Agents of Change: a Close Look at the Peace Corps*, LittleBrown, Boston.

Harrison, D. (1988) *The Sociology of Modernization and Development*, Routledge, London.

Hobsbawm, E. (1995) *Age of the Extremes: the Short History of the Twentieth Century 1914–1991*, Abacus, London.

Hyam, R. (2007) *Britain's Declining Empire: the Road to Decolonisation 1918–1968*, Cambridge University Press, Cambridge.

Kennedy, John, F. (1960) Speech of Senator John F. Kennedy, Cow Palace, San Francisco, CA, November 2 1960. Online by G. Peters and J.T. Woolley, *The American Presidency Project*. Available at http://www.presidency.ucsb.edu/ws/?pid=25928 (accessed 17 October 2014).

Kennedy, John F. (1961) Statement by the President upon signing order establishing the Peace Corps, March 1 1961. Online by G. Peters and J.T. Woolley, *The American Presidency Project*. Available at http://www.presidency.ucsb.edu/ws/?pid=8513 (accessed 17 October 2014).

Kennedy-Pipe, C. (1998) *Russia and the World 1917–1991* (International Relations and the Great Powers), Bloomsbury Academic, London.

Lasch, C. (1979) *The Culture of Narcissism: American Life in an Age of Diminishing Expectations*, Norton, New York.

Lepp, A. (2008) Discovering self and discovering others through the Taita Discovery Centre volunteer tourism programme, Kenya, in *Journeys of Discovery in Volunteer Tourism: International Case Study Perspectives*, (eds) K.D. Lyons, and S. Wearing, CABI Publishing, London, pp.86–100.

Lowther, K. and Lucas, C.P. (1978) *Keeping Kennedy's Promise. The Peace Corps: Unmet Hope of the New Frontier*, Westview Press, Boulder.

Lyons, K. and Wearing, S. (2008a) *Journeys of Discovery in Volunteer Tourism: International Case Study Perspectives*, CABI Publishing, London.

Lyons, K. and Wearing, S. (2008b) Volunteer tourism as alternative tourism: Journeys beyond otherness, in K.D. Lyons and S. Wearing (eds.), *Journeys of Discovery in Volunteer Tourism: International Case Study Perspectives*, pp.3–11. CABI Publishing, London.

Matthews, A. (2008) Negotiated selves: exploring the impact of local–global interactions on young volunteer travellers, in *Journeys of Discovery in Volunteer Tourism: International Case Study Perspectives*, (eds) K.D. Lyons and S. Wearing, CABI, London, pp.101–17.

McGehee, N.G. (2002) Alternative tourism and social movements, *Annals of Tourism Research*, 29 (1), 124–43.

McGehee, N.G. (2012) Oppression, emancipation, and volunteer tourism: research propositions, *Annals of Tourism Research*, 39 (1), 84–107.

McGehee, N. and Andereck, K. (2008) 'Pettin' the critters': exploring the complex relationship between volunteers and the voluntoured in McDowell County, WV, USA and Tijuana, Mexico, in *Journeys of Discovery in Volunteer Tourism: International Case Study Perspectives*, (eds) K.D. Lyons and S. Wearing, CABI, London, pp.3–12.

McGehee, N. and Santos, C. (2005) Social change, discourse, and volunteer tourism, *Annals of Tourism Research*, 32 (3), 760–76.

Meisler, S. (2011) *When the World Calls: The Inside Story of the Peace Corps and its First Fifty Years*, Beacon Press, Boston.

Miller, A. (2012) *Timebends*, Bloomsbury, London.

Mostafanezhad, M. (2014) *Volunteer Tourism: Popular Humanitarianism in Neoliberal Times*, Ashgate, Farnham.

Nkrumah, K. (1965) *Neocolonialism: the Last Stage of Imperialism*, Nelson, London.

Painter, D. (2003) *The Cold War: an International History*, Routledge, London.

Palacios, C. (2010) Volunteer tourism, development, and education in a postcolonial world: conceiving global connections beyond aid, *Journal of Sustainable Tourism*, 18 (7), 861–78.

Peace Corps (2011) *Peace Corps Milestones Fact Sheet*. Available at http://files.peacecorps.gov/multimedia/pdf/about/pc_milestone_factsheet.pdf (accessed 17 October 2014).

Popke, J. (2006) Geography and ethics: everyday mediations through care and consumption, *Progress in Human Geography*, 30 (4), 504–12.

Preston, P.W. (1996) *Development Theory: an Introduction*, Blackwell, Oxford.

Raymond, E. and Hall, X. (2008) The development of cross-cultural (mis)understanding through volunteer tourism, *Journal of Sustainable Tourism*, 16 (5), 530–43.

Redmond, C. (1986) *Come as You Are: the Making of the Peace Corps*, Harcourt, San Diego.

Rees, D. (1967) *The Age of Containment: the Cold War 1945–1965*. Macmillan, London.

Roberts, T. (2004) Speeches of Sargent Shriver (1961), Washington DC cited in Anti-heroes versus new colonialists: modern volunteers as agents of reciprocal participation in development intervention, unpublished thesis. University of Manchester.

Sennett, R. (1986) *The Fall of Public Man*, Penguin, London. Original 1977.

Shriver, S. (1961) *The Shiver Report*, February. Available at http://www.jfklibrary.org/Asset-Viewer/Archives/JFKPOF-085-014.aspx (accessed 17 March 2014).

Shriver, S. (1963) *Foreign Affairs*, July, 41 (4), 694–707.

Simpson, K. (2004) Broad horizons: Geographies and pedagogies of the gap year, unpublished PhD thesis, University of Newcastle.

Simpson, K. (2005) Dropping out or signing up? The professionalisation of youth travel, *Antipode*, 37 (3), 447–69.

Sin, H.L. (2009) Volunteer tourism: 'Involve me and I will learn'?, *Annals of Tourism Research*, 36 (3), 480–501.

Sin, H.L. (2010) Who are we responsible to? Locals' tales of volunteer tourism, *Geoforum*, 41 (6), 983–92.

Sorensen, T.C. (1965) *Kennedy*, Hodder and Stoughton, London.

Tickell, A. (2001) Footprints on the beach: traces of colonial adventure in narratives of independent tourism, *Postcolonial Studies*, 4 (1), 39–54.

Tomazos, K. and Cooper, W. (2012) Volunteer tourism: at the crossroads of commercialisation and service? *Current Issues in Tourism*, 15 (2), 405–23.

Waldorf, S. (2001) My time in the Peace Corps, *The Public Interest*, Winter, 72–82.

Wearing, S. (2001) *Volunteer Tourism: Experiences that Make a Difference*, CABI Publishing, Wallingford.

Wearing, S., Deville, A. and Lyons, K. (2008) The volunteer's journey through leisure into the self, in *Journeys of Discovery in Volunteer Tourism: International Case Study Perspectives*, (eds) K.D. Lyons and S. Wearing, CABI, London, pp.65–71.

Wearing, S., McDonald, M. and Ponting, J. (2005) Building a decommodified research paradigm in tourism: the contribution of NGOs, *Journal of Sustainable Tourism*, 13 (5), 424–39.

Wickens, E. (2010) Journeys of the self: volunteer tourists in Nepal, in *Volunteer Tourism: Theory Framework to Practical Applications*, A. Benson (ed.), Routledge, Oxon. pp.42–52.

Womack, S. (14 August 2007) Gap-year students 'wasting time on projects'. *The Daily Telegraph*. Available at http://www.telegraph.co.uk/news/uknews/1560244/Gap-year-students-wasting-timeon-projects.html

Zimmerman, J. (2001) *Innocents Abroad: American Teachers in the American Century*, Harvard University Press, London.

3 Volunteer tourism in development perspective

Volunteer tourism is a prominent part of what has recently been called the travellers' philanthropy movement. For Wangari Maathai, 2004 Nobel Peace Laureate and founder of the Kenyan green development non-governmental organisation the Green Belt Movement, travel philanthropy is 'a form of development assistance flowing from the travel industry and travellers into local conservation and community projects and organisations' (cited in Honey, 2011: 1). The claim to be a 'form of development assistance' seems doubtful, but it is nonetheless implicit, and sometimes explicit, in the advocacy of volunteer tourism.

Many decry volunteer tourism on the grounds that it is not really development at all, and that it is all about the volunteers' self-image and the volunteer tour operators' profits. Others counter that it can make a significant difference on the ground to people's lives, or turn tourists into global citizens who can understand and act upon development imperatives in their daily lives.

However, what is far less often, if at all, considered is the way development thinking itself has laid the basis for volunteer tourism to become a noteworthy phenomenon. The emphasis on the personal encounter, empathy, localism, the eschewing of professional knowledge in favour of 'experience' and a decrying of 'western' development – all characteristic of volunteer tourism – also all feature in mainstream rural development thinking. Given this, it is hardly surprising that volunteer tourism can be talked up as development.

Here we look briefly at the changes in development thinking since the Second World War, and argue that the conflation of development with ethical holidays is best understood in this context. It is disingenuous to blame volunteers for poor development outcomes or comment cynically on their efforts. Rather it is the promotion of a degraded alternative development politics that has led to tourism being talked about as development. Volunteer tourism is symptomatic of that agenda, not its cause.

Trends in development thinking

The personalised take on development that volunteer tourism represents is not, as is sometimes suggested, a product of the capacity for pro-market ideology to generate neoliberal subjects out of youthful idealists. Rather broad trends in development thinking – trends that are widely accepted and championed amongst those who see themselves as radicals on the question of development – have set the scene for the personalisation of development. Volunteer tourism is exemplary of this trend.

After the Second World War, following the insecurities of the immediate post-war years, there was a sense of optimism with regard to development in relation to what came to be known as the third world (Hettne, 1995: 52). This optimism was shaped by a number of factors.

First, the commencement of economic development in both the developed and less developed countries following two world wars and recession provided a basis for optimism. Economic growth in the developed capitalist world suggested the possibility of a generalised shift towards prosperity, particularly in the 1960s. For the third world, development was promised from both the communist East and capitalist West, who sought to secure the influence of their respective economic and political blocs (Hettne, 1995; Preston, 1996).

United States' President Truman's famous speech of 1949 established the modern context for the use of the term 'development'. He talked of the duty of the West to bring development to those who did not have it (Potter *et al.*; 1999; Preston, 1996; Hettne, 1995). Technical knowledge, coupled with investment and rising markets, could help third world nations move through Rostow's 'stages of development' – part economic model and part Cold War propaganda – and become part of the developed world. From the East, the communist states played on anticolonial sentiment to establish their credentials as a force that could liberate colonies from oppression and former colonies from poverty. Both sides in the Cold War promised economic transformation – modernity – to the non-aligned, unstable and aspirant countries in the third world (Hettne, 1995).

Second, anticolonial struggles in the post-Second World War decades sought sovereignty and economic growth. The achievement of national sovereignty in most cases was accompanied by high hopes of rapid economic development, and the aspiration to join the richer nations on a more equal footing (Preston, 1996). Notably, the demands from newly sovereign states were for national economic development on a transformative scale – localism and ecodevelopment were not part of the development debates (ibid.). According to two authors, many developing world nations

> took it for granted that western industrialised countries were already developed and that the cure for 'underdevelopment' was, accordingly, to become as much as possible like them. This seemed to suggest that the royal road to 'catching up' was through an accelerated process of urbanisation.
>
> (Friedman and Weaver, 1979: 91)

Third, there was optimism regarding the role of the state, which was set to play a central role, as it had during the Second World War, in achieving economic development. In many cases the state was also seen as having the potential to compensate for the inability of markets to provide employment, peace and prosperity, an inability exposed by a period of fifty years of economic instability and two devastating world wars. There was little divergence from Keynesianism and the role it suggested for the state in the post-Second World War decades from either the Left or Right of the political spectrum. That the state could lead development and shape prosperity was orthodoxy (Hettne, 1995; Preston, 1996; Potter *et al.*, 1999).

This optimism was also reflected in the view of the public. Bjorn Hettne describes a 'missionary and Peace Corps mood' prevailing in the 1950s and 1960s (1995: 66). The period gave rise to a certain idealism, from both the political Left and Right, linked to the potential for economic development to liberate people from poverty. Cobbs-Hoffman's account of the Peace Corps, *All You Need Is Love* (1998), indicates how the idealism of young Americans was harnessed by a volunteering initiative that presented itself as part of a wider mission to transform poverty and ignorance into wealth and knowledge. According to Cobbs-Hoffman, whilst initiated by Kennedy, the Peace Corps was subject to a popular demand (1998). It symbolised a spirit of reform and a desire to pursue 'universal values and progress' (ibid.: 26). This involved the 'belief in the right of all peoples to self determination ... such was the spirit of the sixties' (ibid.: 259). Development as modernity – much critiqued today – was the aim of these idealistic volunteers.

Notably, this mission of the Peace Corps pioneers is in clear contrast to today's public face of development, the latter associated with charity telethons, community ecotourism, Fairtrade, the emphasis on the African child and localism.

Moreover, Cobbs-Hoffman argues that the Peace Corps reflected a sense of American moral leadership in world affairs (1998). By contrast, volunteer tourism eschews claims to moral leadership. The moral narratives of the latter are in evidence only at the level of the individual in their daily lives (see Chapter 4), and these narratives avoid a firm commitment to development.

Optimism to pessimism

This optimism has been replaced by a distinctive pessimism within development thinking that began to set in in the 1970s and consolidated in the 1980s (Hettne, 1995; Rist, 2009). Recession and the failure of transformative development in the third world in the 1970s punctured some of the optimism of the 1960s. Stalled growth and the resulting debt, alongside the attendant views of dependency from politically engaged development thinkers, contributed to a more pessimistic view of the prospects for economic growth (Hettne, 1995; Rist, 2009). Also, cultural and environmental critiques of growth began to question the *desirability* of economic growth, even if it were possible (Sutcliffe, 1999).

According to postdevelopment thinker Wolfgang Sachs, by the 1980s:

> The idea of development stands like a ruin in the intellectual landscape. Delusion and disappointment, failures and crimes have been the steady companions of development and they tell a common story: it did not work. Moreover, the historical conditions which catapulted the ideas into prominence have vanished:

development has become outdated. But above all, the hopes and desires that made the idea fly, are now exhausted: development has grown obsolete.

(cited in Peet and Hartwick, 2009: 227)

The extent to which this fashionable pessimism is fully justified is questionable. In the period since the Second World War developing world economies have grown substantially and per capita wealth along with key indicators of development such as literacy and infant mortality have improved substantially. It is certainly true that the 1980s witnessed debt and structural adjustment and a consequent decline in living standards for many in the developing world, and also there has been a great deal of divergence over recent decades (compare South Korea with Ethiopia, North Africa with sub-Saharan Africa). However, the last two decades have witnessed economic growth in many parts of the world associated with the label 'third world' well in excess of that in Europe or North America.

The pessimism is less with the impact of development upon the developing world, and more a part of a general pessimism with development per se. With reference principally to the influence of alternative development thinking, Sutcliffe argues that:

Because the destination, which in the West we experience every day, seems so unsatisfactory, then all aspects of it are rejected as a whole: along with consumerism out goes science, technology, urbanisation, modern medicine and so on and in sometimes comes a nostalgic, conservative postdevelopmentalism.

(1999: 151–52)

In fact many strands of modern intellectual thought reflect a pessimistic view of modernity, which has for critical writers become associated with destruction, human arrogance and excess rather than advancement and liberation (Ben Ami, 2010; Taverne, 2006). Even the orthodoxy of sustainable development often embodies a dim view of economic development (Williams, 2008). This is certainly the case with regard to tourism development, where sustainable tourism has often been equated with ecotourism or other small, green niches (Butcher, 2003). As explored elsewhere, a critical take on development, often akin to post or even antidevelopment, is characteristic of the views of the advocates of volunteer tourism (Wearing, 2001) and many accounts from volunteers themselves (see contributions to Apale and Stam, 2011).

Hettne (1995: 10) describes a crisis and gloom in development thinking in the 1990s, arising out of the collapse of faith in both the mainstream and alternatives: a dual crisis.

On the Left, the project of social transformation through planned development had seemed increasingly untenable through the 1970s and 1980s. When the planned economies of eastern European states gave up on their own planned societies, and communism collapsed, socialist paths to development stood discredited. Parties of the Left have distanced themselves from notions of state-led planned development, as well as class (Giddens, 1994).

Notwithstanding a little self-conscious market triumphalism following the collapse of communism and the fall of the Berlin Wall, the victory of the market in the Cold War has been pyrrhic. The end of the Cold War marked the end of a historical cycle: the attempt at an alternative, communist society following the Russian Revolution, its protracted degeneration and failure, its collapse. Yet whilst communism or any state-led alternatives to the market seemed untenable at the end of this cycle, capitalism itself stood exposed (Laidi, 1998; Jacoby, 1999). The old insult thrown at the Left, 'if you don't like it here, get back to Russia' – hardly an inspiring symbol of capitalist virility itself – no longer held. The mantra of Thatcherism in the UK in the 1980s – 'There is No Alternative' – sums up the new status of the market system. It exists, it is unchallenged, it has acquired an eternal, natural feel due the lack of any tenable alternative (ibid.). Yet capitalism lacks a systematic, progressive dynamic, and contrary to some accounts of neoliberalism, it lacks cultural support (Fukuyama, 1992; Hartwich, 2009; Furedi, 2014). This dual crisis in political identity is important in shaping discussions on development.

The new 'alternative' politics of development

With apparently no alternative to the market at the level of state policy from the 1980s, the search for alternatives focused away from the state. According to Rajni Kothari:

> The assumption after the second World War, by both elites and radicals, that the state would be a liberator and equaliser, is no longer avidly held, and there is a creative reconsideration of the relationship between state and civil society. There is a rediscovery of civil society as an autonomous expression of human and social will.
>
> (1984, cited in Hettne, 1995: 33)

Such a sentiment has contributed to a 'new politics' of the 'third system' (Hettne, 1995: 33), much of it focused on 'alternative development' (Friedman, 1992; Hettne, 1995; Preston, 1996; Rist, 2009). In particular, disillusioned radicals have turned towards post and antidevelopment (Potter *et al.*, 1999: 9). This new radical-sounding politics of development has focused on the community (almost always local) as the appropriate spatial unit for development and the impact of human development on nature (Hettne, 1995).

Many volunteer tourism projects take this line – there is little if any reference to the macro economy or national economic development. The difference is to be made in 'the community'. It is there that the volunteer experiences poverty and can, personally, act upon it and witness first hand the result of their actions.

Moreover, very often the focus is on the *relationship between* community and the Earth, with the aim of promoting a sustainable relationship between people and nature. Linking culture and environment within specific local areas as the basis for development is quite different from previous views which implied that progress involved transforming that relationship. Despite its rhetorical radicalism, it has been argued that this new, 'alternative' outlook – often associated with sustainable development in the rural third world – adopts a very restricted conception of development, effectively tying people to localised natural limits in a fashion alien to the experience of economically developed societies (Sutcliffe, 1999). However, it is often talked up as innovative and superior to previous conceptions of development that prioritised economic growth and the transformation of the relationship between communities, nations and natural environments.

The argument is apposite for ethical tourism niches. These have been pioneered on the basis of their capacity to create a symbiotic relationship between conservation and development, but in so doing fail to envisage development as in any sense transformative of human–environment relationships (Butcher, 2007, 2005).

Neopopulism

The new politics of the community draw heavily on neopopulism. Neopopulism refers to a rhetorical emphasis on 'the people' rather than the state or big business. It is associated with demands for 'bottom-up' rather than 'top-down' approaches to development. There is normally an implied criticism of large, distant bureaucracies and an assumption of the benefits of localism and a local cultural sensitivity. Neopopulism generally involves three interrelated aspects: emphasis on community, a stress on primary production and a distaste for industrial civilisation. There are new factors too: environmental consciousness and commitment to a just world order (see Hettne, 1995).

Against the impersonality of the state and grand theories, the personal involvement characteristic of volunteering appeals to the neopopulist desire to achieve a 'human' dimension to development (Hettne, 1995; Chambers, 1983, 1997). The volunteer has neither state interest nor financial imperative to constrain and shape their dialogue with societies subject to their benevolence. Volunteer tourists themselves often articulate a distinctly neopopulist view of their activities.

Eric Hobsbawm, adopting the terminology of Ferdinand Tonnies, argued that globalisation turns the planet into a remote kind of *Gesellschaft* (society) in which people relate to each other indirectly through formal and impersonal institutions. By contrast, informal and personal aspects of life, *Gemeinschaft* (community), have been squeezed out. The increasingly formalised and institutionalised nature of life, Hobsbawm argues, has led many to try to rediscover *Gemeinschaft* through identity politics. Despite the association of *Gemeinschaft* with authentic human experience, Hobsbawn argues that this search for community is itself fictitious, very limited and often far from progressive (Hobsbawm, 2007).

Volunteer tourism at times reflects this sense of an over-formalised global society and a lack of community, with a consequent desire to reconnect with other people on a more authentic basis. The sense of community in volunteer tourism projects, and the authentic relationships within these communities, are evident in the accounts from tourists and also in academic analyses. Many of these emphasise personal and intimate encounters and friendships (Conran, 2011), and others also draw a contrast with the lack of community at home (Apale and Stam, 2011).

With reference to development debates, Hettne concurs. Alternative development strategies also seek to build *Gemeinschaft* – communities that are locally defined and not determined by a distant, uniform global market; communities that are in a sense authentic (1995).

The desire for authentic, personal bonds with people around the world is no doubt heartfelt, but the link to development and global citizenship should be viewed with caution. Writing with reference to development volunteering one analysis notes that 'the focus on the local as the site of empowerment and knowledge circumscribes consciousness and action' (Mohan and Stokke, 2000: 251). Just as the local and personal open up as arenas for social agency, this is at the expense of any wider political reckoning. That is apt with regard to volunteer tourism's social aspirations, where affect trumps any political framing.

The search for authenticity has long been associated with forms of travel outside of the mainstream, from writers such as Jack Kerouac and Robert Pirsig through sociologists such as Dean MacCannell and John Urry. Volunteer tourism, with a foot in both the tourism and development camps, combines the individual search for authenticity with neopopulist currents in development thinking. This certainly resonates with the promotion of volunteer tourism and the views of volunteer tourists who seek something akin to what Dutch Aid agency SNV describe as 'people to people' development (SNV/ de Jong, 1999).

A prosaic assessment

If tourism's lifestyle politics of development is narcissistic or limited in political vision, arguably that would be less pressing if the outcomes of projects were significantly beneficial to the communities concerned. The actual contribution to development amounts to very little. Indeed, the impacts on local people are often assumed rather than researched (ATLAS/TRAM, 2008: 39). Whilst volunteer tourists can get involved in building homes or schools, or engage in conservation work with the local community, they have usually paid a significant fee for the opportunity to do this (an average of $3,000 per trip in 2007 (ibid.)). This money, if donated to a local community directly, could potentially pay a greater amount of labour than the individual volunteer could ever hope to provide. This is especially so given the level of technical skill or professional experience required of volunteers is negligible. Simpson (2005) suggests the lack of requirement for any particular expertise is an element of the appeal of many gap projects. Volunteer tourists are able to experiment with identity and take on varying roles within the host community with little or no qualification or skill beyond being an enthusiastic volunteer (Hutnyk, 1996: 44).

The problem with little white girls, boys and voluntourism

'Our mission while at the orphanage was to build a library. Turns out that we, a group of highly educated private boarding school students, were so bad at the most basic construction work that each night the men had to take down the structurally unsound bricks we had laid and rebuild the structure so that, when we woke up in the morning, we would be unaware of our failure. It is likely that this was a daily ritual. Us mixing cement and laying bricks for 6+ hours, them undoing our work after the sun set, re-laying the bricks, and then acting as if nothing had happened so that the cycle could continue.

Basically, we failed at the sole purpose of our being there. It would have been more cost effective, stimulative of the local economy, and efficient for the orphanage to take our money and hire locals to do the work, but there we were trying to build straight walls without a level.

Before you sign up for a volunteer trip anywhere in the world this summer, consider whether you possess the skill set necessary for that trip to be successful. If yes, awesome. If not, it might be a good idea to reconsider your trip. Sadly, taking part in international aid where you aren't particularly helpful is not benign. It's detrimental. It slows down positive growth and perpetuates the "white savior" complex that, for hundreds of years, has haunted both the countries we are trying to "save" and our (more recently) own psyches. Be smart about traveling and strive to be informed and culturally aware.'

(Biddle, 2014)[1]

Guttentag lists some other straightforward, logical limits to volunteer tourism's development pretentions. First, volunteers can be in lieu of local labour, potentially distorting local labour markets. Second, it carries a negligible potential for knowledge transfer, as skill and expertise are rarely in evidence. Third, local business may be squeezed by volunteer projects that replace potential demand for their skills and services. Finally, as volunteer tourism is the product of the demands of tourists, albeit concerned ones, the development assistance that takes place need in no way resemble the priorities of the people it purports to help. Rather, it is shaped by the volunteers and what is attractive to them (Guttentag, 2009; see also Mitchell, 2011).

Guttentag also refers to the potential for volunteer tourism, in so far as it has a local economic impact, to promote dependency (Guttentag, 2009). Where charity becomes influential in determining the priorities in a project, then sovereign government and local commerce may become less of a focus for people's struggles. This is a theme that has been raised widely in relation to the foreign aid industry generally (Moyo, 2010). It applies here too, especially given the narrative of benevolent giver and grateful receiver prominent in much volunteer tourism marketing.

It is surprising that we have a discourse around assisting the developing world to develop that involves no development, at least in the sense development has been generally understood until recently. The answer to this lies in the reworking and redefinition of development away from macroeconomic transformation through economic growth and better use of modern technology towards a localised focus on wellbeing.

From development to wellbeing

Volunteer tourism suggests wellbeing rather than development. This might initially seem to invalidate looking at volunteer tourism's relationship to development. However, wellbeing itself has become an influential theme in development thinking – think tanks, influential writers and non-governmental organisations focused on development hold wellbeing as an important innovation (McGregor and Gough, 2010). Sen, in his seminal *Development as Freedom*, also invokes wellbeing, seeing it as closely related to the extension of freedoms and capabilities. Most, though, adopt a more growth wary and psychological perspective (Chambers, 2005; White, 2008; McGregor and Gough, 2010).

According to Allister McGregor, a professorial fellow at the Institute of Development Studies and director of the Bellagio Initiative (an initiative seeking to promote wellbeing in international development thinking):

> At the heart of the wellbeing approach is the recognition that we all aspire to live well – whether we are pastoralists in Somalia, factory workers in China or middle managers in the UK. True, it is clear that across the globe and between generations we all perceive wellbeing differently, but this general need to live well – to be content with the things that we have, the relationships that enable us to achieve our goals, and our feelings that we have about how well we are doing in life – is not bound by geography, culture, religion, age, politics or any other factor defining us.
>
> (McGregor, 2011)

In this vein one advocate of wellbeing in development refers to 'doing well, feeling good and doing good, feeling well' to sum up wellbeing (White, 2008: 3). 'Doing well' refers to material aspects of life, 'feeling good' to the subjective. 'Doing good' refers to the relational aspects of life and 'feeling well' to health and happiness.

Theories of wellbeing describe it in terms of a relationship between three of these concepts: material, subjective and relational. Material factors are objective, a more traditional view of development. But combined with these are the subjective and relational: how people feel about their lives and the importance of how a society or community relates beyond the individual respectively. Relational aspects of development are often expressed through discussions of social capital, like wellbeing, a concept originating in modern western societies now applied to the developing world.

There are a number of key aspects of the rise of wellbeing generally that are evident in volunteer tourism. First, wellbeing is generally viewed as being 'ground[ed] in a particular social and cultural location' (ibid.: 4). It is a product of the varied ways that societies are structured and the way they operate. This is a retreat from a more universal notion of development that is applicable to all societies on the basis that human societies, whilst differentiated, share common aspirations in relation to material betterment and freedom.

Second, the relational emphasis of wellbeing has been viewed by its advocates as taking in love, care and social capital (ibid.). This suggests that interventions in development could usefully be at the level of private and personal encounters – they need not be focused on material transformation at all.

Third, wellbeing is commonly associated with a cultural reaction to the routines of modern life in the West. Many volunteer tourists seem to be influenced by a disillusionment with modern development at home, and their activities abroad also reflect this.

It has been noted by some astute writers on development that development thinking has tended to separate itself off from the large-scale infrastructural and transformative industrial changes that have historically been a precondition for major advances in science, health and wealth. Aiming for localised wellbeing as 'development' is certainly a case in point. Economist Ha-Joon Chang argues that this mode of development thought is akin to 'Hamlet without the prince of Denmark' – a narrative that omits its central character (2010).

Volunteer tourism's contribution fits the wellbeing model of development, and Chang's criticism applies. It is striking that the public face of development, the public focus for making a difference to the world, is so radically divorced from the material transformation needed to improve people's lives. However, as Chang's analysis makes clear, it is development thinking itself that establishes this, not attempts at ethical lifestyle, as the former has retreated from macroeconomic transformation as a precondition for liberation from poverty. As he points out, even the millennium development goals, whilst establishing measurable goals to improve people's lives, omit any strategy to achieve the economic transformation that would make these goals realisable.

Robert Chambers, guru of rural development and one of the most influential figures in his field, refers to 'responsible wellbeing' (2005). Wellbeing already assumes development as culture specific and downplays the central role of economic development in liberating people from want. By adding 'responsible' to this, Chambers emphasises the obligations he believes local communities have to the local environment. Here wellbeing is about improving one's lot within locally determined natural limits, as to go beyond these limits is to fail to be 'responsible'.

The linking of development for human populations to local natural limits is a feature of ecotourism and a significant amount of alternative development (Butcher, 2007). Communities (invariably 'local') are regarded less in the context of the national and global economy (sometimes deemed an unwelcome imposition on local culture) and more in relation to how they interact with their local environment. A lot of volunteer tourism projects focused on assisting rural communities adopt this ecodevelopment outlook. It is based upon working within existing relationships between people and their local environment rather than in any way offering up the prospect of transforming these relationships.

Parallel to its growth in development debates, wellbeing has also emerged as a reference point in domestic culture in recent years. One study, looking at newspaper coverage in the 1980s and 1990s, finds that whilst wellbeing generally referred to the body politic in the 1980s, in the 1990s the focus became the body personal (Sointu, 2005). Wellbeing holidays are marketed as a retreat from the stresses and strains of modern life and affluence itself. Whilst of course wellbeing is associated with enjoyable and relaxing activity, it can also reflect a cultural reaction away from modern life towards spirituality (a 'retreat'). When used in the development context it encapsulates the divorce of development from economic growth (Butcher, 2007). To 'feel well' in this context emphasises non-economic and post-material values.

Social inclusion is another example of a term that contributes to the shifting of the focus away from transformative economic development and onto wellbeing. Social inclusion places objective indices of wealth or unemployment alongside relational aspects such as community and subjective notions such as self-esteem in its conception of human welfare. Volunteer tourists claim to be boosting the self-esteem of poor children, a claim sometimes made in relation to teaching and orphanage-based projects. As with social capital, social inclusion is a concept that has come out of western societies and is widely used in relation to economically poorer societies in debates on development (Rawal, 2008).

The growth of 'happiness' as central to progressive development is a further example of the broad influence of wellbeing-type concepts and their influence vis-à-vis objective measures of economic wealth. Richard Layard's *Happiness: Lessons From a New Science* (2006) is the most notable of a number of books and surveys putting happiness up against wealth as a measure of wellbeing. The happiness approach chimes with the development aspirations of volunteer tourism. As one volunteer tourism advocate reflects, 'maybe happiness is not about affluence' (Mahrouse, 2011: 373). Images of happiness are replete in volunteer tourism marketing. The aspiration to 'bring a little happiness' or to 'bring a smile' to someone is common in volunteer tourists' accounts of their travels.

Robert Chambers and rural development

To illustrate the nature and influence of the new development politics, and how they set the scene for volunteer tourism, it is worth looking further at the ideas of Robert Chambers. Chambers has been an influential figure in rural development for many decades now. Through his books *Rural Development: Putting the Last First* (1983) and *Whose Reality Counts? Putting the First Last* (1997), and many other contributions to rural development thinking and development professional training, Chambers has consistently argued a line that shares important features with modern volunteer tourism.

The most striking thing about Chambers' view is the consistent emphasis placed upon the individual, or more precisely the personal. For Chambers, the project of development workers should be a personal one, in which personal transformation and relationships are paramount. Professionals should be learners and facilitators – learning from the societies in which they work and facilitating local, traditional knowledge as the basis for development (1983, 1997, 2005).

This learning and facilitation approach shares common ground with volunteer tourism. Advocates argue that the tourists learn and transform themselves through facilitating projects based around local strengths and knowledge. They often eschew the idea they are bringing new ways of life or new technologies or that they intend to change very much at all other than themselves.

Volunteer tourists sometimes stand accused of a lack of expertise and a naivety regarding the impact they can make. However, if professional development workers disavow expert knowledge themselves, are they so different?

Chambers' constant emphasis on interpersonal encounters in development presents development as something individuals understand and achieve through a combination of empathy and experience of others' lives (1997, 2000). For example, he advocates 'improvisation' involving 'fun' and 'playfulness' as important for development workers, to enable barriers to be broken down, and surprisingly also as a respite from the stresses of modern life (Chambers, 1997: 207; 2000). That Chambers encourages 'being nice to people' (1997: 207) in the context of development indicates the extremely personalised character of this outlook. Fun, playfulness and being nice are qualities associated with tourism. Here they are part of a serious and influential view of rural development. They are ways of getting to local knowledge, which for Chambers is not only the starting point for local development, but its very basis.

Volunteer tourism is often seen as part of a counter to grand development schemas with their attendant political and financial interests, or a way of generating 'third spaces' within which power relations and cultural assumptions can be challenged (Wearing and Ponting, 2009; Wearing *et al.* 2010; Wearing and Darcy, 2011). Many of the projects involved tend to be small scale and linked to green development.

In similar vein Chambers' view of rural development involves a critique of 'top-down' development, the efficacy of modern technology, and 'western' culture and its standards for development. His questioning of the whole premise of development as previously understood places him amongst the postdevelopment thinkers, writers who are hostile to development, seeing it as transmission mechanism for imposed, alien and ultimately damaging values onto societies denied the opportunity to choose their own cultural path (Peet and Hartwick, 2009).

If that is accepted, then humble attempts of volunteer tourists to challenge their own 'western' views through an immersion in poverty could be seen as commendable. However, Chambers is advocating development devoid of the possibility of social and economic transformation. It is those low horizons rather than western arrogance that are in dire need of being challenged, and volunteer tourism does not aspire to do that.

Chambers' writing has a tendency to treat poor rural societies with a presentism – taking the societies as they are, and viewing any incremental changes as destructive of that. Development always has a destructive side – it destroys old ways. It also has a creative side – it leads to new ways of life, at higher levels of material development. By highlighting the destructive aspects of incremental changes to a society, and seeing these as a justification for decrying the role of modern technology and the benefits of economic development on a large scale, he defends the present against change. Qualities such as community and happiness are assigned to the present. This present is portrayed as under threat from modernity, the community from outside influences.

These are sentiments widely shared with volunteer tourists. In a recent collection of volunteers' reflections, *Generation NGO*, the volunteers expressed their distaste for 'western' development, their disillusionment with their home societies and their desire to learn from rather than impose upon the communities visited (see contributions to Apale and Stam, 2011). They expressed a sensitivity to change rather than a desire for change. Many volunteer projects are motivated precisely by a desire to protect communities from the perceived excesses of development rather than to demand its benefits be generalised.

Rather than divisions of class or nation, or social categories such as capitalism or the state, for Chambers the key social demarcation is between 'uppers' (those with power) and 'downers' (those without power) (Chambers, 1997). The relationship he seeks is one of understanding, empathy and respect (for difference, never for common aspirations) on the part of the uppers. It is an intercultural, interpersonal view of the world, devoid of politics, devoid of context beyond the village. Chambers' view is moralistic rather than political, again reflecting the decline of politics and its replacement by a personalised conception of agency, manifested in ethical consumption, ethical lifestyles and volunteer tourism.

If personal empathy, experience, reducing distance, localism and playfulness are important, and if professional knowledge, scientific knowledge and development itself are 'western' and therefore circumspect, then volunteer tourism seems to have potential. That potential may be to generate an understanding of and empathy for the rural poor that could contribute over time to better development outcomes. However if these characteristics are a poor excuse for a development agenda, then criticism is well justified.

However, it is not the tourists or the volunteer tour operators who deserve the criticism. Development thinking itself has laid the basis for holidays to be confused with development.

Chambers' philosophy is put into practice through his innovation in development work, Participatory Rural Appraisal (PAR), which is now a staple idea in rural development. This method encapsulates his views on knowledge and development. The development worker's role is to facilitate the agency of the local people, drawing upon local knowledge and understanding. As such, the interpersonal skills of the worker, such as empathy and friendliness, are important. Development workers are encouraged to 'hand over the stick' to local people, so, following the metaphor, they can sketch out their own views in the dust. For Chambers this is a process the development worker must learn from, rather than superimposing 'western' views and knowledge onto the communities they work with.

Through PAR, Chambers' emphasis is on the life-changing and awareness-raising character of development workers' experiences – his is a politics of the interpersonal encounter. He refers to the 'primacy of the personal' in rural development interventions (1997: 2). Yet PAR, according to Mohan, 'circumscribes consciousness and action' through its 'focus on the personal and local as the site of empowerment and knowledge' (Mohan and Stokke, 2000: 253). This limiting micropolitics is commonplace in the discussions of volunteer tourism's benefits for both host and tourist.

Rahnema argues that when PAR became influential, its principal function was to change the lives of the idealistic development workers coming from privileged urban backgrounds rather than those of the communities themselves (cited in Peet and Hartwick, 2009: 217). The new face of development was 'the face of a repentant saint, ready to amend, to work in a new fashion with the poor, and even to learn from them' (ibid.). Rahnema's criticisms of PAR apply to volunteer tourists too. Although rural development workers would baulk at the comparison, where expertise is eschewed, where knowledge is relativised, and with the emphasis on empathy and friendliness, it seems justified.

A tale of three schools

One of the problems with volunteer tourism is that it is 'development' based upon the demand to buy into ethical holidays rather than the aspirations or efforts of local populations. The following is from a prominent volunteer tourism blog.

'It started with one school – the village banded together and back in the day built their own schoolhouse, complete with a roof and classrooms and blackboards. The school was running well when an NGO funded by donors and with time donated by foreign volunteers decided that the school needed to be bigger.

So next to school one, let's call it, now stands school two, a very pretty building made of expensive materials and smattered with a ton of Anglo-Saxon sounding names thanking them for their donations. Now school one sits vacant next to school two and is used for storage by locals.

Then another group came in and said this community of maybe 500 villagers needed another school – so school three construction began with donor funded materials and volunteers. However, the funding ran out for school three (because the volunteer company couldn't sell the trip well to volunteers) so school three sits half finished.

So this small community now has three schools – one that was functioning but now sits vacant, one that is smattered with foreign names that is used, one that is half built and probably will never be finished.'

(VoluntourismGal, 2011)

Conclusion

Post-Second World War optimism at the possibility of social and economic transformation through development has been replaced by a pessimism with development thus constituted. This pessimism is less with the possibilities for modern development and more with development itself and its capacity to make the world a better place for people. Alternative 'people-centred' views of development have emerged that redefine it as best conceived of at a local level, premised upon the distinctiveness of local cultures and their relationship with the environment. Whilst this does not describe the practice of much development (development on the basis of large-scale investment and infrastructure has remained an important reality) it is influential in discourses on the developing world and in policy. In terms of the public face of development – the way development is conceived of and the debates framed in public consciousness – these developments are very influential, and are reflected in the growth of ethical consumption, Fairtrade, 'sponsor a child' initiatives and volunteer tourism.

There is a considerable amount of criticism of volunteer tourists and gap year project participants on the basis that they do not really help the societies they visit. Yet in an important sense the criticism is misdirected. Volunteer tourism can be associated with development only because influential 'alternative' development ideas themselves have become aligned with small-scale, local interventions and personal change.

Note

1 Pippa continues to work in the Dominican Republic and sits on the Board of Onwards, a 501(c)3 organisation that is transforming the travel industry by empowering individuals and connecting communities.

References

Apale, A. and Stam, V. (2011) *Generation NGO*, Between the Lines Books, Toronto.
Association for Tourism and Leisure Education/Tourism Research and Marketing (ATLAS/ TRAM) (2008) *Volunteer Tourism: a Global Analysis*, Association for Tourism and Leisure Education, Arnhem.
Ben-Ami, D. (2010) *Ferraris for All: in Defense of Economic Progress*, Policy Press, Bristol.
Biddle, P. (23 February 2014). The problem with little white girls, boys and voluntourism. *Huffington Post Blogs*. Available at http://www.huffingtonpost.com/pippa-biddle/little-white-girls-voluntourism_b_4834574.html (accessed 12 March 2014).
Butcher, J. (2003) *The Moralization of Tourism*, Routledge, London.
Butcher J. (2005) The moral authority of ecotourism: a critique, *Current Issues in Tourism*, 8 (2), 114–24.
Butcher, J. (2007) *Ecotourism, NGOs and Development: a Critical Analysis*, Routledge, London.
Chambers, R. (1983) *Rural Development: Putting the Last First*, Longman, London.
Chambers, R. (1997) *Whose Reality Counts? Putting the First Last*, Intermediate Technology Publications, London.

Chambers, R. (2000) *Fun with 21s: a Sourcebook for Workshop Facilitators – 21 Sets of 21 Ways to Approach Participatory Events*. Wageningen Centre for Development Innovation. Available at http://portals.wi.wur.nl/files/docs/ppme/Chambers_21s_ workshops.pdf (accessed 14 March 2014).

Chambers, R. (2005) *Ideas for Development*, Routledge, London.

Chang, H. (2010). Hamlet without the Prince of Denmark: how development has disappeared from today's 'development' discourse, in *Towards New Developmentalism: Market as Means Rather than Master*, (eds) S. Khan and J. Christiansen, Routledge, Abingdon.

Cobbs-Hoffman, E. (1998) *All You Need Is Love: the Peace Corps and the Spirit of the 1960s*, Harvard University Press, Cambridge, MA.

Conran, M. (2011) They really love me! Intimacy in volunteer tourism, *Annals of Tourism Research*, 38 (4), 1454–73.

Friedman, J. (1992) *Empowerment: the Politics of Alternative Development*, Blackwell, Oxford.

Friedman, J. and Weaver, C. (1979) *Territory and Function: Evolution of Regional Planning*, Hodder & Stoughton Educational, London.

Fukuyama, F. (1992) *The End of History and the Last Man*, Penguin, Harmondsworth.

Furedi, F. (2014) *The First World War: Still No End in Sight*, Bloomsbury, London.

Giddens, A. (1994) *Beyond Left and Right: the Future of Radical Politics*, Polity, Oxford.

Guttentag, D.A. (2009) The possible negative impacts of volunteer tourism, *International Journal of Tourism Research*, 11 (6), 537–51.

Hartwich, O. (2009) *Neoliberalism, the Genesis of the Political Swearword*. Centre for Independent Studies. Available at www.cis.org.aus/publications/ (accessed 20 September 2014).

Hettne, B. (1995) *Development Theory and the Three* Worlds, *second edition*, Longman, London.

Hobsbawm, E. (2007) *Globalisation, Democracy and Terrorism*, LittleBrown, London.

Honey, M. (ed.) (2011) *Travelers' Philanthropy Handbook*. Centre for Responsible Travel, Washington DC.

Hutnyk, J. (1996) *The Rumour of Calcutta: Tourism, Charity and the Poverty of Representation*, Zed Books, London.

Jacoby, R. (1999) *The End of Utopia: Politics and Culture in an Age of Apathy*, Basic Books, New York.

Laidi, Z. (1998) *A World Without Meaning: the Crisis of Meaning in International Politics*, Routledge, Abingdon.

Layard, R. (2006) *Happiness: Lessons From a New Science*, Penguin Books, London.

McGregor, A. (8 August 2011) The promotion of global wellbeing can drive the development agenda. *Guardian* blogs. Available at http://www.theguardian.com/global-development/ poverty-matters/2011/aug/08/global-wellbeing-drive-development-agenda (accessed 20 August 2013).

McGregor, J.A. and Gough, I. (2010) *Development as the Pursuit of Human Wellbeing*, Institute of Development Studies, Brighton.

Mahrouse, G. (2011) Feelgood tourism: an ethical option for socially conscious westerners? *ACME: An International E-Journal for Critical Geographies*, 10 (3), 372–91.

Mitchell, H. (25 March 2011). Adventures in Humanitarian Travel. *New York Times (Travel)*.

Mohan, G. and Stokke, K. (2000) Participatory development and empowerment: the dangers of localism, *Third World Quarterly*, 21 (2) 247–68.

Moyo, D. (2010) *Dead Aid: Why Aid is Not Working and How There is Another Way for Africa*, Penguin Books, London.

Peet, R. and Hartwick, E. (2009) *Theories of Development: Contentions, Arguments, Alternatives, second edition*, Guilford Press. Guildford.

Potter, R., Binns, T., Elliot, J. and Smith, D. (1999) *Geographies of Development*, Longman, London.

Preston, P.W. (1996) *Development Theory: an Introduction*, Blackwell, Oxford.

Rawal, N. (2008) Social inclusion and exclusion: a review, *Dhaulagiri Journal of Sociology and Anthropology* 2, 161–80.

Rist, G. (2009) *History of Development: from Western Origins to Global Faith, third edition*, Zed Books, London.

Sen, A. (1999) *Development as Freedom*, Oxford University Press, Oxford.

Simpson, K. (2005) Dropping out or signing up? The professionalisation of youth travel, *Antipode*, 37 (3), 447–69.

SNV/de Jong, A. (1999) *Cultural Tourism in Tanzania*, SNV, The Hague.

Sointu, E. (2005) The rise of an ideal: tracing changing discourses of wellbeing, *The Sociological Review*, 53 (2), 255–74.

Sutcliffe, B. (1999) The place of development in theories of imperialism and globalization, in *Critical Development Theory Contributions to a New Paradigm*, (eds) R. Munck and D. O'Hearn, Zed Books, London, pp.135–54.

Taverne, D. (2006) *The March of Unreason: Science, Democracy, and the New Fundamentalism*, Oxford University Press, Oxford.

VoluntourismGal. (2011) A tale of three schools, *VoluntourismGal*. Available at http://voluntourismgal.wordpress.com/2011/01.18/a-tale-of-three-schools/ (accessed 17 March 2014).

Wearing, S. (2001) *Volunteer Tourism: Experiences that Make a Difference*, CABI Publishing, Wallingford.

Wearing, S. and Darcy, S. (2011) Inclusion of the "othered" in tourism, *Cosmopolitan Civil Societies Journal*, 3 (2), 18–34.

Wearing, S. and Ponting, J. (2009). Breaking down the system: how volunteer tourism contributes to new ways of viewing commodified tourism, in *The Sage Handbook of Tourism Studies*, (eds) T. Jamal and M. Robinson, Sage, London, pp.254–69.

Wearing, S., Stevenson, D. and Young, T. (2010) *Tourist Cultures: Identity, Place and the Traveller*, Sage, London.

White, S.C. (2008) *What is Wellbeing? A Framework for Analysis in Social and Development Policy and Practice*, Centre for Development Studies, Bath.

Williams, A. (2008) *Enemies of Progress: Dangers of Sustainability*, Imprint Academic, London.

4   The personal and the political in volunteer tourism

The rise of ethical tourism's latest incarnation, volunteer tourism, tells us more about wider social and political consciousness – how people make sense of their place and their possibilities in the world – than it does about a surfeit or lack of ethical behaviour. This chapter focuses on the language through which ethical tourism is advocated and discussed, and considers it as a social construct, a product of the times we live in. We note the growth of a discourse of personal qualities such as 'care', 'awareness' and 'responsibility'. These narratives of personal virtue occupy the terrain once held by a distinctly political debate on what people can do about a lack of development in the global South. In order to consider this change we look at the rise of this language of personal virtue and its significance in debates on development that have previously taken political ideologies, perspectives and interests as their principal point of reference.

There is a long tradition in political thought of considering the relationship between the private, intimate and personal aspects of our everyday lives, and the public and political arenas through which societies are constituted. We draw on the perspectives of key thinkers – Hannah Arendt, Jurgen Habermas, Richard Sennett and Christopher Lasch – to argue that the growth of private sentiment in the public face of development contributes to a limited and limiting morality and politics.

We look at the prospects for volunteer tourism, with its attendant focus on personal identity and selfhood, to generate greater political understanding and engagement, and argue that in fact the lifestyle politics that it represents reinforces antipolitics. Finally, we critically consider the view that the closeness and intimacy with people and places characteristic of this niche confers understanding and humanises politics.

In conclusion we argue that the elevation of private virtues, unmediated by political framing, into the public understanding of development politics, does no favours to development or politics.

Care, responsibility and politics

With the rise of ethical lifestyle strategies such as Fairtrade, the advocacy of organic food and localism, personal attributes have become the stuff of politics. These attributes are directly linked to desirable development outcomes. Questions such as, 'Are you "responsible"?' 'Do you "care"?' Or maybe, 'Do you lack "awareness"?' are implicit in much of this (Barnett *et al.*, 2011). However, up until fairly recently narratives of care and responsibility did not feature prominently in development or politics at all. Instead, development politics was informed by competing visions of social transformation through growth backed up by macroeconomic theories and critiques (Chang, 2010). The politics of Left and Right, albeit encompassing a diverse set of positions, framed development politics and animated distinctly social movements and beliefs (Chouliaraki, 2013; Glaser, 2014).

It is important to note that the emphasis on responsibility and care is not only the prerogative of 'alternative' initiatives such as Fairtrade. 'Responsible capitalism' and 'caring capitalism' have both been part of the rhetoric of western governments and big business in recent years. Ben Cohen and Jerry Greenfield, co-founders of Ben & Jerry's *Homemade* ice cream, have championed 'responsible capitalism', a phrase that has found favour in boardrooms and company mission statements around the world. George Bush in his 2000 presidential campaign adopted the label 'caring conservatism' as his big idea. In the UK think tanks and the main political parties have all widely adopted the prefixes 'responsible' and 'caring'. This rise of the rhetoric of care, responsibility and ethics in business has been argued to be in part a reaction to the exhaustion of political ideologies and the consequent imperative to search for a shared moral purpose (Hunt, 2003).

The way development is presented to the public through the media and in everyday life, or the 'public face of development' (Smith and Yanacopulos, 2004), emphasises these personal traits. High-profile telethons, charity challenges, Fairtrade and ethical consumption generally are examples of this trend. The 'caring' approach to development gained prominence through Bob Geldof's 1984 Live Aid concerts. This does not mean that people began to or were prompted to care more or less, or to be more or less responsible (both admirable personal qualities), but that these private virtues came to shape discussions on development unmediated by political and ideological perspectives (Chouliaraki, 2013). Since then the humanitarian impulse has increasingly come to be shaped by a distinctly personal morality as opposed to finding expression in politics (ibid.).

You care we care

Mainstream cruise ship travel company Crystal Cruises run a volunteer programme called 'You Care We Care'. Passengers can take time out from their luxury cruise to take part in complimentary on-shore excursions to aid communities in need, including: assisting orphans with homework in Langa Township, South Africa and helping troubled youth from the St. Joseph's youth club, Dublin.

Volunteers have 'bonded with young burns victim over cards and a "jam" session in Lima's burn rehab unit' and 'planted trees to restore Hkikino Conservation Reserve in New Zealand'.

> John Stoll, Vice-President, land and port operations, says of the project: 'Whether from the hugs from the village children or the tears from grateful adults, our volunteers always leave these places moved by the experience.'
>
> (Crystal Cruise Line, undated)

Appeals to care, responsibility and awareness are also evident, and often explicit, in much of the advocacy of a self-consciously moral approach to tourism consumption (Butcher, 2003). In *The Holiday Makers: Understanding the Impact of Leisure and Travel* (1987), Krippendorf focuses on personal behaviour, awareness and attitudes as key to the role of tourism in development. Since Krippendorf placed personal ethics at the heart of tourism's development impact, care, awareness and responsibility have loomed ever larger. Charities such as Tourism Concern in the UK see their role as raising awareness of injustices (see www.tourismconcern.org.uk). The assumption here is that if people are 'aware', then they might consider moral questions relating to their impact on other cultures and the natural environment, leading to more 'responsible' and 'caring' social outcomes. Laudable goals, such as the livelihoods of Nepalese porters, and more debatable ones, such as codes of conduct for travellers, are frequently discussed in terms of care, awareness and responsibility on the part of private consumers.

'Responsible Tourism' has become a well-known brand courtesy of academic and ecotourism promoter Harold Goodwin and former Body Shop marketing executive Justin Francis, through their ResponsibleTravel.com web site (www. responsibletravel.com) (the late Anita Roddick, formerly prime mover in ethical consumption with her Body Shop stores, was part of originating the brand). For these advocates of ethical holidays, responsible tourism 'simply means holidays that *care* about local communities and culture as well as wildlife conservation and the environment' (ibid.; italics added). Goodwin and Francis – ethical lifestyle entrepreneurs – have also turned their attention to volunteer tourism, seeking to endorse what they see as good, 'responsible' practice.

The laudable personal qualities of care and responsibility are explicitly linked to the social project of development in the campaigning and academic literature. Responsibletravel.com and Tourism Concern are examples of the former, and the academic volume *Responsible Travel* edited by rural development expert Anna Spenceley (2012) is indicative of the latter. Indeed, the adjective 'responsible' has been widely adopted, including from the mid 1990s by the world's biggest conservation body, the World Wide Fund for Nature (WWF). They use it as a label for their attempts at utilising tourism to link conservation and development in economically poor, biodiversity rich destinations (Woolford, 2002).

Two books in the ethical tourism tradition share the title *The Good Tourist* (see Wood and House, 1992, and Popescu, 2008). This is indicative of the replacement of political categories such as Left and Right, class interest, modern development and green development, with abstract moral categories. Being 'Good' or 'Bad' is directly linked to good and bad development outcomes for the holidaymakers' hosts in these books.

The link between personal qualities and social outcomes is clearest with volunteer tourism. Here the impulse to act upon the world privileges personal experience and reflection over any political framing of the issues being addressed (Butcher and Smith, 2010). Attempts to assist others are mediated through a self-conscious process of identity formation, a process focused on personal rather than political identities and morality (Chouliaraki, 2013). The very term 'volunteer tourism' would have seemed odd a generation ago precisely because of its conflation of private behaviour and political agency. Today it seems unremarkable.

The ethical-sounding adjectives (responsible, caring, green, aware ...) that are commonplace in the above examples suggest personal qualities, not political categories. To describe oneself as 'caring' or 'ethical' gives nothing away as to your politics and beliefs about society and the people in it. Likewise, to say your policy is 'responsible' gives no indication of its position on any wider political spectrum. Neither does it place it on a moral spectrum beyond what Chouliaraki refers to as a 'self-oriented morality' (2013), one that is only capable of framing the attendant issues in terms of the identity and feelings of, in this case, the tourist. It does, however, serve to place the view on the moral high ground. This is especially the case vis-à-vis mass package tourism, the consumers of which are implicitly less moral, less responsible (Butcher, 2003).

Responsible tourism is a rhetorical orthodoxy amongst campaigners, academics and many commentators. The ethical lobby now colonise the moral high ground, which can on occasion have the effect of closing down debate on contrasting development choices and visions. After all, who could be against care and responsibility?

What is taken to be 'responsible', or what makes one a 'Good Tourist' is generally discussed, argued over and decided amongst a milieu of non-governmental organisations, academics and campaigners and codified in statements ranging from the United Nations' *Quebec Declaration on Ecotourism* (UNEP/WTO 2002) through to numerous codes of conduct and declarations such as the International Centre for Responsible Tourism's 2002 *Cape Town Declaration* (ICRT, undated).

What does and does not qualify as responsible or ethical tourism is, however, contested. For example, the accusation of 'greenwashing' is commonly made against corporate attempts to develop ethical tourism (Robbins, 2008). Volunteer tourism in particular attracts praise for its development potential and enlightening role (Wearing, 2001) alongside criticism that it can be a conduit for neoliberalism and neocolonial attitudes (Simpson, 2005; Brown and Hall, 2008; McGehee and Andereck, 2008; Sin, 2009; Baillie Smith and Laurie, 2011; Vrasti, 2012). Nonetheless, the tenor of all these discussions is very much how we can make our holidays truly moral pursuits, rather than a questioning of the efficacy of the lifestyle politics central to ethical travel.

Ethical behaviour and the ethical climate

There are plenty of advocates and critics of different variations on the theme of ethical tourism. Some look at material outcomes from specific attempts at being ethical (see contributions to Benson, 2011). Some attempt to formally apply ethical theory to how people behave on holiday (Fennell, 2003). There has also been a growth in debate on ethical certification and on codes of conduct for tourists (Fennell and Malloy, 2007). The former is often viewed as important, but with the potential to constitute tokenism or 'greenwashing' (Honey, 2002: 370; Buckley, 2003: xiv). The latter reflects an impulse to regulate 'unethical' behaviour (Butcher, 2003).

These features of the analysis of ethical tourism are manifest in academic discussions of volunteer tourism. Currently there are a number of attempts to establish what is to be regarded as good and ethical and what is bad and unethical in volunteer tourism practice (Wearing and McGehee, 2013). For example, in recent years prominent UK-based campaigners for ethical tourism such as Tourism Concern and ResponsibleTourism.com have codified their own guidelines for good practice. Books, papers and reports look towards good practice and attempt to identify bad (see various contributions to Benson, 2011).

Yet lacking in the debates is a critical analysis of the ethical climate itself, the context of these attempts at ethical lifestyles. This refers to the way right and wrong are posed in a society at a particular time: the assumptions of the time, the political standpoints debated, the way people relate to social and political issues (Blackburn, 2001). It is important to step back from the debate as it is presented and consider an ethical climate in which personal qualities feed into a discussion of development, unmediated by a political framing. Looked at from this perspective, the question is less 'which types of tourism are ethical?', and more 'why is the language of care, responsibility and awareness so prominent in social and political questions?'

Today's ethical climate is characterised by a dearth of political debate. Political issues tend to be interpreted through the prism of personal ethical behaviour, divorced from contested views of development and opposing ideologies. This situation has been described by some thinkers as 'postpolitical' (Zizek, 1999; Swyngedouw, 2009). One of the characteristics of a postpolitical world is the substitution of ethical discourse for politics, as moral parameters of right and wrong come to replace the political ones of Right and Left (Mouffe, 2005).

The portrayal of volunteer tourism as 'ethical' (and also the implication that package tourism is unethical) is indicative of this. The dual crisis of both capitalism and any alternative to it has emptied politics of competing visions of social change – the very stuff of politics. The fall of the Berlin Wall and the collapse of eastern European communism exposed the exhaustion of Left alternatives to capitalism and also, ironically, of capitalism itself (Jacoby, 1999). The latter had justified itself in relation to its communist opponent throughout the period of the Cold War, and hence the victory of the market in the Cold War was pyrrhic. For Jacoby, the search for better forms of society, or 'utopias', had been linked to the political projects of Right and Left (ibid.). In the absence of these utopias and future-oriented political ideologies, a dull managerialism generally pervades all manner of public institutions, from parliaments to universities. The saying associated with British Conservative leader Margaret Thatcher in the 1980s, 'There is No Alternative', accompanied by the failure of the market (the thing that it was claimed there is no alternative to), left a vacuum which has been filled by trends such as the politics of behaviour (e.g. Thaler and Sunstein's *Nudge: Improving Decisions about Health, Wealth, and Happiness* (2009)), lifestyle politics (e.g. Giddens' (1991) concept of 'Life Politics') and the politics of ethical consumption (e.g. Barnett *et al.*, 2011). These are associated with hitherto private aspects of life (shopping, personal behaviour, everyday life), now thrust into the public sphere, and hence into political life.

The rise of volunteer tourism – really a sort of lifestyle politics (with the emphasis firmly on lifestyle) – is strongly indicative of these trends. Volunteer tourism's association with development and development politics may be tenuous, but in the absence of a political focus for people's social and political aspirations and impulses it is, along with ethical lifestyles generally, pervasive.

The public and private spheres

The issue is not at all whether people should care or act responsibly. Rather, it is the prominence of these code words for goodness and correct ethical behaviour in the public realm of political debate on development that is significant. The elevation of a discourse of responsibility and care into the realm of the politics of development is indicative of an important trend in politics: that of the diminution of public life and the consequent extension of private emotions and personal qualities into the centre of hitherto political debate (Lasch, 1979; Nolan, 1998). Therefore in order to situate 'new moral tourism' (Butcher, 2003) brands such as volunteer tourism it is worth considering the relationship between personal qualities and private reflection on the one hand, and debate in the public sphere as an expression of politics on the other.

There is a long tradition in political thought of considering the relationship between the private aspects of life, and the public and political world through which society is constituted. Historically, the establishment of a public life outside of the private realm of the home marked the rise of a sense of society, of a social order constructed out of and subject to the wishes of the people (Habermas, 1989).

Aristotle in the *Politics* was arguably the first thinker to consider a distinctive public sphere beyond the individual: the *polis* or political community in contrast to the *oikos*, or household. The household was where the necessities of life were dealt with which, once satisfied, enabled involvement in public realm of the *polis*. For Arendt, without this separate and distinct public world beyond necessity and beyond the household, freedom in any meaningful sense cannot exist (Arendt, 1958). Hence classical Greek society laid the basis for the development of conceptions of the individual and society, and of the agency of the former in the latter (Arendt, 1958).

For Aristotle, man is by nature a political animal and it is through this public sphere that man acts as a rational and moral being (Meiksins-Wood, 2008). The Roman forum, an arena for trade and the discussion of public affairs, is a further example of the public sphere. The Italian city states in the Renaissance, the eighteenth-century urbanisation of Paris and London, the development of parliamentary authority and political parties and subsequent demands to democratise in line with the ideas of the Enlightenment are all indicative of the rise of an active public sphere (Skinner, 1978; Van Creveld, 1999; Ryan, 2012). The forms taken by the public sphere are historically specific, yet all demonstrate a developing sense of humans as individuals with private, intimate, and personal lives increasingly able to speak and act in public, alongside others, in pursuit of shared goals.

Richard Sennett and Jurgen Habermas argue that the modern version of public life took form in the eighteenth century. Sennett traces the emergence of the modern public sphere through a social history of the city in eighteenth-century Europe, citing examples such as the coffee houses and salons of Paris and London (1986). The patrons drank coffee and talked about the public affairs of business and politics. These 'social structures of the public sphere' established a bourgeois claim to public space based on property and private law, rupturing the previous monopoly of responsibility for public matters held by absolutist authority (Habermas, 1989: 27–28).

Sennett argues that the private and public realms are in an important sense distinct: intimacy and self-disclosure are the preserve of the private, while the public realm demands a degree of civility and self-control (Sennett, 1993). Public conversation and cooperation required a reining in of the individual's innermost feelings in the interests of clear communication, considered thinking and debate in a common public space on matters relating to business affairs and the organisation of society. The language of the public sphere is one in which interests, ideologies and perspectives feature strongly whilst affect, emotion and personal experience are secondary.

The form taken by public life, in the salons, the societies and in political institutions, separated it off from private, intimate life to the benefit of each. Public involvement is dependent upon, but at the same time removed and different from the private life of the family, intimates and individual reflection (Sennett 1993). Based on this analysis Sennett argued that the blurring of boundaries between the private and public spheres marked a diminution of public life, and of politics. He noted the rise of an 'ideology of intimacy' through which political categories were transmuted into psychological ones, and argued that public culture was threatened by this (ibid.: 259).

Sennett thought that the distinction between public and private began to break down from the middle of the nineteenth century, but noted the acceleration of this process in the 1960s. In the closing chapter of *The Fall of Public Man*, titled 'The Tyrannies of Intimacy', Sennett argues the balance between an impersonal public world and a private intimate one has tilted far more towards the latter. The study concludes that psychological interpretations of the self and society triumphed over social ones. The erosion of political debate in the public sphere Sennett noted in the 1960s has gone much further since.

The emptying out of the public sphere in the last few decades is stark. Ideologies that framed political debate have collapsed following the end of the Cold War. Institutions that facilitated public, political debate (such as political parties and trade unions) have declined in membership and more importantly in their ability to inspire and cohere support. Politics invites cynicism and disbelief. The emptying of the public sphere clears the way for private virtue, unmediated by any political framing, to influence discussions of societal issues such as international development. The invocation of care in volunteer tourism, and the implicit linking of this to the politics of development, is symptomatic of a diminished public sphere and, by default, the extension of private virtue into erstwhile political issues.

Writing in the late 1950s Arendt was concerned about this diminishing public world and the increasing importance placed on private concerns. Her argument for the importance of recognising the private and public spheres as notionally separate spheres of human existence was made in the light of the experience of the Second World War and the totalitarian regimes of fascism and Stalinism. These regimes did not afford the private individual freedoms from the politics of the state, nor did they see politics as an arena separate from private reflection where diverse humanity could strive for a 'world in common' (Arendt, 1958: 57–58). Arendt argues that the enlargement of the private sphere did not constitute a wider public realm, more inclusive of experience, but meant only that the public realm, and hence political judgement, were diminishing. She suggests that a withdrawal from public life and association with others in the public sphere led simply to an 'intercourse with one's self' and concern with an 'inward domain' (Arendt, 2006: 155).

It is of course true that in the classical world of Athenian democracy venerated by Arendt, entering the public world was the preserve solely of an elite of free citizens and relied on slavery to take care of the private household. However, whilst citizenship had been the preserve of the few in ancient Greece, in the post-Enlightenment world it was a universal aspiration and 'a right for all' (Arendt, 1958: 15).

Arendt's analysis supports the view that political contestation and judgement are a necessary part of a democratic society and of republican citizenship. They create the potential to strive for a 'world in common' out of the diversity of individual experience. A discourse that majors in allusions to private virtues such as care, awareness and responsibility lacks the capacity to achieve this. The concern with personal ethical identity and biography, characteristic of volunteer tourism, is analogous to an 'intercourse with one's self' (Arendt, 2006: 155). It disavows interests, perspectives, ideologies – in short, politics – and replaces it with personal virtues such as care, awareness and responsibility.

Further, whilst volunteer tourism can be presented as the widening of freedom to act upon the world in the realm of culture and consumption, Arendt's analysis suggests the opposite. Arendt shows that the development of the public sphere historically represented the extension of human freedom to live in and act upon society rather than simply in relation to one's immediate desires and needs (Arendt, 2006). Through politics, in the public sphere, we acquire and extend freedom. For Arendt, '[f]reedom is actually the reason that men live together in political organization at all. Without it, political life as such would be meaningless. The raison d'être of politics is freedom' (ibid.: 145).

The expansion of freedom to act on the world that volunteer tourism suggests through creatively harnessing one's privilege through the market is hence indicative of an attenuated freedom and a diminished political subject.

Christopher Lasch's seminal book *The Culture of Narcissism* (1979), like Sennett's *Fall of Public Man* (1993 original 1977), was similarly concerned with the turn to psychology and the self in politics. For Lasch the political upheavals of the 1960s involved progressive political demands (the Civil Rights movement) but also a retreat into primarily personal preoccupations through a 'projection of the search for self into politics' (1979: 28) which became more evident in the 1970s. Lasch argued that self-realisation rather than social change became the defining feature of this politics (ibid.: 4). In making this charge he attracted much criticism from many on the Left who saw vocal social movements as holding potential for radical social change or even revolution. Whilst Lasch shared some of the formal aims of the Left, he viewed the radical lifestyle politics of the period as a diminished public politics and a form of therapy for the individual. Conspicuous lifestyle expressions of politics expanded, but political possibilities at the level of society diminished.

This is apposite for today's lifestyle politics, and arguably is a process that has gone much further. For example, it is striking in studies of volunteer tourism how the self and personal identity are constantly invoked (Wearing, 2001; Callanan and Thomas, 2005; Pearce and Coghlan, 2008; Sin, 2009, among others). Certainly the emphasis on transforming the consciousness of the volunteers is suggestive of this take on politics. These experiential, personal missions are closely associated with acting on the issue of development in much advocacy of volunteer tourism, but social change through development is barely on the agenda.

Is the personal political?

The extension of personal qualities (awareness, care, responsibility) associated with private actions (individual purchases, lifestyle, behaviour) directly into the realm of politics is central to the claims made for volunteer tourism. That is not to suggest that these qualities in themselves are corrosive in any way, but that a healthy public, political scene involves both a recognition of a world beyond the individual, and the capacity of the individual to involve themselves in understanding, commenting upon and negotiating issues that cannot be explained or understood through a discourse focused on personal qualities and private interventions.

However, some view the developments Sennett describes in a positive light. For example, feminists have long politicised the private sphere as a site of the oppression of women, and the slogan 'the personal is political', originating from feminist Carole Hanisch's oft quoted 1969 essay, neatly sums up the desire to view the intimate and private world of relationships as a directly political issue for discussion in the public sphere (Hanisch, 1969). Similarly, it is argued that the politicisation of lifestyle opens up new avenues for a politics more relevant to everyday experience (Barnett *et al.*, 2011). That just about everything is political has become a hallmark of poststructuralist political thought, drawing upon neo-Foucauldian ideas of dispersed power. For radical human geographers, 'affect' and 'care' are very much a part of an expanded realm of the political (Smith, 1998; Silk, 2004; Madge, Raghurama and Noxolo, 2009).

The argument that 'the personal is political' presupposes a clear recognition of the social roots of personal struggles. The defining difference today is a lack of influence of social critiques – the public sphere has been emptied out by the apparent exhaustion of both mainstream and alternative political philosophies (Leys, 1996; Laidi, 1998; Furedi, 2005; Chouliaraki, 2013). For Laidi (1998) the end of the Cold War destroyed the principal framework through which politics of the Left and Right were defined. Chouliaraki (2013) concurs – the grand narratives of Left and Right, flawed as they were, mediated between private experiences, emotions and reflections on the one hand, and a public realm of political contestation on the other. Their decline has not been paralleled by new ideas that facilitate political reflection and judgement. We might meet in the coffee shop, but it is unlikely we will talk politics when politics seems devoid of principle and passion. The nearest we might get to politics, if we accept the ethical consumption agenda, is to worry about what brand of coffee we are drinking, or whether our offspring's gap year is ethically compromised.

Can volunteer tourism be political?

The trend towards a politics that revolves around responsibility, awareness and care – indicative of a blurring of the private and the public as discussed above – is clearly reflected in human geography's 'moral turn'. 'Geographies of care' (Silk, 1998) and 'responsibility' (Popke, 2006; Massey, 2004) hold that through an awareness of our place in global trade, which can be developed through a focus on the commodity chains that link producer and distant consumer, we may be able to extend a 'care' normally associated with those close to us (by family ties, geography or nationality) to distant others (Barnett and Land, 2007: 5). We can buy ethically here to extend care globally. Giddens, for example, comments:

> Our day to day activities are increasingly influenced by events happening on the other side of the world. Conversely, local lifestyle habits have become globally consequential. Thus my decision to buy a certain item of clothing has implications not only for the international division of labour, but for the Earth's ecosystem.
>
> (1994: 5)

This argument has been developed quite extensively in relation to Fairtrade (e.g. Lyon, 2010; Nicholls and Opal, 2005). One recent intervention, *Globalising Responsibility: the Political Rationalities of Ethical Consumption*, sees recognition of these links between everyday consumption and global, often distant, impacts as part of developing of a new progressive politics (Barnett *et al.*, 2011). However, aware of the charge that this is a consumer politics with limited horizons the authors further argue that such an approach can lead to wider 'political' recognition of how to change society (ibid.). In other words, they understand some of the limitations of ethical trade but consider it as more prepolitical than postpolitical, looking forwards towards new forms of social and political agency.

A number of writers on volunteer tourism also assert the potential for the experience to feed into a new progressive politics. McGehee considers volunteer tourism as a 'conduit for the development of social movements' (2012: 92). She considers that this as not solely about support for others in less fortunate situations, but as a reaction of westerners to their own oppression. Oppression in this formulation is not in the more traditional sense of the denial of equal rights, but a generalised oppression of the human spirit brought about by modern capitalism. She argues that people are 'expected to work longer hours and consume more, often having no space for genuine human interaction' in a world in which 'the TV, cell phone, iPod and the computer all fight for our attention, distracting us from the cultivation of human exchange in both our homes and in our communities' (Hollinshead, 1998, cited in McGehee, 2012: 94). The political focus here is anticonsumerism.

Conran accepts that 'the politics of personal feeling cannot address the institutional … reasons for injustice' (2011: 1463). Yet rather than questioning the efficacy of volunteer tourism and consumer politics, she seeks a more politically aware version of the same. For Conran, critical refection on the right type of experience through volunteer tourism can contribute to an 'emerging social conscience' which is 'at the heart of volunteer tourism's potential as a platform from which to develop structural change' (ibid.: 1467). This is wishful thinking. Whilst it may prompt questions, experience, in and of itself, provides no basis for how to answer them.

Sin also wants to politicise volunteer tourism – she feels that 'if it continues to be organised in an apolitical manner that neglects critical engagement with issues of democracy and active citizenship, it could easily fail to achieve its purported intentions of being "pro poor" or addressing social inequalities' (2009: 497). The flaw with Sin's analysis is not her call for a more enlightened volunteering, but the way she frames the issue. Sin wants volunteer tourism to be more responsible so it can address social inequalities. This fails to differentiate between politics and experience. In fact tourism cannot address social inequalities. The notion of seeing leisure travel as a part of one's political identity in this sense can only diminish politics and make it a personal project rather than a social one, focused on private qualities such as responsibility and awareness rather than subject to public debate and contestation.

Simpson's argument that gap year projects need to engage with structural relationships is akin to saying that holidays need to be political (Simpson, 2004: 689). This formulation tries to tie lifestyle and politics closer together, or to make lifestyle more political. This misses the point that the close association between lifestyle and politics is itself the limiting characteristic. Deproblematising lifestyle – freeing it from a close association with social and political ambitions – could contribute to a reproblematising of development as a social question involving interests, perspectives and power – in short, politics.

'Volunteer vacations'

'As a volunteer you can begin to halt the tide of the nasty effects of globalisation and instead promote the benefits of international understanding and cooperation.

Volunteer vacations change your perspective on the world, teach you new skills, and greatly affect the lives of others.

See a new part of the United States, or a completely different country. Help other people. Relax. Make new friends. Learn a few words in a new language or resurrect the Spanish that you haven't used since high school. Change your perspective on what it means to be rich or poor, first world or third world, developed or underdeveloped. Consider what it might mean to be "overdeveloped".

How? Take a volunteer vacation.

You're only likely to experience some kind of paradigm shift and to look at yourself, our country, or the world in a new way.'

(McMillon *et al.*, 2009)

'The 100 best volunteer vacations to enrich your life'

'Ask any seasoned volunteer. People in developing countries have a depth of joy, a richness to which those of us consumed with material things are often blind.

The reasons for wanting to volunteer vary. Some do it to gain experience, to add some heft to the old resume. Others want to test themselves or to act out a fantasy. Still others are tired of waiting for their government to act. They want to stand up and be counted. Now.

You'll see a country for what it really is, neither a sound bite nor a statistic of those who died in the last tragedy. You'll get to know real people. You'll work beside them, share their struggles, learn what it feels like live in a village where no men are over 50, and experience what it's like to be invisible to outsiders.'

(Grout, 2009: 9)

Writing out politics

Rather than responsible or caring approaches to consumption having political potential, or being in need of a more political or structural focus, the focus on private virtue tends to rule politics out of court. *Globalising Responsibility* (Barnett *et al.*, 2011) attempts to link ethical consumption to wider political goals.

Yet what is considered responsible and ethical (organic agriculture, Fairtrade, green tourism) is a given. Political contestation of ideologies of development (the substance of politics) is completely absent from the analysis. Those who do not act in the prescribed ethical manner are deemed to lack awareness and the opportunity to act responsibly (ibid.). This is antipolitical and also patronising.

An example of this trend from the advocacy of ethical tourism is responsible tourism guru Harold Goodwin's casual equating of being responsible with the promotion of organic agriculture and localism: 'You just have to look at the growth in ethical consumption. People buy into Fairtrade, organics and local produce, so why would you not take that mindset with you when you go on holiday?' (Cited in Rowe, undated.) The political, contested question of agricultural production can be ignored as the 'responsible' side of the argument is simply assumed as for organic agriculture and localism. Politics is circumvented by a prescriptive discourse of responsibility.

There is hence an implicit assumption in the politics and geographies of care that buying non-Fairtrade food – for example factory farmed or genetically modified food – means you do not care (or lack 'awareness', a slightly less pejorative characterisation). That you may believe farming utilising genetic modification to be a better option for the future of the developing countries, or that you may not believe consumption can really address political issues of development, is outside of the framing of this debate. Similarly, buying a cheap package holiday is not failing to care. It could reflect the view that holidays are a poor vehicle for advancing social and political aspirations. It could legitimately reflect the opinion that the eco-options that go under the heading 'responsible' more often than not have nothing much to offer by way of development (Butcher, 2003 and 2007).

In this way the 'moralisation of tourism' leads away from a political framing of the issue of development (Butcher, 2003). 'Caring and uncaring', 'responsible and irresponsible', 'aware and lacking awareness' not only reproduce a discourse of personal qualities as the key to acting on the world, but they close down debate on other development perspectives that do not conform to the characteristics favoured by the ethical lobby. In this sense the rise of personal ethics mirrors the decline of both politics and an attendant public discussion of political morality.

Is closer better?

Ethical consumption has been viewed as a progressive humanising of politics (see Shah *et al.* 2012), although it could more accurately be characterised as a *personalising* of politics. In contrast to abstract theories and grand narratives, it appears to bring political issues down to everyday human relationships. This is attractive in postpolitical times. For example, Fairtrade is assumed absolutely central to ethical consumption (Barnett *et al.*, 2011). Consumers are encouraged to consider the impact of their consumption upon the producer, and to pay more to support them, very often on the basis that they are small-scale and organic producers. Fairtrade favours small-scale production over large, and organic over modern methods such as the use of genetically modified organisms. The latter is barred from being certified as Fairtrade. Cafés and Fairtrade packaging and publicity carry pictures of the farmers and their names – the connection is personal.

In similar vein, the clientele of 'ethical' holiday companies are also encouraged to make a difference to the individuals they meet. Through tourism, the care associated with ethical consumption is experienced personally. If care is seen as bonds associated with those close to us (family, friends, neighbours) then tourism is an exemplary case as tourists are both literally and metaphorically developing a closeness to the objects of their care (Meletis and Campbell, 2007; Smith, 2014).

Volunteer tourism is the clearest example of all these aforementioned trends: it links holidays *directly* to the *active* promotion of wellbeing of the people *personally* encountered. Consumers not only see and learn a little of the workers producing their product – their village, their names, their farms – but also visit them and work with them on projects to assist their livelihoods.

This personalised aspect of volunteer tourism plays well at a time when government and business are often prefixed by 'big', 'distant' or even 'dirty', and in the social sciences 'grand narratives' are not only not in evidence, but are regarded as untenable by many (Minca and Oakes, 2011).

Volunteer tourism fits well with contemporary antipolitics and, as with almost all ethical tourism, often adopts a populist rhetoric – 'the local community' are often contrasted favourably to the perceived impersonality of governments and global trade (Butcher, 2007, 2011; see for an example Scheyvens, 2002).

Yet the closeness to the object of our care, in itself, provides no moral guidance. If we encounter a poor trader selling coral necklaces whilst on holiday, should we buy it to help the man and his family (but contribute to the destruction of the coral) or refuse to buy to discourage damage to the reef (but leave the man and his family poorer)? Holiday encounters, like all consumption-based ethical strategies, seem to expand the possibilities for moral action, but in doing so narrow the scope for moral agency.

A similar argument is well made by Mohan with regard to development volunteers. He points out that being over-reliant upon personal contact for one's view of development tends to encourage a conception of development and inequalities based upon a fetishised view of culture, rather than through an emphasis on fundamental historical and material inequalities (Mohan, 2001). The personal touch – 'being there' – is no substitute for politics. The intimate and 'can do' approach of volunteer tourism seems to encourage this fetishised view of culture as personally experienced, cut adrift from a wider political framing.

Whilst reducing literal distance between the subject and object of care does not lead to enlightenment, the same can be argued with regard to metaphorical distance. Chouliaraki argues that the immediacy of emotional and personal responses to humanitarian issues – for example a response to a poster of a poor orphan, a half built village school or a film showing poor children – without the mediating influence of a healthy 'agonistic' public sphere, leave us with a 'posthumanitarianism': an inability to think and act beyond a 'self-oriented' moral framework in relation to the suffering of others (Chouliaraki, 2013). She argues, in effect, to re-establish some metaphorical distance between the humanitarian individual and the object of their humanitarian impulse. That distance makes possible a framing of the issues in social and political terms, and a contestation of the roots of the humanitarian matter at hand. It enables people to see others as having agency within the context of their lives and society, rather than collapsing this into their own search for ethical identity.

Without this distance, Chouliaraki argues that solidarity will be fleeting, fitting around the lifestyle of the humanitarian, reacting to the surface rather than the substance of the issue. This is the limit of lifestyle, personalised politics informed by the language of responsibility, awareness and care. Ultimately, as Chouliaraki shows, the best intentions can feed in to a narcissism, where the issues we wish to act upon are a backdrop for a western search for selfhood and purpose – a 'self-oriented' moral project (Chouliaraki, 2013).

This argument is illustrated by the controversies over volunteer tourism to orphanages in poor countries such as Cambodia (Pitrelli, 2012; Al Jazeera, 2008). The impulse to help a poor child motivates volunteer tourism, and this, alongside the personal benefit the tourist will get through the experience, is what is promised by volunteer tourism operators. Yet the political and economic roots of poverty, the social struggles of families to get by, the construction of childhood in different circumstances – issues in many ways for the public sphere and for Chouliaraki's metaphorical distance from the object of concern – appear beyond the individual (2013). The social agents are the tourists alone, and the children, their families and societies are presented as victims and bystanders. Most children in the orphanages are reported as having at least one surviving parent, but in Cambodia tourist dollars and the emotions of well-meaning volunteers can push desperate families apart (Pitrelli, 2012).

Effectively, albeit unwittingly, help is available if you give up your child, but unavailable if you do not. Care from a western volunteer attracts money, but care for your own children does not. Outcomes for the children in some orphanages are reported to be poor to the extent that some volunteer tourism companies have recently withdrawn from this area of work (Francis, 2013). Beyond the material outcomes, orphanage volunteer tourism reinforces damaging political assumptions of a dependent, vulnerable third world in need of the benevolent, caring westerner (Guiney, 2013).

That is to neither condemn nor praise volunteering in foreign orphanages, but to point out the poverty of such actions as social or political interventions in development. Charity is always an admirable impulse. However, the Good Samaritan who crosses the road to help someone in need is quite different to the volunteer tourist. One simply acts in a charitable manner; the other claims to be a player in development whilst gathering valuable life experience. Private charity as conspicuous lifestyle politics diminishes politics. It may also diminish charity as a selfless act for others.

Intimacy, friendship and private reflection

Given the importance of 'being there' in volunteer tourism, and the emphasis on personal encounters, it is unsurprising that tourists' accounts focus on intimacy.

Heart-rending moments with children, winning the trust or respect of local people and vignettes featuring poignant personal encounters are all prominent. Marketing literature for volunteer tourism often features pictures of volunteers holding children or enjoying leisure time with happy, smiling youths.

There is a sense in much commentary on modern society that social intimacy has declined as societies have become richer. We may be richer materially, but whether societies are happier or more caring has been called into question. The sentiment is well expressed in McMichael's influential text *Development and Social Change*:

> The 'development debate' is re-forming around a conflict between privileging the global market and privileging human communities: Do we continue expanding industry and wealth indefinitely, or do we find a way that human communities (however defined) can recover social intimacy, spiritual coherence, healthy environments, and sustainable material practices?
>
> (2000, xiii)

Volunteer tourism is one way to try to rediscover social intimacy. The quest for intimacy is also linked to smallness of scale and sustainability (McMichael, 2000), both typically characteristic of volunteer tourism projects. The sense of a dearth of social intimacy at home is projected onto the project of development abroad.

Intimacy in volunteer tourism

Lea, a 21-year-old Norwegian volunteer in Thailand:

'I think for me it has been holding the kids' hands and, like one of them grabbed my arm and it is just things like that that makes it worth it'.

(cited in Conran, 2011: 1460)

Jen, a 22-year-old American woman:

'[Thailand is] a land of smiles, I will miss that. When I reach America, I am going to hate it, everyone walks with their heads down, they don't look at each other. Lots of love, there is so much love here. I want to bring that back with me.'

(cited in ibid.)

Tracy, a community volunteer in Mongolia:

'There were many "gifts" that I brought home with me, none of them that you could see or touch. I gave them "things". What they gave was more precious than gold. Whenever I need courage to live this life back in "civilisation", I think of the nomads.'

(Projects Abroad, undated)

Inspire Volunteer Abroad volunteer, India:

'If you really engage with the people and the teaching you will bond with the villagers and children in ways you never imagined, becoming part of a culture and community which you never heard of before.'

(Inspire Volunteer Abroad, undated)

Giddens (1991) argues that modern bureaucratic institutions appear to have diminished social intimacy. Capitalism relies on abstract and bureaucratic structures, the private sphere more upon intimacy and private judgement. He argues that the private sphere itself has been crowded out by modern society. This also means that we then endow human intimacy with a magical quality it may not possess – just as the family can act as a haven in a heartless world, so intimacy can be respite from the big, distant institutions of modern society.

Today, when these institutions attract little loyalty or support, the search for intimacy has a distinct edge. Development linked to grand narratives and big business or government is out of fashion in the public face of development. The public world of political contestation has turned into a dry landscape where people passively fulfil obligations (Negreiros, 2010).

Development that comes with intimacy and personal development on the other hand is reflected and affirmed in public culture. Sennett argued that due to the demise of the public sphere: 'Social relationships of all kinds are real, believable and authentic the closer they approach the inner psychological concerns of each person' (1986: 259). The private sphere has become the social place, the place to act, the place where belief and commitment are possible. Volunteer tourism, with its personal and experiential take on agency and on development, caters for the desire for intimacy and a private route into social issues. This, however, severely limits the potential for it to contribute to any actual material development.

With reference principally to the family, Bauman argues that the destruction of the divide between the private and the public realms profoundly affects personal relationships. These relationships have lost their distinctive intimate and private quality. No longer shielded from the interests and judgements of the public world, personal relationships can become another form of investment (Bauman, 2000).

The analysis can be extended to private relationships and encounters, such as those involved in volunteer tourism. Here, the construction of meaningful personal friendships may be hindered by the fact they are immediately a part of the calculation implicit in the market for cultural capital and desire to gain global citizenship. Prospective private friendships are at once development interventions in the lives of those prospective friends, interventions shaped by prior cultural and political assumptions. The open ended and exploratory character of personal encounters, through which private individuals may develop autonomy (and indeed friendships), may be curtailed.

So just as Sennett argued that the diminished boundary between the private and public spheres erodes politics, it also erodes distinctive private space where personal relations can develop shielded from the logic prevailing in the public realm. The private sphere, thus constituted, is, in turn, a prerequisite for the performance of an active individual role in the public sphere.

Hence not only does ethical volunteer tourism and the claims made for it mark a diminished politics and public sphere, it also does nothing to benefit our capacity to reflect and act in our private lives. This is striking given the claims of volunteer tourism to contribute to personal transformation. In everyday life we are constantly confronted with moral dilemmas – do we castigate the naughty child, do we give the beggar some money, do we tell our friend that they are in a bad relationship? Do we volunteer at the Cambodian orphanage, send a donation or redouble our attempt to understand and challenge the reasons why Cambodia is a poor country? We develop and exercise our own moral autonomy in these everyday encounters. There is no benefit in prescribing or proscribing private, lawful individual behaviour in the name of ethical conduct.

In the past travel was associated with escape from the formal institutions of family, education and work. Now, through the language of modern volunteer tourism it is closely aligned with each – families are encouraged to be involved with their offspring's volunteer project, universities accredit it and regard it as a measure of global citizenship, and it is deemed a valuable intercultural learning process to fit young people for employment in ethical business. It is worth considering whether the baggage of ethics, safety and citizenship that volunteer tourists are obliged to carry around with them actually inhibits the capacity of travel to be life changing or transformative for the individual.

The thrill of travel is to negotiate new people, new places, cultures and relationships. It may well provide opportunity for critical reflection on one's life and prompt moral reflection on the issues of the day. However, making the exciting private journey of the traveller subject to a set of ethical imperatives linked to a particular political outlook cuts down the potential for personal development – or in Sennett's terms, the development of moral autonomy through reflection in the private sphere (1993).

Conclusion

Contrary to the claims that volunteer tourism is or points towards progressive politics, it diminishes politics in two senses. First, politics is diminished as personal qualities replace political categories in public development discourse. This reflects and reinforces the emptying of the public sphere in postpolitical times. Second, ethical tourism is a particular outlook masquerading, via terms such as 'care' and 'responsibility', as a universal ethics for all. It narrows discussion of different development options by, a priori, placing some (ethical tourism) on a moral pedestal and consigning others (mass tourism) to the ethical wilderness.

References

Al Jazeera. (8 November 2008) Cambodia's 'fake' orphans (video). Available at http://www.youtube.com/watch?v=emYlQf-7piA (accessed 17 September 2014).

Arendt, H. (1958) *The Human Condition*, University of Chicago Press, Chicago.

Arendt H. (2006) *Between Past and Future: Eight Exercises in Political Thought*, Penguin, London.

Baillie Smith, M. and Laurie, N. (2011) International volunteering and development: global citizenship and neo-liberal professionalisation today, *Transactions of the Institute of British Geographers*, 36, 545–59.

Barnett, C., Clarke, N., Cloke, P. and Malpass, A. (2011) *Globalising Responsibility: the Political Rationalities of Ethical Consumption*, Wiley-Blackwell, London.

Barnett, C. and Land, D. (2007) Geographies of generosity: beyond the 'moral turn', *Geoforum*, 38 (6), 1065–1075.

Bauman, Z. (2000) *Liquid Modernity*, Polity, Oxford.

Benson, A. (ed.) (2011) *Volunteer Tourism: Theoretical Frameworks and Practical Applications*, Routledge, London.

Blackburn, S. (2001) *Being Good: a Short Introduction to Ethics*, Oxford Paperbacks, Oxford.

Brown, F. and Hall, D. (2008) Tourism and development in the global south: the issues, *Third World Quarterly*, 29 (5), 839–49.

Buckley, R. (2003) *Case Studies in Ecotourism*, CABI, Wallingford.

Butcher, J. (2003) *The Moralization of Tourism*, Routledge, London.

Butcher, J. (2007) *Ecotourism, NGOs and Development: a Critical Analysis*, Routledge, London.

Butcher, J. (2011) Volunteer tourism may not be as good as it seems, *Tourism Recreation Research*, 36 (1), 75–76.

Butcher, J. (2012) Putting the personal into development. *Spiked Review of Books*, May. Available at http://www.spiked-online.com/review_of_books/article/12487 (accessed 17 October 2014).

Butcher, J. and Smith, P. (2010) 'Making a difference': volunteer tourism and development, *Tourism Recreation Research*, 35 (1), 27–36.

Callanan, M. and Thomas, S. (2005) Volunteer tourism, in *Niche tourism*, (ed.) M. Noveli, Butterworth-Heinemann, Oxford, pp.183–200.

Chang, H. (2010) Hamlet without the Prince of Denmark: how development has disappeared from today's 'development' discourse, in *Towards New Developmentalism: Market as Means Rather than Master*, (eds) S. Khan and J. Christiansen, Routledge, Abingdon.

Chouliaraki, L. (2013) *The Ironic Spectator: Solidarity in the Age of Post Humanitarianism*, Polity, London.

Conran, M. (2011) They really love me! Intimacy in volunteer tourism, *Annals of Tourism Research*, 38 (4), 1454–73.

Crystal Cruise Line (undated), Crystal Cruise Line web pages. Available at www.crystalcruiseline.com/infoDetails.php?newsID=371&newsCode=news (accessed 17 September 2014).

Fennell, D.A. (2003) *Ecotourism: an Introduction, second edition*, Routledge, London.

Fennell, D. and Malloy, D.C. (2007) *Codes of Ethics in Tourism: Practice, Theory, Synthesis*, Channel View, Bristol.

Francis, J. (2013) *Orphanage Volunteering Holidays Removed*. Responsibletourism.com. Available at http://blog.responsibletravel.com/orphanage-tourism/ (accessed 17 October 2014).

Furedi, F. (2005) *Politics of Fear: Beyond Left and Right*, Continuum, London.

Giddens, A. (1991) *Modernity and Self Identity: Self and Society in the Late Modern Age*, Polity, Oxford.

Giddens, A. (1994) *Beyond Left and Right: the Future of Radical Politics*, Polity, Oxford.

Glaser, E. (21 March 2014) Bring back ideology: Fukuyama's 'end of history' 25 years on. *Guardian* blogs. Available at http://www.theguardian.com/books/2014/mar/21/bring-back-ideology-fukuyama-end-history-25-years-on (accessed 21 March 2014).

Grout, P. (2009) *The 100 Best Volunteer Vacations to Enrich Your Life*, National Geographic Books, Washington DC.

Guiney, T. (2013) Constructive development or commodification of orphans? Orphanage tourism impacts in Cambodia, unpublished paper presented at the American Association of Geographers conference, Los Angeles, March.

Habermas, J. (1989) *The Structural Transformation of the Public Sphere: an Inquiry into a Category of Bourgeois Society*, Polity Press, Cambridge.

Hanisch, C. (1969) The personal is political. Available at http://www.carolhanisch.org/CHwritings/PIP.html (accessed 17 October 2014).

Hollinshead, K. (1998) Tourism, hybridity and ambiguity: the relevance of Bhabha's third space cultures. *Journal of Leisure Research*, 30 (1), 121–56.

Honey, M. (2002) Conclusions, in *Ecotourism and Certification*, (ed) M. Honey, Island Press, Washington DC, pp.357–71.

Hunt, B. (2003) *The Timid Corporation: Why Business is Terrified of Taking Risk*, Wiley, Chichester.

Inspire Volunteer Abroad (undated) Inspire Volunteer Abroad web pages. Available at http;//www.inspirevolunteer.co.uk/countries/india/volunteer-in-india/ (accessed 17 October 2014)

International Centre for Responsible Tourism's (undated) From the Cape Town Declaration to an international network. International Centre for Responsible Tourism. Available at http://www.icrtourism.org/who-is-the-icrt/

Jacoby, R. (1999) *The End of Utopia: Politics and Culture in an Age of Apathy*, Basic Books, New York.

Krippendorf, J. (1987) *The Holidaymakers: Understanding the Impact of Leisure and Travel*, Butterworth-Heinemann, London.

Laidi, Z. (1998) *A World Without Meaning: the Crisis of Meaning in International Politics*, Routledge, Abingdon.

Lasch, C. (1979) *The Culture of Narcissism: American Life in an Age of Diminishing Expectations*, Norton, New York.

Leys, C. (1996) *The Rise and Fall of Development Theory*, James Currey, London.

Lyon, S. (2010) *Coffee and Community: Maya Farmers and Fair-Trade Markets*, University Press of Colorado, Colorado.

Madge, C., Raghuram, P. and Noxolo, P. (2009) Rethinking responsibility and care for a postcolonial world. *Geoforum*. Themed Issue: *Postcoloniality, Responsibility and Care*, 40 (1): 1–126, 5–13.

Massey, D. (2004) Geographies of responsibility, *Geografiska Annaler*, 86B, 5–18.

McGehee, N.G. (2012) Oppression, emancipation, and volunteer tourism: research propositions, *Annals of Tourism Research*, 39 (1), 84–107.

McGehee, N. and Andereck, K. (2008) 'Pettin' the critters': exploring the complex relationship between volunteers and the voluntoured in McDowell County, WV, USA and Tijuana, Mexico, in *Journeys of Discovery in Volunteer Tourism: International Case Study Perspectives*, (eds) K.D. Lyons, and S. Wearing, CABI, London, pp.3–12.

McMichael, P. (2000) *Development and Social Change: a Global Perspective*, Pine Forge Press, Thousand Oaks, CA.

McMillon, B., Cutchins, D. and Geissinger, A. (eds) (2009) *Volunteer Vacations*, Chicago Review Press, Chicago.

Meiksins-Wood, E. (2008) *Citizens to Lords: a Social History of Western Political Thought from Antiquity to the Middle Ages*, Verso, London.

Meletis, Z.A. and Campbell, L.M. (2007) Call it consumption! Reconceptualising ecotourism as consumption and consumptive, *Geography Compass*, 1 (4), 850–70.

Minca, C. and Oakes T. (2011) Real tourism, in *Real Tourism: Practice, Care, and Politics in Contemporary Travel Culture*, (eds) C. Minca and T. Oakes, Routledge, Abingdon.

Mohan, G. (2001) Beyond participation: strategies for deeper empowerment, in *Participation: the New Tyranny*, (eds) B. Cooke and U. Kothari, Zed Books, London, pp.153–67.

Mouffe, C. (2005) *On the Political*. Routledge, London.

Negreiros, J. (2010) Democracy and intimacy: contrasting views on a controversial connection, in *Problems of Democracy: Probing the Boundaries* (e-book), (eds) N. Bechter and Gabriele de Angelis, Inter-Disciplinary Press, Oxford, pp.169–75.

Nichols, A. and Opal, C. (2005) *Fair Trade: Market-Driven Ethical Consumption*, Sage, London.

Nolan, J.L. (1998) *The Therapeutic State: Justifying Government at Century's End*, New York University Press, New York and London.

Pearce, P.L. and Coghlan, A. (2008) The dynamics behind volunteer tourism, in *Journeys of Discovery in Volunteer Tourism: International Case Study Perspectives*, (eds) K.D. Lyons and S. Wearing, CABI, London, pp.130–43.

Pitrelli, M. (3 February 2012) Orphanage tourism: help or hindrance? *Daily Telegraph*. Available at http://www.telegraph.co.uk/expat/expatlife/9055213/Orphanage-tourism-help-or-hindrance.html (accessed 17 September 2014).

Popescu, L. (2008) *The Good Tourist*, Arcadia Books, London.

Popke, J. (2006) Geography and ethics: everyday mediations through care and consumption, *Progress in Human Geography*, 30 (4), 504–12.

Projects Abroad (undated) Volunteer abroad with children in orphanages and care centres. *Projects Abroad* web site. Available at http://www.projects-abroad.co.uk/volunteer-projects/care/ (accessed 17 October 2014).

Robbins, T. (6 July 2008). Are you being greenwashed?, *The Observer*. Available at http://www.theguardian.com/travel/2008/jul/06/green.ethicalholidays (accessed 17 October 2014).

Rowe, M. (undated) Future of tourism dossier. Available at http://www.responsibletravel.com/resources/future-of-tourism/dossier.htm (accessed 14 January 2014).

Ryan, A. (2012) *On Politics: a History of Political Thought from Herodotus to the Present*, Allen Lane, London.

Scheyvens, R. (2002) *Tourism for Development: Empowering Communities*, Prentice Hall, Harlow.

Sennett , R. (1986) *The Fall of Public Man*, Penguin, London. Original 1977.

Sennett , R. (1993) *The Fall of Public Man*, Penguin, London.

Shah, D.V., Wells, C., Friedland, L.A., Kim, Y.M. and Rojas, H. (eds) (2012) *Communication, Consumers, and Citizens: Revisiting the Politics of Consumption* (The Annals of the American Academy of Political and Social Science Series), Sage, London.

Silk, J. (1998) Caring at a distance, *Ethics, Place and Environment*, 1, 165–82.

Silk, J. (2004) Caring at a distance: gift theory, aid chains and social movements, *Social and Cultural Geography*, 5 (2), 229–51.

Simpson, K. (2004) 'Doing development': the gap year, volunteer-tourists and a popular practice of development, *Journal of International Development*, 16 (5), 681–92.

Simpson, K. (2005) Dropping out or signing up? The professionalisation of youth travel, *Antipode*, 37 (3), 447–69.

Sin, H.L. (2009) Volunteer tourism: 'Involve me and I will learn'?, *Annals of Tourism Research*, 36 (3), 480–501.

Skinner, Q. (1978) *The Foundations of Modern Political Thought: Volume 1, The Renaissance*, Cambridge University Press, Cambridge.

Smith, D.M. (1998) How far should we care? On the special scope of beneficence, *Progress in Human Geography*, 22 (1), 15–38.

Smith, M. and Yanacopulos, H. (2004) The public faces of development: an introduction, *Journal of International Development, Special Issue: The Public Faces of Development*, 16 (5), 657–64.

Smith, P. (2014) International volunteer tourism as (de)commodified moral consumption, in *Moral Encounters in Tourism*, (eds) K. Hannam and M. Mostafanezhad, Ashgate, London, pp.31–45.

Spenceley, A. (ed.) (2012) *Responsible Travel: Critical Issues For Conservation and Development*, Routledge, Abingdon.

Swyngedouw, E. (2009) The antimonies of the postpolitical: in search of a democratic politics of environmental protection, *International Journal of Urban and Regional Research*, 33 (3), 601–20.

Thaler, R.H. and Sunstein, C.R. (2009) *Nudge: Improving Decisions about Health, Wealth, and Happiness*, Penguin Books, London.

UNEP/WTO (2002) *The Quebec Declaration on Ecotourism*, UNEP and WTO, Paris (forms pp.65–73 of the Final Report).

Van Creveld, M. (1999) *The Rise and Decline of the State*, Cambridge University Press, Cambridge.

Vrasti, W. (2012) *Volunteer Tourism in the Global South: Giving Back in Neoliberal Times*, Routledge, Abingdon.

Wearing, S. (2001) *Volunteer Tourism: Experiences that Make a Difference*, CABI Publishing, Wallingford.

Wearing, S. and McGehee, G. (2013) *International Volunteer Tourism: Integrating Travellers and Communities*, CABI Publishing, Wallingford.

Wood, K. and House, S. (1992) *The Good Tourist: A Worldwide Guide for the Green Traveller*, Mandarin, London.

Woolford, J. pers. comm. (2002) Tourism policy officer in international policy unit of WWF-UK, on 30 May 2002, telephone interview to WWF-UK offices in London.

Zizek, S. (1999) *The Ticklish Subject: the Absent Centre of Political Ontology*, Verso, London.

5　The lifestyle politics of volunteer tourism

It is, on the face of it, odd to write about tourists in the context of a discussion about development in the global South. Yet the last three decades have witnessed a growing literature on an ethical tourism that links the personal conduct and purchasing habits – the lifestyle – of holidaymakers to development outcomes (Krippendorf, 1987; Poon, 1993; Patullo, 1996; Wearing and Neil, 1999; Scheyvens, 2002; Hickman, 2007; Pattulo and Minelli, 2009). This literature almost invariably focuses on small-scale, community-oriented tourism that explicitly aims to promote both conservation and community wellbeing.

This growth is part of a more general trend – the invocation of ethical consumerism as an important way to assist communities in less developed countries (Harrison *et al.* 2005). Volunteer tourism is exemplary of such attempts to 'make a difference' (Simpson 2004; Raymond, 2008). At issue is the lifestyle politics through which this noble impulse is channelled.

The politics of lifestyle is far from new – many associate the counterculture of the 1960s with the heyday of radical and experimental lifestyle. We argue that as the political ideologies that influenced the 1960s have waned, lifestyle has become less overtly political but, counterintuitively, more central to politics.

Giddens, through his concept 'life politics', developed a useful perspective on what is novel about contemporary lifestyle and politics (1991, 1994). This is a politics that involves a reconfiguration of the relationship between individuals and political issues, away from the grand narratives of Left and Right, in favour of one that takes individual identity as its starting point. Life politics revolves around individuals' attempts to reposition themselves culturally in the context of their own lives and through this to try to act upon their immediate environment and also more broadly in society and politics (Giddens, 1991).

Such attempts most often shun grand political projects or ambitious visions of the future, setting them apart from earlier lifestyle politics of the 1960s and 1970s. However, they have become central to social and political agency precisely because of the exhaustion of grand political narratives and the consequent crisis of political identity, and even crisis of meaning, characteristic of contemporary society (Furedi, 2014).

The roots of tourism's lifestyle politics

Tourism's lifestyle politics has a long pedigree. Leisure travel seems to carry its own tourism culture wars reflecting divisions of ideology and class. According to Feiffer, with reference to the Grand Tour of the eighteenth century: 'In the era of the "lifestyle", one expressed oneself more at leisure than at work; by one's hobbies, one's possessions, one's tastes. The tour represented all of them' (1985: 224). These tastes were markers of privilege, the tour a cultural rite of passage for the landed aristocracy.

In the 1840s Wordsworth sought to preserve the Lake District from tourists by opposing the building of the Kendal to Windermere railway. He wanted to preserve not only the beauty of the Lakes, but also something intrinsic to human culture that he thought was being destroyed by the industrial revolution (Urry, 1996). The Romantic reaction to the industry and urbanisation of the industrial revolution sought a sense of selfhood in tradition and in nature in the midst of fundamental change in the mode of life.

A fear of mass society was often evident. Thomas Cook, pioneer of mass tourism, was held in low regard by those who felt the masses were ill equipped to benefit from travel. The rise of Cook's seaside tourism in the UK prompted the clergyman and diarist Francis Kilvert to write in the 1870s that, 'of all noxious animals, the most noxious is a tourist' (Fussell, 1982: 40).

Yet more influential at that time was a positive attachment to the benefits of industrialisation, including leisure travel. Cook's sentiment was widespread amongst all classes, evidenced by the popularity of his tours. For him travel was: 'for the millions [who could] o'erleap the bounds of their own narrow circle, rub of rust and prejudice by contact with others, and expand their sales and invigorate their bodies by an exploration of some of nature's finest scenes' (cited in Withey, 1997: 145). Cook sold thousands of tickets to the Great Exhibition of 1851. Many of humble means committed their meagre disposable income to travel on the recently established railways to the Crystal Palace in Hyde Park, London, to witness a celebration of science and industry as progress.

For the newly mobile masses, and for the Romanic critics, how people chose to spend their leisure time – their lifestyle – reflected different beliefs and values relating to how society should be.

Lifestyle politics: counterculture and travel

Dean MacCannell's sociology has expressed more modern roots, post-Second World War, for today's tourism lifestyle politics. MacCannell's seminal *The Tourist: a New Theory of the Leisure Class* (1976) and his reflections in *Empty Meeting Grounds: the Tourist Papers* (1992) suggest that in a modern world in which authentic human contact is stymied by the market some tourists seek more human and humane personal and cultural relations through tourism. However, all too often this search for authenticity is doomed to be in vain as tourism itself becomes subject to ever greater commercialisation. Nonetheless, he argued that this process holds out possibilities for greater understanding and a better world.

MacCannell was influenced by the turn of the Left in the early 1970s, from analysing production and the social relations emerging from this to a focus on consumption and culture. MacCannell himself shifted his allegiance from the working class as a force for progressive change on the world stage, to cultural encounters and the possibility of new subjects arising from these (1992). In effect, the cultural subject is substituted for the political subject, a development characteristic of much radical thought on the Left (Gitlin, 1995; Heartfield, 2002).

MacCannell considers the encounters between tourist and host and suggests that they can have positive outcomes for cultural understanding leading to progressive social and political consequences. Tourism in this analysis is also a metaphor for society. MacCannell is interested in wider possibilities through intercultural and interpersonal encounter. This notion is central to Wearing's study *Volunteer Tourism: Experiences That Make a Difference* (2001), and much of the wider advocacy of the benefits of volunteer tourism since. Much of the writing around volunteer tourism looks critically, but hopefully, at the potential for this niche to contribute to a greater level of understanding and empathy, leading to a more progressive politics.

Sometimes presented in contrast to MacCannell's thesis is historian Daniel Boorstin's critique of inauthentic travel in his 1962 collection of essays, *The Image: a Guide to Pseudo-Events in America* (1992 – originally published 1962). The essays were a response to what Boorstin saw as the superficial consumption-based culture in post-1945 America. MacCannell's radical search for agency is sometimes contrasted to Boorstin's conservative bemoaning of America's loss of authenticity. The coincidence of conservative and radical thinking here over the emptiness of modern mass consumer society is itself notable.

The countercultural character of the tourists described by MacCannell (although they would have identified themselves as travellers and baulked at the notion that they were tourists) is reflected in sociologist Erik Cohen's categorisation of leisure travellers. Cohen sees a section of tourists as looking for a 'spiritual centre', either at home or in another society, and classifies them in this way (1979). Cohen's spiritual centre is a place where the individual finds meaning to their life, and where they feel part of something authentic. He identifies, amongst other categories, 'experiential tourists' and 'existential tourists', both alienated from and critical of their home culture, both seeking meaning through travel in places and relationships deemed more authentic, more human. Cohen identifies these 'alternative' tourists with the counterculture (ibid.).

MacCannell's thesis, and Cohen's discussion of the search for a spiritual centre, mirror influential political analyses of the times. Most notably Marcuse, in his *One Dimensional Man* (1964), sets out a radical cultural critique of mass consumption, technological rationality and the bureaucracy of modern capitalism. These are sentiments that prefigure the critique of mass consumption so influential today and evident in the advocacy of ethical tourism niches such as volunteer tourism, albeit the latter lacking the radical political perspective of Marcuse.

Wolin in *The Wind from the East: French Intellectuals, the Cultural Revolution and the Legacy of the 1960s* also concurs with MacCannell's characterisation of the times. For Wolin: 'The 1960s was a period of acute disenchantment with western modernity'. Opposition, such as the revolts in Paris in May 1968 'targeted impersonal, bureaucratic and highly formalised modes of socialisation' that operated 'without regard for persons' (2012: 11). A number of prominent French intellectuals were at the forefront of developing poststructuralism as a key reference point in the social sciences. Rather than capitalism as a system that held back historical progress, it was rationalism and progress itself – the legacy of the Enlightenment – that were increasingly the target of poststructuralist analyses.

Bell, in *The Cultural Contradictions of Capitalism*, had already by 1964 described the cultural mood and its relationship to the economic system and its values: 'The social structure today is ruled by an economic principle of rationality, defined in terms of efficiency in the allocation of resources; the culture, in contrast, is prodigal, promiscuous, dominated by an antirational, anti-intellectual temper' (1964: 432–33). Given the diagnosis of society's ills as emanating from lived experience in a modern, soulless bureaucratic society, it is unsurprising that the reaction to this took an at times 'antirational' cultural form, through lifestyles associated with the counterculture.

The protests of May 1968 in Paris threw up an example of tourism's culture wars. Situationist-inspired protestors smashed the windows of Club Med's offices in Paris and wrote 'Club Med: a cheap holiday in other people's misery' in the street. The bourgeois lifestyle, characterised by affluence and luxury, was the target for these protestors (their graffiti later reprised by punk band The Sex Pistols, in the 1977 hit 'Holidays in the Sun'). Club Med epitomised despised bourgeois culture and the protesters represented the counterculture.

Others expressed their countercultural opposition to 'the system' in the spirit of the phrase 'turn on, tune in, drop out', popularised by hippie icon Timothy Leary. The hippie trail to India and Nepal of the 1960s and 1970s, in reality practised by few, led young critics of the system to seek alternative ways to live through cannabis, mysticism and a rejection of authority. Separating one's self from the mainstream, spiritually and materially, was characteristic of Jack Kerouac's *On the Road* (1957). Kerouac, an icon to a generation of travellers, refused to buy in to the American dream, and lived and wrote on the margins, seeking an alternative consciousness to that of mainstream America.

The Lonely Planet guide books were originally associated with a countercultural rejection of mainstream society and carried a similar radical caché for a while in the 1970s. The first official guide to the hippie trail, published in 1974, included advice on cannabis use and how to obtain fake identification. It followed the success of a makeshift stapled-together edition designed to raise cash to enable its writers, Tony and Maureen Wheeler, to get home. Hippies on the trail were trying to free their minds, and whilst the revolution remained in their heads, there was an association with societal as well as personal change.

The relationship of this countercultural rejection of bourgeois values, and often Enlightenment values, to political ideology is key. There is much truth in Bell's argument in *The End of Ideology* (1960) that the ideologies that had defined the preceding 150 years were exhausted and unlikely to define the post-Second World War period. Two world wars fought amongst the developed powers and the failed attempt at radical social change in the USSR made grand ideologies less tenable. Also, relative stability and economic growth after the war opened up possibilities for some to embrace culture as a realm within which they could experiment and promote alternatives to bourgeois norms (Furedi, 2014).

Lifestyle nonetheless retained a connection to radical social change. The 1960s in particular is closely associated with radicalism and cultural experimentation (Markwick, 1999), and trends in tourism lifestyles reflected that. The politics of Left and Right, as competing social and economic systems, continued to animate politics. The existence of an alternative system in the USSR (albeit one that had degenerated and lost any claim to be a higher form of society in the eyes of most people), the post-Second World War growth of the state vis-à-vis the market, relatively strong class allegiances through political parties and trade unions in many countries, and the demands for freedom made by national liberation struggles all sustained a belief in societal change in radical thought. Countercultural lifestyle retained a future orientation – radical and utopian visions of how society could and should be were in evidence (ibid.). A sizeable rebellious section of principally middle-class youth in this period not only exhibited their disdain for bourgeois culture as they saw it, but also sought to develop a political consciousness that could challenge the system (ibid.).

Anarchist green thinker Murray Bookchin's ideas are indicative of how lifestyle was seen by some as intimately linked to social change, even revolution, in the 1970s. He argued the following:

> [T]he revolutionary movement is profoundly concerned with lifestyle. It must try to live the revolution in all its totality, not only participate in it. It must be deeply concerned with the way the revolutionist lives, his relations with the surrounding environment, and his degree of self-emancipation.
>
> (1986: 67, original 1971)

For Bookchin the 'personal is political' in that it was linked to distinctly political movements for substantial or even revolutionary change. This is in stark contrast to today, when the idea of societal change and a movement to bring it about are neither on the agenda nor on the horizon. Green lifestyles today would be more closely associated with shopping for organic food, utilising solar panels and perhaps looking to make your holiday an ethical one. Personal behaviour and consumption are linked to ethical imperatives, but not social change of any sort.

From lifestyle politics to lifestyle in place of politics

Published eleven years after MacCannell's *The Tourist: a New Theory of the Leisure Class* (1976) was a further influential book addressing tourism's lifestyle politics, Jost Krippendorf's *The Holiday Makers: the Impacts of Leisure and Travel* (1987). Krippendorf pioneered the now more widely developed critique of mass tourism. For Krippendorf mass tourism has become a 'restless activity that has taken hold of the once sedentary human society' (ibid.: xiii) and results in damage to host communities and the local environment as mass migration encounters social and environmental limits. Krippendorf's study, along with Turner and Ash's prescient *The Golden Hordes* (1975) published fifteen years earlier, set the tone for the academic critiques of mass tourism that now add up to a significant body of work across a range of related disciplines, probably constituting an orthodoxy (Butcher, 2003).

Krippendorf not only criticised mass tourism, he also suggested that consumption is an area where individuals can adopt lifestyle patterns that are more favourable both to host communities and the wider environment. His view was that consciousness of consumption can lead to a more aware and ethical individual thus humanising travel (1987). In making this argument he draws a clear link between tourists' consumption and development outcomes for their hosts. This sentiment is a key element of the advocacy of volunteer tourism and ethical tourism more broadly.

In spite of commonalities – both are critical of mass consumption and advocates of lifestyle politics – the shift from MacCannell (1976) to Krippendorf (1987) is important. MacCannell writes in the context of the Cold War and the end of the post-war boom (the Oil Crisis of 1973 is often cited as an event that marked the end of the post-war 'golden years' of consistent economic growth and optimism). By the 1980s, however, the belief in the state to reform society was far less tenable, and the USSR from being a symbol of another system being possible came to represent the impossibility and undesirability of attempts at social change on a grand scale, a view brought vividly into relief by the fall of the Berlin Wall in 1989 (Giddens, 1994, 2000; Jacoby, 1999). The influence of class had waned, with its political expression in unions and parties of the Left greatly diminished. Capitalism's erstwhile critics accepted and even embraced market forces as 'no one any longer has any alternatives to capitalism' (Giddens, 1998: 43).

Yet the collapse of alternatives did not vindicate capitalism and the market. Anti-communism had proved important in cohering conservative and social democratic elites who were able to present their politics favourably vis-à-vis their Cold War opponents. For Laidi (1998) the end of the Cold War precipitated a far-reaching 'crisis of meaning'. Similarly Judt notes that in Europe 'after 1989 there was no ideological project of Left or Right on offer' (2005, 33). There are no longer narratives-based competing ideologies and positive visions of the future that connect the individual to their society. Moreover, new political narratives have not emerged. Consequently the market has taken on the appearance of an eternal reality in political and social debates (Heartfield, 2002). Fukuyama's *End of History* thesis (1992), following soon after the end of the Cold War, presenting a contemporary world in which all the big ideological issues have been settled, is emblematic of the sense of closure of grand politics.

Hence by the late 1980s – when Krippendorf's assertions on the theme of ethical holidays start to become mainstream – the scene was set for lifestyle to become in one sense less, and in another more, political. In contrast to the radicalism and political conflict of the 1960s, by the 1980s there are few pretensions to radical social change. Today's ethical lifestyle tourists articulate their aspirations in terms of care, awareness and helping rather than reform or revolution. In this respect tourist lifestyles are far less political, and in fact are conveyed in terms of ethics rather than politics. This bears out the view of political theorist Chantal Mouffe, who argues that moral issues have become central to contemporary political rhetoric and the struggle between 'right and wrong' has replaced the struggle between 'right and left' (2005: 5). The common portrayal of volunteer tourism as 'ethical' (and also mass tourism as unethical) is indicative of this.

Yet at the same time, the demise of erstwhile narratives of the Left and of the Right mean that today ethical lifestyle has come to define public life in a way not evident in the past. Volunteer tourists, along with Fairtrade shoppers and ethical consumers generally, try to make their mark on the world directly through lifestyle. Whereas in the 1960s and 1970s lifestyle was linked to political ideologies, today lifestyle *is politics*, with ideology absent.

Also it is notable that when compared to the 1960s and early 1970s – the frame of reference of MacCannell's and Cohen's original ideas – lifestyle politics in the last thirty years has lost much of its critical and experimental character. In the earlier period alternative travel was aligned to a counterculture, to an implied critique of the prevailing norms and values of society. Kerouac-inspired and Lonely Planet-guided travellers stood outside of the contemporary modes of citizenship. From the 1990s onwards – the period in which Krippendorf's *The Holiday Makers* has found resonance in academic writing and popular culture – alternative tourism is applauded and even sponsored by governments, industry, school and university as a route to responsible global citizenship.

Claims for a more overtly political lifestyle politics are still in evidence, but in today's climate are unconvincing. For example, one contemporary advocate of lifestyle politics asserts that: 'The way one dresses, the food one eats, even the people one chooses to have sex with, can become overtly political acts. Radical lifestyle politics reconfigures the everyday life of the individual into an ongoing struggle against domination' (Portwood-Stacer, 2013).

Yet it is difficult to envisage anything being 'overtly political' in times that are distinctly postpolitical (Zizek, 1999). Rather, lifestyle politics is a useful idea today in the sense that people are trying to act upon the wider world through consumption and in the context of their everyday lives. It is 'political' in that it fills the space vacated by the retreat of politics as previously understood.

Secondly, the idea that lifestyle politics is part of an 'ongoing struggle against domination' suggests that there is a committed and coherent movement with a common identifiable enemy, an oppressor. Again, this is not useful as it does not at all describe political consciousness today. Volunteer tourists and others engaged in similar lifestyle political acts often do have a sense of injustice, and a desire to promote fairness, justice and wellbeing. Their politics may make reference to tyranny and 'the West', but their focus is on responsibility, caring for others and 'checking' their own privilege. The oppressor is rarely if ever identified. When it is, it would be more accurate to describe it as a moral deficit residing in business, government and people generally (volunteer tourists would include themselves in this – they seek to challenge their own prejudices, check their own privilege and enlighten themselves through experience).

Lifestyle as politics or even *lifestyle in place of politics* would be suitable terms for what we describe. We retain the term lifestyle politics for three reasons. First, this term (or similar) is in common usage, so it is useful to clarify what it really represents today.

Second, governments, lacking purpose and clarity over their own role, and in search of ways to connect with their electorates, have adopted lifestyle and behaviour as key themes. No longer are western governments focused upon macroeconomic policy, and certainly not ideology. Healthy living, 'happiness', pro-social behaviour and community have become established over the last thirty years as important focuses for mainstream politics in the West.

Alternative politics is even more focused on lifestyle. Radical debates on the Left were once configured around 'reform or revolution' and which would provide the best path towards a new way of organising society in the interests of the working class. Support for national liberation abroad was a major focus of radical campaigning in the post-Second World War period up to the 1980s. Today neither reform nor revolution appear tenable. As for campaigns focused abroad, ethical consumption via Fairtrade is the most prominent focus for public concern over poverty in the global south (Darnton and Kirk, 2011). 'Alternative' politics are strongly focused on lifestyle. Where and how one holidays is part of this.

Third, reflecting the changes in society, influential thinkers in sociology (e.g. Giddens) and human geography (e.g. Barnett) have theorised lifestyle on the basis of its political import. Whilst accepting consumption in and of itself may be limited as a form of politics, they see its potential in a wider remoralisation of political life spurred through a recognition of a lack of fairness in trade. Some see it as prefiguring a wider shift in political consciousness well beyond lifestyle (Barnett *et al.*, 2011). This case is made in relation to volunteer tourism by, amongst others, Wearing (2001) and Higgins-Desboilles and Mundine (2008).

What you need to know about humanitarian tourism

'As a volunteer, you will soon realize that helping others is actually just a way of helping yourself. If you strip away all the luxury and convenience of your everyday life, you will get the chance to really do some introspection. Seeing the sunset from the other side of the world might just give you that perspective and outlook on life that you were craving.'

(Simmons, 2013)

Life politics and ethical consumption

Giddens' category of 'Life Politics' describes well the contemporary relationship between lifestyles and the realm of politics. Giddens identified a shift from the traditional politics of emancipation, embodied in collective identities informed by the politics of Left and Right, towards 'life politics' (Giddens, 1994, 1998, 2000). For Giddens, contemporary society is no longer bound by the fixities of tradition or custom, as we are living in a 'post-traditional' world. Life politics represents the attempt to create morally justifiable lifestyles, and to bridge the gap between the individual and social change, when we are no longer guided by traditions such as class or religion. Hence life politics is a reconfiguration of the relationship of the individual to their society, through which individual identity becomes the key site of political change (Giddens, 1994, 1998, 2000; Kim, 2012). This certainly chimes with the literature on volunteer tourism (Wearing, 2001), and also with the publicity put out by gap year companies (Bindloss *et al.*, 2003).

It is worth noting that it also chimes with the much more extensive literature on ecotourism and development. Ecotourism promotes the view that inspiring experiences that deepen an appreciation of the value of nature also promote good, 'sustainable' development outcomes, and hence the prefix 'ethical' is often applied (Wearing and Neil, 1999; UNEP/WTO, 2002a and b; Fennell, 2003). Many of the conservation projects on which tourists can volunteer could be regarded as ecotourism, as they often attempt to bring benefits to sustain communities and environments (Coghlan, 2006). The volunteer tourist simply takes this to its logical conclusion, structuring their visit around conservation and community development directly rather than assisting simply this through their spending whilst on holiday.

Life politics, as advocated by Giddens, urges a reconfiguration of the relationship of the individual to society against a historical backdrop where 'the terms left and right no longer have the meaning they once did, and each political perspective is in its own way exhausted' (1994: 78). For Kim, life politics 'emphasises the demise of dichotomous ideologies (capitalism versus socialism or liberalism versus socialism) and the rise of pluralistic, diverse, lifestyle concerns and value systems' (Kim, 2012: 149).

This new relationship focuses on consumption. Ethical consumption – what and where we buy the things we need and desire – is not only a part of the process of negotiating our own identities, but can also connect with the lives of others who have produced these same things, as well as with other issues such as the environment (Giddens, 1991). For example, it is argued that consumers can force a more ethical agenda onto companies through exercising choice in favour of products that are deemed more sustainable or that involve a fairer outcome for workers (Hertz, 2001; Nicholls and Opal, 2005; Jackson, 2006; Paterson, 2006).

An early example of life political ethical consumption was *The Green Consumer Guide* (Elkington and Hailes, 1988) which sold some 350,000 copies in 1988. It was illustrative of the growth of this ethical strategy as a focus for people's aspirations. It is from around this time that gap year companies have grown greatly in number and size (ATLAS/TRAM, 2008: 5), and ethical tourism has become a significant issue amongst human geographers and others studying tourism and development.

Of course, engaging in social action through consumption may be social action only for those who can afford to pay. This is certainly the case with many volunteer tourism placements which given their cost are generally the prerogative of the middle class (ATLAS/TRAM, 2008: 39). As a result ethical tourism has been labelled, albeit with some cynicism, as 'trendies on the trail' (Mowforth and Munt, 1998: 115). Some volunteers are candid about their relative prosperity, and express a desire to harness their privilege creatively to help others.

However, the impulse to volunteer is widely held amongst young people, and encouraged through schools, universities and government (Jones, 2004, 2011). It is a pervasive agenda, often seen as a part of developing citizenship or, in the case of international volunteering, global citizenship. Gap years are accredited, structured and even praised by politicians for their contribution to citizenship (Heath, 2007; Jones, 2011). Simpson has argued that the gap year experience is increasingly seen by employers as desirable and can thus be considered, in part, as a training ground for future professionals, who accumulate 'cultural capital' through their volunteer work (2005). This is in stark contrast to the associations of travel in the 1960s and 1970s, in which a year out was more likely to be taken in the spirit of Kerouac, dropping out rather than signing up for global citizenship (Butcher, 2003).

The primacy of the politics of consumption is a result of the collapse of the contestation of production, the questioning of capitalism as a social and economic system (Kim, 2012). Baptista goes as far as to argue that: 'Consumption of commodities is becoming the purpose of human existence and thus a major determinant of both identities and self-cultivation, at least in most of the "North"' (2012: 640).

This shift to the politics of consumption is also often regarded as in part due to changes in production in western economies and the nature of work. Andre Gorz (1982, 1985) identified a shift in the technical organisation of production that led to a more individuated, less collective 'postindustrial' experience in the workplace, contributing to a decline in traditional collective allegiances relating to work. This is mirrored by the post-Fordism thesis, developed in the pages of the left journal, *Marxism Today* (Hall and Jacques, 1989; Kumar, 1995). For Bauman the result of these trends is that contemporary society engages its members primarily as consumers rather than producers (1996). As a consequence of these changes Bauman characterises contemporary society as moving from 'heavy' and 'solid' modernity to 'light' and 'liquid' modernity (Bauman, 2000).

Post-Fordism and 'liquid modernity' are notable in that they mark a shift from the politics of production (and social class) to consumption (and individual identity) in radical thinking. The consumption of alternative tourism brands is just one example of the wider politics of consumption and the ethical and even radical credentials of these activities are prominent in the debates (Paterson, 2006; Butcher, 2007).

This process, through which the world of consumption and lifestyle has become prominent in the search for selfhood, and also in social and political issues, can only be outlined here. But it is in this spirit that many volunteer tourists seek to effect change as a part of a self-conscious shaping of their own identity, their own sense of self. The trip can be a prominent part of a person's 'biography' in this respect. Indeed, a biographical approach to selfhood is associated with life politics generally (Bauman, 2000) and travel specifically (Heath, 2007). The narrative is that of the individual rather than of the society visited. The self-reflexive character of the trip is evident too. It is suggested that as part of the volunteer experience, 'interactions occur and the self is enlarged or expanded, challenged, renewed or reinforced', and as such, the experience becomes an 'ongoing process which extends far beyond the actual tourist visit' (Wearing, 2001: 3). Similarly, for McGehee and Santos (2005) participation in the volunteer project is the key element in the consciousness raising of the individual participant, and their route to an ethical life. To misquote the old feminist slogan, 'the personal becomes (life) political'.

Kim usefully describes life politics as 'private *yet public*' (2012: 150; italics added). Hitherto private aspects of life, focused on consumption, acquire the public status of a politics of sorts. As discussed in Chapter 4, this association of private virtues such as care and responsibility with politics is contradictory. In endowing everyday activities like shopping and holidays with political meaning, politics appears enlarged. Yet the apparent growth of ways in which to act upon society represents a narrowing of human subjectivity away from collective solutions to social problems towards individual life choices, and away from democratic and potentially democratic state governments towards companies and non-governmental organisations that have no democratic remit. The political subject can act in new and innovative ways through lifestyle, yet the content of these actions is fleeting and shallow.

A 'private yet public' politics effectively facilitates what Christopher Lasch referred to as a 'projection of the search for self into politics' (1991: 28). In his well-known polemic *The Culture of Narcissism*, Lasch describes the growing role of the private in the public realm, and the decline of deliberation and judgement beyond individual feelings and identity. This, for Lasch, diminishes public politics to a form of therapy for the individual – political possibilities at the level of society lose out. Certainly, the emphasis on transforming the consciousness of the volunteers invoked earlier by Wearing and others is suggestive of the wider trend towards a therapeutic outlook on politics.

Making a difference

i-to-i Travel: *'make a difference whilst creating memorable experiences'.*

Antipodeans Abroad: *'enrich your travels and benefit a small country'.*

Real Gap Experience: *'there are people, places and creatures all over the world who could do with any time and effort that you are willing to give to help make their lives a little better'.*

(cited in Ingram, 2008)

Conclusion

Lifestyle has consistently been invoked in tourism's very own culture wars, be that the disdain for the ascendant industrial capitalist class on holiday by the grand tourists of the aristocracy, the disparagement of Cook's tours by Victorian

Romantics, the contempt for Club Med's luxury by protesting Parisian students in May 1968 or the moral authority over mass tourism assumed by 'ethical' brands such as volunteer tourism today.

Today the exhaustion of the political ideologies of liberalism and collectivism leaves these culture wars not as reflections of the political landscape but as a central aspect of it. Alternative tourism lifestyles revolve around moral distinctions (ethical, unethical) premised on a search for selfhood, and in the absence of ideology these moral distinctions are at the expense of political reflection. Volunteer tourism is indicative of this.

As a way of describing volunteer tourism, life politics is apposite. As a strategy for promoting politics it is ineffective. The narcissistic search for meaning and political progress through ethical lifestyle only reinforces antipolitics and an antidevelopment outlook.

References

Association for Tourism and Leisure Education/Tourism Research and Marketing (ATLAS/TRAM) (2008) *Volunteer Tourism: a Global Analysis*, Association for Tourism and Leisure Education, Arnhem.

Baptista, J.A. (2012) The virtuous tourist: consumption, development, and nongovernmental governance in a Mozambican village, *American Anthropologist* 114 (4), 639–51.

Barnett, C., Clarke, N., Cloke, P. and Malpass, A. (2011) *Globalising Responsibility: the Political Rationalities of Ethical Consumption*, Wiley-Blackwell, London.

Bauman, Z. (1996) *Life in Fragments: Essays in Postmodern Moralities*, Polity, Oxford.

Bauman, Z. (2000) *Liquid Modernity*, Polity, Oxford.

Bell, D. (1960) *The End of Ideology*, Free Press, Glencoe, IL.

Bell, D. (1964) *The Cultural Contradictions of Capitalism*, Basic Books, New York.

Bindloss, J., Hindle, C. and Fletcher, M. (2003) *The Gap Year Book: Lonely Planet Gap Year Guide*, Lonely Planet Publications, London.

Bookchin, M. (1986) *Post-Scarcity Anarchism, second edition*, Black Rose Books, Montreal.

Boorstin, D. (1992) *The Image: a Guide to Pseudo-Events in America*, Vintage, London. Original 1962.

Butcher, J. (2003) *The Moralization of Tourism*, Routledge, London.

Butcher, J. (2007) *Ecotourism, NGOs and Development: a Critical Analysis*, Routledge, London.

Coghlan, A. (2006) Volunteer tourism as an emerging trend or an expansion of ecotourism? A look at potential clients' perceptions of volunteer tourism organisations, *International Journal of Nonprofit and Voluntary Sector Marketing*, 11 (3), 225–37.

Cohen, E. (1979) Rethinking the sociology of tourism. *Annals of Tourism Research*, 6 (1), 18–35.

Darnton, A. and Kirk, M. (2011) *Finding Frames: New Ways to Engage the UK Public in Global Poverty*, Oxfam/DFID, London.

Elkington, J. and Hailes, J. (1988) *The Green Consumer Guide: From Shampoo to Champagne, How to Buy Goods That Don't Cost the Earth*, Gollancz, London.

Feiffer, M. (1985) *Going Places: the Ways of the Tourist from Imperial Rome to the Present Day*, Macmillan London.

Fennell, D.A. (2003) *Ecotourism: an Introduction, second edition*, Routledge, London.

Fukuyama, F. (1992) *The End of History and the Last Man*, Penguin, Harmondsworth.

Furedi, F. (2014) *The First World War: Still No End in Sight*, Bloomsbury, London.

Fussell, P. (ed.) (1982) *Abroad: British Literary Traveling between the Wars*, Oxford University Press, Oxford.

Giddens, A. (1991) *Modernity and Self Identity: Self and Society in the Late Modern Age*, Polity, Oxford.

Giddens, A. (1994) *Beyond Left and Right: the Future of Radical Politics*, Polity, Oxford.

Giddens, A. (1998) *The Third Way: the Renewal of Social Democracy*, Polity, Oxford.

Giddens, A. (2000) *The Third Way and Its Critics*, Polity, Oxford.

Gitlin, T. (1995) *The Twilight of Common Dreams: Why America is Wracked by Culture Wars*, Henry Holt Books, New York.

Gorz, A. (1982) *Farewell to the Working Class*, Pluto, London.

Gorz, A. (1985) *Paths to Paradise: on the Liberation from Work*, Pluto, London.

Hall, S. and Jacques, M. (eds) (1989) *New Times: the Changing Face of Politics in the 1990s*, Lawrence and Wishart, London.

Harrison, R., Newholm, T. and Shaw, D. (eds) (2005) *The Ethical Consumer*, Sage Publications, London.

Heartfield, J. (2002) *The 'Death of the Subject' Explained*, Perpetuity Press, London.

Heath, S. (2007) Widening the gap: pre-university gap years and the 'economy of experience', *British Journal of Sociology of Education*, 28 (1), 89–103.

Hertz, N. (2001) *The Silent Takeover*, Heinemann, London.

Hickman, L. (2007) *The Final Call: In Search of the True Cost of Our Holidays*, Eden Project, London.

Higgins-Desboilles, F. and Russell-Mundine, G. (2008) Absences in the volunteer tourism phenomenon: the right to travel, solidarity tours and transformation beyond the one-way, in *Journeys of Discovery in Volunteer Tourism: International case study perspectives*, (eds) K.D. Lyons and S. Wearing, CABI, London, pp.182–94.

Ingram, J.M. (2008) Volunteer tourism: does it have a place in development? Hons thesis, University of Tasmania.

Jackson, T. (ed.) (2006) *The Earthscan Reader on Sustainable Consumption* (Earthscan Readers Series), Earthscan, London.

Jacoby, R. (1999) *The End of Utopia: Politics and Culture in an Age of Apathy*, Basic Books, New York.

Jones, A. (2004) *Review of Gap Year Provision*, Department for Education and Skills (DfES), University of London. Available at www.dfes.gov.uk/research/ (accessed 17 October 2014).

Jones, A. (2011) Theorising international youth volunteering: training for global (corporate) work?, *Transactions of the Institute of British Geographers* 36, 530–44.

Judt, T. (2005) *Postwar: a History of Europe Since 1945*, Heinemann, London.

Kerouac, J. (1972) *On The Road*, Penguin Books, London. Original 1957.

Kim, Y.M. (2012) The shifting sands of citizenship toward a model of the citizenry in life politics, *Annals of American Academy of Political and Social Science*, 644 (1), 147–58.

Krippendorf, J. (1987) *The Holiday Makers: Understanding the Impact of Leisure and Travel*, Butterworth-Heinemann, London.

Kumar, K. (1995) *From Post-industrial to Post-modern Society: New Theories of the Contemporary World*, Blackwell, Oxford.

Laidi, Z. (1998) *A World Without Meaning: the Crisis of Meaning in International Politics*, Routledge, Abingdon.

Lasch, C. (1991) *The Culture of Narcissism: American Life in an Age of Diminishing Expectations*, Norton, New York. Original 1979.

MacCannell, D. (1976) *The Tourist: a New Theory of the Leisure Class*, University of California Press, Berkley and Los Angeles.

MacCannell, D. (1992) *Empty Meeting Grounds: the Tourist Papers*, Routledge, London.

Marcuse, H. (1964) *One Dimensional Man: Studies in the Ideology of Advanced Industrial Society*, Routledge & Kegan Paul, London.

Markwick, A. (1999) *The Sixties: Social and Cultural Transformation in Britain, France, Italy and the United States, 1958–74*, Oxford Paperbacks, Oxford.

McGehee, N. and Santos, C. (2005) Social change, discourse, and volunteer tourism, *Annals of Tourism Research*, 32 (3), 760–76.

Mouffe, C. (2005) *On the Political*, Routledge, London.

Mowforth, M. and Munt, I. (1998) *Tourism and Sustainability: New Tourism in the Third World*, Routledge, London.

Nicholls, A. and Opal, C. (2005) *Fair Trade: Market-Driven Ethical Consumption*, Sage, London.

Paterson, M. (2006) *Consumption and Everyday Life*, Routledge, London.

Patullo, P. (1996) *Last Resort: the Cost of Tourism in the Caribbean*, Cassell, London.

Patullo, P. and Minelli, O. (2009) *The Ethical Travel Guide: Your Passport to Exciting Alternative Holidays*, Earthscan, London.

Poon, A. (1993) *Tourism, Technology and Competitive Strategy*, CABI Publishing, Wallingford.

Portwood-Stacer, L. (2013) *Lifestyle Politics and Radical Activism*, Bloomsbury, London.

Raymond, E. (2008) Make a difference! The role of sending organizations in volunteer tourism, in *Journeys of Discovery in Volunteer Tourism: International Case Study Perspectives*, (eds) K.D. Lyons, and S. Wearing, CABI, London.

Scheyvens, R. (2002) *Tourism for Development: Empowering Communities*, Prentice Hall, Harlow.

Simmons, K. (2013) What you need to know about volunteer tourism, *Journal of Humanitarian Affairs*, 6 February. Available at http://journalofhumanitarianaffairs. blogspot.co.uk/2013/02/what-you-need-to-know-about.html (accessed 23 June 2014).

Simpson, K. (2004) 'Doing development': the gap year, volunteer-tourists and a popular practice of development, *Journal of International Development*, 16 (5), 681–92.

Simpson, K. (2005) Dropping out or signing up? The professionalisation of youth travel, *Antipode*, 37 (3), 447–69.

Turner, L. and Ash, J. (1975) *The Golden Hordes: International Tourism and the Pleasure Periphery*, Constable, London.

UNEP/WTO (2002a) *The Quebec Declaration on Ecotourism*, UNEP and WTO, Paris (pp.65–73 of the Final Report).

UNEP/WTO (2002b) *The World Ecotourism Summit Final Report*, UNEP and WTO, Paris.

Urry, J. (1996) *The Tourist Gaze*, Sage, London.

Wearing, S. (2001) *Volunteer Tourism: Experiences that Make a Difference*, CABI Publishing, Wallingford.

Wearing, S. and Neil, J. (1999) *Ecotourism Impacts, Potentials and Possibilities*, Butterworth-Heinemann, London.

Withey, L. (1997) *Grand Tours and Cooks Tours: a History of Leisure Travel 1750–1915*, Aurum, London.

Wolin, R. (2012) *The Wind from the East: French Intellectuals, the Cultural Revolution and the Legacy of the 1960s*, Princeton University Press. Princeton.

Zizek, S. (1999) *The Ticklish Subject: the Absent Centre of Political Ontology*, Verso, London.

6 Volunteer tourism and global citizenship

It has been argued that development volunteering's value may not and need not be in remarkable development outcomes, but that it resides in the creation of global citizens (Palacios, 2010). Global citizenship, in turn, is associated with a better world, and hence with development. Global citizens should, it is commonly argued, be best placed to discharge their responsibilities to others in distant lands, as they are less constrained by national interests.

Yet global citizenship involves a reworking of the concept of citizenship not only spatially from nation to globe, but also politically from nation and polity to non-governmental organisations and consumption. This chapter reflects on the association of volunteer tourism with global citizenship and suggests that this involves outsourcing citizenship to 'the globe' in a manner unlikely to benefit global understanding or development politics.

What is global citizenship?

The concept of citizenship originated with the *polis* in ancient Greece, and has always subsequently referred to membership of a political community. Modern citizenship is associated with modern nation states, and people's formal membership of these. The notion of a social contract is implicit in citizenship – citizens have rights within the state, sometimes inscribed in a constitution, as well as obligations under the law. The civic republican conception of citizenship emphasises the individual operating in the public sphere, an active part of political determinations.

Global citizenship offers a different model of citizenship. Here identification with a 'global community' is emphasised above that as a citizen of a particular nation (Bianchi and Stephenson, 2014). Global citizenship transcends geography or political borders and assumes that responsibilities or rights are or can be derived from being a 'citizen of the world'. This does not deny national citizenship, but the latter is often assumed to be more limited, morally as well as spatially (Dower, 2003). The advocacy of global citizenship is premised upon the straightforward view that important political issues such as environmental damage, climate change and development are global in nature. That it may not be possible to address global development-related issues from the perspective of national politics is a common assumption (ibid.). Issues are often presented as requiring private initiative (recycling, buying Fairtrade) linked to the globe (global poverty, globally unsustainable consumption), mediated through a global civil society of non-governmental organisations and globally oriented campaigns (Standish, 2012).

Global citizenship as a concept has emerged principally through discussions about the role of education (ibid.). Advocates argue that children should learn about the world within a framework of global citizenship, and be encouraged to see themselves as having obligations towards environmental, human rights and development issues well beyond their own nation. This is especially the case in geography, but also true elsewhere in the curriculum.

According to one typical definition, global citizenship means:

> enabling young people to develop the core competencies which allow them to actively engage with the world, and help to make it a more just and sustainable place. This is about a way of thinking and behaving. It is an outlook on life, a belief that we can make a difference.
>
> (Oxfam, undated).

The definition is typical of very many others emanating from school boards, educationalists and non-governmental organisations, and it is one that has been taken on by advocates of gap year projects and volunteer tourism.

Global citizenship and volunteer tourism

Volunteer tourism is very strongly associated with the development of global citizenship (Lyons and Wearing, 2011; Lyons *et al.*, 2012). It is argued that it can forge global citizenship by building long-term relationships and networks that promote activism in new social movements (McGehee 2002; McGehee and Santos, 2005), and through promoting the understanding of other cultures (Crabtree, 2008; Devereux, 2008; Howes, 2008; McGehee, 2012). Palacios has argued strongly that volunteer tourism should drop any pretences to development and in effect become about promoting intercultural understanding leading to greater global awareness (2010). Effectively, volunteer tourism is held to have the potential to contribute to the forging of a global conscience and understanding key to the nurturing of ethical, global citizenship.

Volunteer companies and non-governmental organisations have pushed this line in their advertising. The non-profit Yanapuma Foundation offers a global awareness programme in Ecuador and the Galapagos Islands with the following statement on global citizenship:

> The concept of Global Citizenship encompasses sociocultural, political, economic and environmental factors as students experience at first hand the reality of being from the 'other side' of the development process. As such it implies critical and transformative elements as students develop their understanding on both social/political and personal experiential levels. The experience of immersion in a new context in combination with relevant

academic support provides an intense learning environment that will transform both social/political awareness and personal awareness, informing future academic and professional development.

(Yanapuma Foundation, undated)

A recent scheme promoted by a leading UK volunteer company asserts the link to employability from global citizenship, stating that volunteering overseas 'will help boost the employability skills and global citizenship of young adults' (Raleigh International, 2009).

Politicians and commentators too have promoted the global citizenship benefits of a well used gap year or a volunteer tourism project. For example in the UK the International Citizen Service was launched in 2011 by the British Prime Minister, working through charities such as Raleigh International and Lattitude Global Volunteering. International Citizen Service volunteers are expected to contribute to sustainable development abroad (including addressing the millennium development goals) and also to their own global citizenship via short unskilled volunteer placements.

Such initiatives are part of a wider orientation of politics towards volunteering which has been promoted strongly by many governments (see various contributions to Paxton and Nash, 2002). In 2001 the UK Prime Minister announced he intended 'to give more young people the chance of voluntary community service at home and abroad between school and university' (Chen, 2002). This contributed to a growth in political interest in the role of volunteering in citizenship. There have been suggestions that volunteering may become a mandatory part of the school curriculum (Paxton and Nash, 2002).

Schools, colleges and universities have also identified with the role of gap year projects and volunteer tourism in producing global citizens (Pearce and Coghlan, 2008). Careers advisors and geography admissions tutors often see it as a boon for employment opportunities in ethically attuned businesses (Standish, 2008). A growing number of universities even give formal academic accreditation to volunteer tourism trips and see it as an important part of creating global citizens (Jones, 2011). In North America there is a long-standing tradition of international service through all levels of education, and this tradition has also adapted to the more commercial and lifestyle orientation of volunteer tourism.

Building a sense of global citizenship

'The theory behind a common humanity and fundamental human rights is closely tied to the idea of Global Citizenship, namely that as humans we all have the right to be treated equally and in turn treat each other equally. Each of these terms is strongly debated among academics and there is no set definition about what constitutes humanity, what (if any) rights are universal and what it means to be a global citizen (or whether such a concept can truly exist).

> *While academics can debate the extent, causes and meaning of this change, many of us feel more connected to others around the world, particularly as the result of the internet and modern communication tools. We are now able to see events from the other side of the world unveiling live, are able to communicate to people thousands of miles away and are able to visit countries more easily and more accessibly. Global Citizenship therefore is the idea that as individuals we should consider our actions and responsibilities in a global context. According to Oxfam Education "Global Citizenship is a way of thinking and behaving. It is an outlook on life, a belief that we can make a difference."*
>
> *At Lattitude Global Volunteering we see our vision of a world where all young people contribute to a more dynamic, caring and tolerant society as responsible global citizens. We see it as our mission to give young people the opportunity to experience the world beyond their community and to truly engage with it, to seek to develop young people's awareness and responsibilities towards themselves and others, and equip them with vital life skills.'*
> (excerpt from publicity, Lattitude Global Volunteering, undated)

Volunteer tourism, and international volunteering generally, lend themselves to the project of global citizenship. Global citizenship education emphasises experiential learning – learning through direct experience and encounter rather than through books and classes (Tiessen and Huish, 2014). Codifications of global citizenship often make reference to the development of 'attitudes' or an 'outlook' as opposed to the acquisition of knowledge about the world per se.

Citizenship divorced from power

There are arguments against global citizenship. Sociologist Bikhu Parekh argues that: 'If global citizenship means being a citizen of the world, it is neither practicable nor desirable' (2003: 12). Such a citizenship is divorced from the actual institutions of politics that matter – national governments. It is in the nation state that citizens can vote, or can strive for the vote, and through that alter the law, campaign for their rights and negotiate a social contract between state and individual (ibid.). The distant notion of a world state that would invalidate his opposition is also criticised as 'remote, bureaucratic, oppressive and culturally bland' (ibid.: 12). Global citizenship is a citizenship divorced from power.

Parekh's view is not to decry a knowledge of international issues, but to confront moral obligations towards others through a strengthened and agonistic relationship to national citizenship. He calls this being a 'globally oriented citizen' (ibid.), a national citizen who views their citizenship in the context of a political worldview.

Geographical education expert Alex Standish argues on a similar premise. He contends that global citizenship tends to bypass national politics in a world in which nations are the principal expressions of power and of democratic potential. Standish cites Heilman, who points out that 'cosmopolitan global citizenship … seeks to shift authority from the local to the national community to a world community that is a loose network of international organisations and subnational political actors not bound within a clear democratic constitutional framework' (cited in Standish, 2012: 66). Hence in bypassing national citizenship, global citizenship in a sense bypasses politics too.

The critiques of Standish and Parekh of the concept of global citizenship are apposite with regard to volunteer tourism's claims to be promoting it. Global citizenship through volunteer tourism means citizenship carried out through private companies and non-governmental organisations. No one, bar shareholders, votes for the directors of companies. Non-governmental organisations and non-profits are accountable to, at most, a self-selecting group of supporters. That is entirely appropriate for commercial companies and for campaigns and pressure groups, but it is not in any direct sense citizenship as previously understood.

If volunteer tourism initiatives are where people look to act in relation to development, then that has to be a restricted form of citizenship, as it bypasses the authority of the state, the latter having the potential to act as the political expression, democratically, of its citizens. The appeal of volunteer tourism to individuals as moral agents is worthy, but unmediated through an agonistic public sphere the parameters of this moral agency are extremely constrained.

As Standish points out, global citizenship rhetorically eschews nationally based political channels (sovereign governments, unions, etc.) (2012). It presents itself as having no axe to grind beyond that of the globe and the people living on it. It does not require political judgement, but instead emphasises awareness, responsibility and caring (see Chapter 4). This personalisation of the issues and the attendant encouraging of such private virtues is characteristic of volunteer tourism.

Hannah Arendt's political philosophy sheds some light on the limitations of global citizenship and on volunteer tourism's capacity to contribute to political enlightenment. She argued that the full realisation of human freedom requires the development of a public realm. Such a realm historically represents the extension of human freedom beyond the private sphere of the family and intimate life. It brings together the diversity of private experience and interest into an agonistic public space. Whilst 'everyone sees and hears from a different position' (Arendt, 1958: 57) through private experience, this public space is the basis for striving for a 'word in common' (ibid.: 58). In modern societies the public realm is defined by the citizenship of a state. Arendt's republican citizen is an active part of the political determinations of states, states being the principal institutions of power and authority.

A citizenship outside of the state is therefore a limited citizenship, unable to truly strive for a common world. Outside of an agonistic public sphere enabling the political contestation of ideas and power, private virtues are projected onto human problems unmediated by a political framing. Without the potential for politics to transcend or mediate differences, private experiences (by their very nature differential and varied) dominate.

For Arendt, 'freedom as a demonstrable fact and politics coincide and are related to each other like two sides of the same matter' (Arendt, 2000: 442). This is apposite with regard to volunteer tourism. Freedom to act without politics is an attenuated freedom. Despite the widespread rhetoric on the theme of developing one's ethical identity through travel and experience, individuality is in fact limited by the emphasis on self-development.

Global citizenship involves a shift away from a potentially political citizenship, seen as vital by Arendt, to a moral one, where morality is set apart from the contestation of ideologies and power. Contrary to the advocacy of global citizenship it is, for Arendt, through the process of politics that different societies and interests can try to achieve a 'world in common', itself a truly moral goal (Arendt, 1958). Global citizenship circumvents political power in the name of 'the globe', replacing it with pre-political virtues such as respect, care and responsibility, exercised by individuals through the market and the non-governmental organisation sector.

Was citizenship parochial? Is global citizenship cosmopolitan?

Underlying the advocacy of global citizenship is a sense that national citizenship is and has been limited and parochial, and that global citizenship has the potential to overcome these limits. This is doubtful. Thomas Paine famously said in *The Rights of Man* (1781): 'The world is my country, all mankind are my brethren, and to do good is my religion', yet spent his adult life agitating for republican citizenship in the USA, France and the UK, precisely so free citizens could shape their destiny and 'do good'. As Parekh argues, global politics may be better approached through a citizenship defined by a focus on political power and the institutions that wield it (2003).

Political campaigns and engagement have often taken the globe as their remit – this was the case well before global citizenship. For example, domestic issues in the nineteenth century such as bread prices were both national and global, influenced by grain imports and the duties levied. The political debates around these were shaped by this truism. Colonialism and imperialism were justified with reference to the globe, as was the opposition to them. On the Left of politics, there is a tradition of internationalism, born out of the belief that workers have no country and are united, globally, by their position in relation to their employers and capitalism, and their potential to advance society. Capitalism too has been justified with reference to its capacity to develop the globe and safeguard freedom around the world. National citizenship has never precluded global concern. The argument that today society faces intertwined and complex so called 'wicked' problems that are best addressed by global citizenship is difficult to sustain – were not the wars, famines and epidemics of the past as complex and severe as those today?

The principal difference between political movements of the past and those influenced by global citizenship today is that the former addressed these global issues through the contestation of politics, not through ethical imperatives to care or act responsibly alone.

It is precisely the crisis of citizenship itself that has led to rise of global citizenship (Standish, 2012). The citizen is no longer linked to society through the institutions of politics, as in the past. The public sphere is empty and uninspiring. Ideologies that facilitated political judgement are exhausted and new ideas and movements that might serve that function have not emerged. Global citizenship bypasses the public sphere and connects private feelings and qualities such as care, empathy and awareness, with the global issues of the day. Hence these issues are reinterpreted as issues of personal ethics rather than political contestation. The antipolitics that defines the period we live in is only reinforced by this trend.

Consider, for example, the category of solidarity, strongly implicit in volunteering overseas (Lewis, 2006). Critical citizens in the past may have shown solidarity (albeit all too rarely) with their peers in poorer countries on a political basis through a common identification of social class or interest, or through a recognition that the oppression of a people elsewhere strengthened the hand of your rulers at home. Solidarity today, through lifestyle political practices such as Fairtrade, is an adjunct to consumption, a fleeting moment of charity towards other individuals (Chouliaraki, 2013). Volunteer tourism arguably involves greater dedication, but the association of social action with leisure travel betrays a similar lack of ambition and commitment.

Citizenship, pre-global citizenship, has never been parochial or limiting with regard to global politics. Nonetheless, if global citizenship coincided with an increased knowledge of the globe and development, that would constitute a very strong argument for the new approach. Using the UK and US geography curricula as a guide, there is evidence that knowledge of the globe has actually declined alongside the elevation of 'global issues' through education for global citizenship (Standish, 2008, 2012). There has been an increased propensity to present environmental issues and poverty as ethical dilemmas and questions of personal responsibility, but on the basis of a declining breadth and depth of subject knowledge (Standish, 2008, 2012). All too often in global citizenship and in volunteer tourism issues are matters for one's personal contemplation and identity rather than social questions requiring a commitment to knowledge and truth seeking beyond the individual.

The claim that volunteer tourism promotes global knowledge draws on a pedagogy of 'experiential learning' that in turn is closely associated with global citizenship (Tiessen and Huish, 2014). Wearing (2001) notes experiential learning as an integral element of volunteer tourism. Raymond (2008) stresses the importance of experiential learning, enabling volunteers to reflect on their experience and to think critically about global issues. This type of learning is also a particular feature of US Service Learning-type volunteerism with universities often accrediting participating students (ibid.; Sin, 2009).

Experiential learning privileges individual experience and affect (Klob, 1984: 41), but deprioritises a commitment to knowledge and truth beyond experience. As one volunteer with WorldActivity Philippines put it 'you will learn more from being there in person than from watching 1,000 hours of documentaries, or reading 100 books about the society' (WorldActivity Philippines, undated). The emphasis on learning through experience is in line with a general elevation of experience over knowledge that is a feature of the claims made for volunteer tourism.

Anyone for a (government-sponsored) gap year?

'In 2009 the UK Department for Business, Innovation and Skills announced an initiative to assist students leaving university. In conjunction with expedition company Raleigh International (famous for arranging Prince William's volunteer placement in Chile in 2000), £500,000 of public funds was made available for 500 young people, under the age of 24, to travel to countries such as Borneo, Costa Rica, Nicaragua and India and participate in development and conservation projects.

Government interest in the gap year is not new – a 2004 UK government-commissioned report into gap years found a growing uptake (between 100,000 and 200,000, depending on the definition you take). The report's author, Professor Andrew Jones of Birkbeck College in London, argued that what is most important is making good use of the time through a structured work placement. Soft skills considered vital for the knowledge economy – team working, leadership and communication, organisational and interpersonal skills – can be developed in a gap year, he argued.

The then Minister of State for Higher Education, David Lammy, who launched the 2009 gap year scheme, reiterated the importance of "soft skills" such as "the communication and leadership skills that are so highly valued in the workplace". These "soft skills" apparently can't be gained through the lecture hall or seminar room, yet are essential for the competitiveness of the economy and for the individual seeking a decent job.

Besides, these "soft skills" have been being promoted in British schools and universities for some time, often to the detriment of subject knowledge. For example, in his recent book Alex Standish pointed out that the school geography curriculum has evolved in the direction of such soft skills, sometimes to the detriment of geographical knowledge. Universities, too, have adapted to the skills and citizenship agendas.

Certainly travel and work abroad can form part of broadening one's knowledge and taking a step into the adult world and taking responsibility for oneself. Such travel can be inspiring, challenging or just simply fun. Yet it seems to us that this sponsorship of the gap year, and encouragement to spend the time brushing up one's life skills with an eye on future employment, reduces the potential for the individual really to gain from taking a year out.

The government's partner in the 2009 initiative, Raleigh International, for a fee, brokered a placement, oversaw it, assessed the risk and even liaised with parents ... thus removing from the process the very things that would constitute growing up, taking initiative and responsibility.'

(Butcher and Smith, 2009)

'Doable' development

Global citizenship most often presents global action in terms of what an individual can do in the context of their daily life, through consumption and lifestyle. In schools global citizenship focuses on recycling, responsible shopping and Fairtrade. Volunteer tourism is another item on the global citizens' shopping list. Relevance to daily life, practicality and pragmatism are attractive features of global citizenship. As a global citizen you can always 'do your bit' for the planet or for others. Volunteer tourism fits this pattern. To buy the right holiday, to help build a school, to hug a distressed child – to *do* something – replaces the more distant, seemingly untenable and for some undesirable collective and political project of shaping transformative development and promoting economic growth.

Personal responsibility in the face of major global threats is a common theme in global development education – 'what would/will you do' is implicit (Standish, 2012). Standish looks critically at the tendency in global citizenship education to personalise and make development issues immediately relevant to the life and lifestyle of the individual. Clearly this approach is attractive. To be able to act and witness or at least visualise the outcome of one's actions can be inspiring and many volunteer tourists find it so. The problem is that what appears 'doable' in antipolitical times is limited. It places agency squarely in the context of one's own biography, one's own lifestyle, rather than in the context of the individual's capacity to challenge entrenched political ideas and institutions. Whilst taking personal responsibility is a progressive impulse, in the advocacy of global citizenship it is also *private* responsibility – responsibility posed in the context of one's lifestyle, consumption decisions and emotions cut adrift from a political framing.

Volunteer tourism appeals to the impulse to act in pursuit of a better world, a commendable impulse at all times. Where that impulse has few inspiring outlets through politics, it manifests itself increasingly through lifestyle and the rhythms of everyday life. The breadth of innovative ways to make a difference through lifestyle – shopping, telethons, wrist bands, volunteer tourism – correspond to the lack of ambition and vision with regard to what that difference might actually be.

The assumption of relativism

Standish points out that strong cultural and political assumptions are often hidden behind a value neutral veneer in the advocacy of global citizenship (2012). It is often a *particular* ethical stance presented as a *universal* ethical imperative for all. Foremost amongst the assumptions of this stance is, Standish points out, cultural relativism. This is often expressed in terms of 'respect' for other cultures (ibid.). Standish is not arguing against the often admirable personal quality of respect. Rather, he is arguing that in the advocacy of global citizenship respect for difference trumps recognition of common aspiration and values, and that this relativism can be a barrier to education and to opportunities for learning about other societies and people.

Malik has argued that cultural relativism reflects not only a lack of common values, but also an inability to aspire to such values (1996). It may be humanistic in the sense that it is rhetorically interested in people and their culture, but it stands against the tradition of humanism that holds that people, regardless of nation or culture, share far more than divides them.

Respect, along with empathy and care, are commendable private virtues prompted by travel and cultural encounter. However, the assumption of cultural relativism restricts the capacity of respect to lead to judgement and questioning, as the relativist can neither judge nor question that which he or she considers fundamentally different from his or her own culture. Rather than a critical cultural engagement, volunteer tourism often carries a cultural deference.

In so far as cultural relativism is a normative political stance central to global citizenship it may inhibit the development of a *critical* citizenship. Volunteering and tourism, as valuable life experiences, may have greater potential to contribute to the development of moral autonomy if freed from the assumption of relativism.

Developing a global moral compass through tourism

Raleigh International (excerpt from publicity)

Via global citizenship it is important to: *'Encourage active citizens who will become long term agents of social change in their own communities in the UK and in overseas developing countries.'*

'Each placement will help Raleigh and the local community to move towards achieving one or more of the United Nations millennium development goals.'
(Raleigh International, undated)

True Ecuador Educational Travel (excerpt from publicity)

According to their statement on global citizenship, *'students develop their understanding on both social/political and personal experiential levels. The experience of immersion in a new context in combination with relevant academic support provides an intense learning environment that will transform both social/political awareness and personal awareness, informing future academic and professional development.'*
(True Ecuador Educational Travel, undated)

Project Trust (excerpt from publicity)

Global citizenship enables you to *'appreciate that your way isn't the only way'*, and to value the ability *'to belong to a country other than the one you were born in, and make a difference.'*
(Project Trust (returned volunteer's view), undated)

'It's about challenging a personal view and considering the world from a different perspective; understanding the world from several angles and accepting differences.'

(Project Trust, undated)

Where There Be Dragons (Excerpt from publicity)

This US company regard experiential learning through travel as a *'cornerstone to global citizenship'.* It involves *'developing empathy for those whose resource-base and opportunity-levels may be less, but whose life-histories and cultures provide often profound lessons that aren't available to those living in more developed countries.'*

(Where There Be Dragons, undated)

Students *'develop a moral compass in which they see more clearly how their actions and decisions impact the people and environment outside of their immediate communities.'*

(Where There Be Dragons, undated a)

The outsourcing of citizenship

Citizenship has historically referred to the relationship between state and individual citizen of that state. The shape of that relationship has changed over time. However, citizenship as a national phenomenon has never precluded global or international political concerns. *National* citizenship has been the focus for *global* political issues.

Citizenship as a normative category assumes that the individual citizen is involved in the politics of their nation state. As we have argued throughout this book, in recent decades the institutions through which this political citizenship functioned remain only as shells. Politics does not inspire. There is a pervasive crisis of meaning and a lack of vision as to what the future could or should look like (Furedi, 2013). There is a no clear moral framework on offer through citizenship. Moral and ethical strategies are unlikely to be linked to national politics, and are far more likely to be associated with disparate campaigns and lifestyles (Giddens, 1994; Kim, 2012).

The crisis of meaning at the heart of politics has led elites to look elsewhere for some sort of moral purpose or justification. As a result, they have been keen to endorse global citizenship as a focus in education and in general. There is a sense in which the process of producing citizens is being outsourced from the nation to the globe, from the institutions of the state to companies and non-governmental organisations.

The growth of volunteer tourism is a good example of this outsourcing of citizenship. The global South has become a stage for the working out of what it is to be an ethical person. A number of writers and commentators on volunteer tourism have noted the way this outsourcing of citizenship functions in terms of a new political elite. Diprose points out through international volunteering the global South acts as a 'training ground' for a new liberal elite for business and politics (2012: 190). For Pearce and Coghlan volunteer tourism enriches the sending society by developing a 'pool of personnel with experiences and an embodied awareness of global issues' (2008: 132). For some, the gap year project is a part of building a portfolio of ethical experiences that shape the individual for a career in business or politics (Heath, 2007). Elsewhere it may be an 'immersion' experience to develop empathy with people who may be affected by decisions the global citizen makes in his or her career.

The process involves very little if any material development benefit to the global South. It is very much a process driven by the crisis of politics in the West and the subsequent search for meaning away from the institutions of politics. In the past if there was no development, then a development project would be said to have failed. Now it is legitimate to see the value in terms of the transformation of the volunteer and their personal journey towards global citizenship.

However, it has been argued that the contribution to development cannot be measured simply in terms of the projects themselves. Rather, the projects play a role in developing people who will, in the course of their careers and lives, act ethically in favour of the poor and the oppressed. Thus, the experience of volunteering becomes 'an ongoing process which extends far beyond the actual tourist visit' (Wearing 2001: 3).

For example, Chris Brown of Teaching Projects Abroad makes the case that a lack of experience of third world societies on the part of the bankers and businessmen of tomorrow contributes to exploitative relationships: 'How much better it might have been if all the people who are middle and high management of Shell had spent some time in West Africa ... how differently they would have treated the Ibo people in Nigeria? (sic)' (cited in Simpson 2004: 190).

Jonathan Cassidy, of Quest Overseas, concurs, arguing that if influential business people could only: 'look back for a split second to that month they spent working with people on the ground playing football with them or whatever' then they would act more ethically in their business lives' (ibid.: 191). Such sentiments are typical: through individual experience we can develop, decision by decision, a more ethical world, with less suffering, more fairness and greater opportunity.

Yet there is a narcissism to this outsourced search for moral meaning. It leads away from addressing the pressing material needs of others in the context of their lives and towards addressing the crisis of political identity in the West. The claim that volunteers' ethical careers post-trip can lead to change is false. It only promotes further lifestyle political initiative and global citizenship, and fails to contribute to debate on development.

Conclusion

The new experiential cosmopolitanism of global citizenship is illusory. Travel can certainly broaden the mind and the impulse to help is of course progressive.

However, global citizenship through volunteer tourism is questionable as a normative goal. It focuses the desire to act away from political citizenship, which in a world of nation states inevitably has a strong national dimension. In its place, the engaged citizen is encouraged to act through the rhythms of their life – lifestyle and consumption – via non-governmental organisations and private companies. Hence even leisure – holidays in this case – is associated with social agency through its contribution to global civil society and global citizenship.

A restatement of the importance of republican citizenship has greater potential than global citizenship. It redirects agency from unaccountable companies and non-governmental organisations to the principal institutions of sovereign democracy and political power, state governments. Republican citizenship assumes a respect for the citizens of other societies as sovereign political actors within a polity, and not recipients of lifestyle largesse through the market or non-governmental organisations.

References

Arendt, H. (1958) *The Human Condition*, University of Chicago Press, Chicago.

Arendt, H. (2000) What is freedom? in *The Portable Hannah Arendt*, Penguin Books, London.

Bianchi, R. and Stephenson, M. (2014) *Tourism and Citizenship: Rights, Freedoms and Responsibilities in the Global Order*, Routledge, London.

Butcher, J. and Smith, P. (2009). 'Who'd go on a government sponsored gap year?' Spiked-online. Available at http://www.spiked-online.com/newsite/article/7233#.VGXYRHlOU88 (accessed 17 October 2014).

Chen, S. (2002) Transitions to civic maturity: gap year volunteering and opportunities for higher education, in *Any Volunteers For the Good Society?* (Eds) W. Paxton and V. Nash, Institute for Public Policy Research, London, pp.67–77.

Chouliaraki, L. (2013) *The Ironic Spectator: Solidarity in the Age of Post Humanitarianism*, Polity, London.

Crabtree, R. (2008) Theoretical foundations for international service-learning, *Michigan Journal of Community Service Learning*, 15 (1), 18–36.

Devereux, P. (2008) International volunteering for development and sustainability: outdated paternalism or a radical response to globalization?, *Development in Practice*, 18 (3), 357–70.

Diprose, K. (2012) Critical distance: doing development education through international volunteering, *Area*, 44, (2), 186–92.

Dower, N. (2003) *An Introduction to Global Citizenship*, Edinburgh University Press, Edinburgh.

Furedi, F. (2013) *Authority: a Sociological History*, Cambridge University Press, Cambridge.

Giddens, A. (1994) *Beyond Left and Right: the Future of Radical Politics*, Polity, Oxford.

Heath, S. (2007) Widening the gap: pre-university gap years and the 'economy of experience', *British Journal of Sociology of Education*, 28 (1), 89–103.

Howes, A.J. (2008) Learning in the contact zone: revisiting neglected aspects of development through an analysis of volunteer placements in Indonesia, *Compare*, 38 (1), 23–38.

Jones, A. (2011) Theorising international youth volunteering: training for global (corporate) work?, *Transactions of the Institute of British Geographers*, 36, 530–44.

Kim, Y.M. (2012) The shifting sands of citizenship toward a model of the citizenry in life politics, *Annals of American Academy of Political and Social Science*, 644 (1), 147–58.

Klob, D.A. (1984) *Experiential Learning: Experience as the Source of Learning and Development*, Prentice Hall, New Jersey.

Lattitude Global Volunteering, (undated), About us. Available at http://www.lattitude.org.uk/about-us/ (accessed 17 October 2014).

Lewis, D. (2006) Globalisation and international service: a development perspective, *Voluntary Action*, 7, (2), 13–26.

Lyons, K. and Wearing, S. (2011) Gap year travel alternatives: Gen-Y, volunteer tourism and global citizenship, in *Tourism and Demography*, (eds) K.A. Smith, I. Yeoman, C. Hsu and S. Watson, Goodfellow Publishers, London, pp.101–16.

Lyons, K., Hanley, J., Wearing, S. and Neil, J. (2012) Gap year volunteer tourism: myths of global citizenship?, *Annals of Tourism Research*, 39 (1), 361–78.

Malik, K. (1996) *The Meaning of Race*. Palgrave Macmillan, London.

McGehee, N. (2002) Alternative tourism and social movements, *Annals of Tourism Research*, 29, 124–43.

McGehee, N.G. (2012) Oppression, emancipation, and volunteer tourism: research propositions, *Annals of Tourism Research*, 39 (1), 84–107.

McGehee, N. and Santos, C. (2005) Social change, discourse, and volunteer tourism, *Annals of Tourism Research,* 32 (3), 760–76.

Oxfam (undated) Global citizenship. Available at http://www.oxfam.org.uk/education/global-citizenship (accessed 17 October 2014).

Paine, T. (2000) *The Rights of Man*, Mineola, NY, Dover Publications. Original 1781.

Palacios, C. (2010) Volunteer tourism, development, and education in a postcolonial world: conceiving global connections beyond aid, *Journal of Sustainable Tourism*, 18 (7), 861–78.

Parekh, B. (2003) Cosmopolitanism and global citizenship, *Review of International Studies*, 29, 3-17.

Paxton, W. and Nash, V. (2002) *Any Volunteers for the Good Society*, Institute for Public Policy Research, London.

Pearce, P.L. and Coghlan, A. (2008) The dynamics behind volunteer tourism, in *Journeys of Discovery in Volunteer Tourism: International Case Study Perspectives*, (eds) K.D. Lyons and S. Wearing, CABI, London, pp.130–43.

Project Trust (undated), accessed at: http://projecttrust.org.uk/global-citizenship/ (accessed 18 December 2014).

Raleigh International (30 July 2009) Raleigh and Department for Business, Innovation and Skills launch bursary award for recent graduates. Available at www.raleighinternational.org/.../Raleigh%20Graduate%20Bursary%20Award%20official%20release (accessed 17 October 2014).

Raleigh International (undated) Why volunteer with Raleigh International. Accessed at http://www.raleighinternational.org/files/Frequently_Asked_Questions_about_ICS.pdf

Raymond, E. (2008) Make a difference! The role of sending organizations in volunteer tourism, in *Journeys of Discovery in Volunteer Tourism: International Case Study Perspectives*, (eds) K.D. Lyons and S. Wearing, CABI, London.

Simpson, K. (2004) Broad horizons: geographies and pedagogies of the gap year, unpublished PhD thesis, University of Newcastle.

Sin, H.L. (2009) Volunteer tourism: 'Involve me and I will learn'?, *Annals of Tourism Research*, 36 (3), 480–501.

Standish, A. (2008) *Global Perspectives in the Geography Curriculum: Reviewing the Moral Case for Geography*, Routledge, London.

Standish, A. (2012) *The False Promise of Global Learning: Why Education Needs Boundaries*, Continuum, London.

Tiessen, R. and Huish, R. (eds) (2014) *Globetrotting or Global Citizenship? Perils and Potential of International Experiential Learning*, University of Toronto Press, Toronto.

True Ecuador Travel (undated) Available at http://www.true-ecuador-travel.org/global-citizenship.html (accessed on 18 December 2014).

Yanapuma Foundation (undated). Global citizenship – concepts and practice. Available at http://www.yanapuma.org/en/resintoverview.php

Wearing, S. (2001) *Volunteer Tourism: Experiences that Make a Difference*, CABI Publishing, Wallingford.

Where There Be Dragons (undated) Accessed at http://wheretherebedragons.com/dragons-position-papers/ (accessed on 18 December 2014).

Where There Be Dragons (undated a) Accessed at http://wheretherebedragons.com/wp-content/uploads/2014/02/PP_2014_LearningService_2.pdf (accessed on 18 December 2014).

WorldActivity Philippines (undated) Testimonials. Available at http://www.worldactivity.ph/ (accessed 17 October 2014).

7 The volunteers: postcolonial, neoliberal or diminished subjects?

As a conspicuous expression of 'making a difference in the world' volunteer tourism's features indicate what is new and distinctive about political and social agency today, specifically with reference to global development.

Discussions of *the subject* in sociology consider the capacity of people to act upon and shape their world, and how that is understood historically and philosophically. *Agency* is an expression of similar at a less abstract level – a reference to the ability of individuals, groups or people in general to act and shape their own destiny in particular circumstances. The liberal conception of the subject assumes the individual can act autonomously, rationally and for the good of themselves and society. Today though, the subject is commonly regarded as profoundly shaped by the legacy of colonialism and neoliberal ideology.

Postcolonialism holds that the aftermath of colonialism leaves an ideological legacy. Moreover, this is an active legacy, a part of cultural and political relations now. It is often argued that volunteer tourism reproduces damaging assumptions that derive from colonialism. These can be notions of western superiority – 'the west knows best' – but equally can be more subtle cultural assumptions such as a romantic view of rural poverty that effectively helps to legitimise inequality and limit the prospects for advancement for former colonies (Loomba, 2005).

A further perspective from postcolonial studies sees progressive possibilities in the spaces where former coloniser and former colonised meet outside of the power structures associated with colonialism (Bhabha, 2004). These 'third spaces' are viewed as having the potential to enable damaging postcolonial assumptions to be challenged through the renegotiation of identities. This perspective has been applied to volunteer tourism (Wearing and Wearing, 1999; Wearing and Ponting, 2009; Wearing, Stevenson and Young, 2010; Wearing and Darcy, 2011).

Hence volunteer tourism features as both neocolonial practice, and radical anticolonial stance in the discussions.

Volunteer tourism (or examples of it deemed to be bad practice) also stands accused of turning youthful idealists into neoliberal subjects (Vrasti, 2012). The tourists may be motivated by altruism or the simple desire to help others, but volunteer tourism trains these aspirations onto market-based possibilities for making a difference, be it to oneself or other societies. In doing so, the market is reinforced as the focus of all human endeavour (Hall *et al.*, 2013). Following this line of argument, if the market as the organising principle of economic and social life is reinforced through volunteer tourism then, in spite of their good intentions, the volunteers are unwittingly complicit in a destructive neoliberal project. In this view, good individual intentions can sit side by side with bad outcomes. In fact it is notable how the market-critical sentiments of volunteer tourists exist alongside academic analyses that view those same volunteers as subject to an insidious neoliberal influence.

As with postcolonial criticism, analyses of volunteer tourism and neoliberalism are contradictory. Volunteer tourism is also invoked on the other side of the argument – as an antidote to the assumed rampant individualism and profit seeking of mass tourism, a counter to neoliberal identity. For Higgins-Desboilles volunteer tourism is a 'chance to contribute to the restoration of natural environments and to address social problems while simultaneously building a self-identity based upon caring relationships, rather than iconoclastic individualism and the isolating selfishness that capitalism fosters' (Higgins-Desboilles and Mundine, 2008: 349). These sentiments are evident in the reflections of volunteer tourists themselves (see contributions to Apale and Stam, 2011).

This chapter will examine these two focuses for critics (and advocates) of volunteer tourism – *postcolonialism* and *neoliberalism*. We argue that each framework has merits, but also considerable limitations, in understanding the significance of volunteer tourism today.

We argue that a further concept needs to be considered, that of *diminished subjectivity* (Heartfield, 2002). This refers to a diminished sense that societies and individuals (either the volunteer or the communities subject to volunteer tourism) can transcend their present culture and level of development, or that they would benefit from doing so. It involves a strong assumption of vulnerability in the face of development and cultural change. The diminished subject, characterised by vulnerability in the face of development, is rooted in a widespread disillusionment with and disorientation towards politics and political agency characteristic of our times (Laidi, 1998; Furedi, 2013, 2014). It is this crisis in political agency that frames volunteer tourism more fundamentally than colonialism's legacy or the power of neoliberal ideology.

Postcolonial subjects?

Postcolonialism examines the legacy of colonialism and how relationships of inequality between societies are continued, adapted and even strengthened through less direct, often cultural mechanisms. In this vein tourism has been seen as a continuation and reinforcing of paternal attitudes or attitudes of superiority rooted in colonialism (Hall and Tucker, 2004). It has also been cited as having the potential to challenge these (Wearing, 2001; Wearing, Stevenson and Young, 2010; Wearing and Grabowski, 2011).

Historically the ideology of colonialism has been premised upon the assumption of the superiority of (usually) the white races over subject peoples. For example, ideas of racial supremacy rationalised the scramble for African colonies on the part of developed European nations in the 1870s. Racial thinking characterised not just the view of the colonies in the nineteenth century, but also the assumption of the inferiority of people of lower classes within the more economically developed countries. People were deemed to be different and inferior by class as well as by race (Malik, 1996; Loomba, 2005).

The notion of the 'white man's burden' presented colonialism as a moral obligation. The West was held to be bringing a higher cultural level, a degree of 'civilisation', to societies defined by their inability to achieve these things for themselves (Malik, 1996) Even though volunteer tourists would never regard themselves as exporting civilisation, the image of the benevolent western volunteer bringing happiness to the African child, so pronounced in volunteer tourism marketing, looms large in criticism of volunteer holidays as neocolonialism.

Colonialism had largely ended by the 1970s, and yet despite the formal equality of nations, uneven development continues to characterise the globe. In contrast to the criticism of volunteer tourism as colonialism, a number of studies indicate that the tourists themselves are conscious of a colonial legacy and see their actions as challenging its contemporary influence (see contributions to Apale and Stam, 2011). Volunteer tourism companies and non-governmental organisations, and their customers, see themselves as addressing certain deficits that arise from uneven development – poverty, lack of education, lack of facilities for a good childhood (Sin, 2010). Lozanski argues that 'travellers' often see themselves as distinctive and morally superior to mass tourists, the latter associated with a colonial legacy (2011: 466). Yet critics argue that in spite of altruistic intent, these worthy tourists perpetuate assumptions about other societies and cultures that legitimised colonialism in the past and continue to rationalise underdevelopment and inequality still.

Tourism equals colonialism

Mass tourism is often described as neocolonial or imperialist in academic analyses. It is no exaggeration to say that 'tourism equals colonialism' is a pretty mainstream view. Volunteer tourism is one of a number of attempts at an ethical tourism that challenges mass tourism's supposed colonial character (McGehee, 2002). Yet in spite of the sentiments of its advocates and some volunteer tourists, it has attracted similar criticism.

There is quite a tradition in comparing modern tourism directly with colonialism. Krippendorf's influential *The Holiday Makers* regards it as having a colonial character 'everywhere and without exception' (1987: 56). Turner and Ash label tourism a 'new form of colonialism' in their often cited *The Golden Hordes: International Tourism and the Pleasure Periphery* (1975: 1). Cohen asserts that tourism is 'always and everywhere, colonialism' (1972: 182) and that '[t]he easy going tourist of our era might well complete the work of his predecessors, also travellers from the West – the conqueror and colonialist' (ibid.). Lozanski argues that independent travel is 'embedded in the implicit hierarchies of colonialism that persist in a neocolonial setting' (2011: 466).

These assertions rely on certain superficial aspects of colonialism – the wealthy foreigner stepping out onto a private beach in the developing world, served by local people who have little immediate prospect of attaining the privileges of their guest. This is less colonialism and more simply the reality of capitalist society everywhere – rich people can afford nice things and others are employed to provide them. Subjective assertions about colonialism such as this, whilst radical in tone, rob it of meaning. They substitute colonialism as a set of attitudes and behaviours for colonialism as a result of political systems and economic structures. In doing so they relativise the horrors of real colonialism by suggesting a moral and political continuum running from holiday making to the oppression of populations.

Tourism has also been accused of 'imperialism'. Anthropologist Dennison Nash invokes imperialism and argues that '[t]he North American vacationer who insists on fast food hamburgers, coffee with his meal, hot running water in his bedroom and the use of the English language' is part of the systematic domination of the third world (1989: 39). This suggestion that the American vacationer has, in effect, an imperialist lifestyle, can only be argued if one takes a subjective and limited view of imperialism. In the past imperialism was viewed as an extension of a nation's interests abroad on the basis of claimed moral authority or as a result of capitalist crisis (Lenin, 1996; Hobson, 2011). There are no useful parallels with the purchase of holidays.

Underlying the charge that tourism is neocolonialism or imperialism is a pejorative view of mass consumption and mass consumers' behaviour. Suggestions of tourism's colonial or imperialist character feature in popular commentaries and texts. In *The Final Call: In Search of the True Cost of Our Holidays* the UK Guardian's lifestyle correspondent, Leo Hickman likens Tallin's budget airline tourists to Estonia's previous Nazi and Soviet invaders (2007: 313). The popular university introductory text *Tourism: A Modern Synthesis* suggests tourists have 'superseded the armies of the colonial powers' (Page *et al.*, 2001: 397).

A recent exposition of the 'tourism as colonialism' view is human geographer Steven Flusty's essay, *Rime of the Frequent Flyer* (2011). He argues that tourism is complicit in the inequalities and oppression, past and present, that he encounters as he travels. For Flusty, tourism is 'inextricably rooted in conquest' (ibid.: 99), a view supported elsewhere through references to colonialism. He goes further in suggesting there is a culpability in all tourism – *our* leisure depends on *their* subjugation.

Modernity is a key point of reference for Flusty. He asserts that 'those who do not subject themselves to modernity's relentless and shifting winds are forever in danger of finding themselves subject to those who have' (ibid.). One could equally argue that those who desperately want more of the benefits of modernity are denied this due to being subject to the macroeconomic and political relationships that prevail.

So are the problems witnessed by leisure travellers a product of modernity, or of capitalism? For all the sympathies with the poor and oppressed, emphasising modernity (a general state) rather than capitalism (a specific set of social and power relations) ends up conflating all modern human activities (such as tourism) with the failings of capitalist societies historically and today. For Flusty, we are all 'playing Elgin' (ibid.) – the humble tourist is linked to British colonialism and the theft of others' property and culture. All things modern become complicit and suspect.

If this were to be accepted, how could one argue that others should have the opportunities enjoyed by many in wealthy nations, such as to travel widely for leisure? Anticolonialism used to be a demand for freedom from subjection by powerful nations, not from tourists' unenlightened attitudes. If colonialism is held to be implicit in modernity, then anticolonial demands for a share in the benefits of modern societies are not likely to gain a hearing.

The claim that tourism is colonialism is not convincing. The overuse of any term can contribute to a blunting of its meaning, and that would seem to be the case here. The fast and loose usage of 'colonialism' and 'imperialism' obscures the specific historical circumstances and experiences of colonialism in the past, and dodges the need to analyse the political roots of poverty and denial of political equality beyond the colonial legacy. Postcolonial analysis is of limited value in times that have aptly been described as postpolitical (Zizek, 1999).

Volunteer tourists themselves often express a rhetorical anticolonial outlook not dissimilar to that of Flusty. It is one of the new 'ethical' tourism niches that claim to address the perceived past injustices of mass tourism and of western consumer societies in general. There is a desire amongst volunteer tourists to ameliorate 'the historical exploitation and environmental mistakes on which their society has been built' (Pearce and Coghlan, 2008: 132). If most tourists are 'playing Elgin' as Flusty asserts, then volunteer tourists are trying to return the Elgin Marbles to Greece! They express a sense of culpability for colonialism, and there is certainly no expressed desire to visit western civilisation upon poorer societies. Rather, any hierarchical notion of civilisation and progress is eschewed in favour of a cultural relativism that holds that the volunteer tourists' own culture has much to learn from the societies visited.

To argue that volunteer tourism is complicit in colonial arrogance, or that it is a counter to such an outlook, is to understate and misunderstand colonialism, and to overplay leisure consumption's political significance. The real problem is the association of the consumption of holidays with colonialism in the first place. Volunteer tourism has little if anything to do with colonialism, either perpetuating or challenging its legacy.

Neocolonialism: from the Peace Corps to volunteer tourism

A second theme to consider is the relationship of post-Second World War volunteering of the United States Peace Corps/UK Voluntary Service Overseas (VSO) variety to colonialism, and to then consider claimed continuities with contemporary volunteer tourism. This is more fully developed in Chapter 2.

Processes of decolonisation involving the big powers in the quarter of a century following the Second World War necessitated attempts to secure influence in the newly independent regimes. Two World Wars, a new post-Second World War balance of power and anticolonial movements made colonialism morally and politically unfeasible (Furedi, 1994). Assistance to the newly independent regimes could prospectively assist in normalising relations and maintaining influence. This was clearly important in the context of the Cold War. Soviet influence in large parts of the third world was feared by the western powers, and volunteering organisations presented a human and benevolent face to what had been occupying powers. The other side in the Cold War, the eastern bloc, developed its own volunteering capacity, as part of its propaganda front.

The establishment of the Peace Corps in the USA, Voluntary Service Overseas in the UK and similar initiatives in other countries in the 1950s and 1960s was seen by some as part of postcolonial politics (Cobbs-Hoffman, 1998). For idealistic volunteers it was an act of altruism to assist poorer nations become richer, in line with positive western values, but for others it was informed by the interests of the former colonisers in retaining political and economic interest in the third world (ibid.). The technical assistance and education on offer from the volunteers fitted with the view that the third world could and should ally with the capitalist world rather than the communist alternative. The organisations involved were established or supported directly by government initiative, and their establishment was linked to clear (albeit contested) narratives of national interest, narratives not evident in volunteer tourism today. These narratives were explicitly a part of national identity. For example, the Peace Corps was held to reflect America's 'altruistic values' as well as 'universal values and progress' (ibid.: 26).

The questioning of that narrative ultimately led to the questioning of volunteering itself. In the USA the Vietnam War and the fraught issue of race in the late 1960s caused many young Americans to question these values and even to accuse their own country of colonialism. The Peace Corps itself was subject to the charge of being an instrument of colonialism and American imperialism (Cobbs-Hoffman, 1998). Some of its volunteers contravened policy and publically criticised American values during the Vietnam War, whilst private doubts were commonplace (Zimmerman, 2001).

The receivers of aid were not universally grateful for the assistance offered and anticolonial sentiment questioned America's claim to be promoting anything other than America's geopolitical interests. Kwame Nkrumah, Ghanaian freedom fighter and the country's first President, labelled Peace Corps and US policy in general as neocolonialist in his book *Neocolonialism: The Last Stage of Imperialism* (1965). The State Department responded to the Ghanaian government in writing and aid was cut as a direct result.

Whilst a relationship between the volunteering organisations of the 1950s and 1960s and western interests in the post-Second World War decades is clear, modern volunteer tourism's relationship to national or other interests is far less so. What characterises the sentiments of volunteer tourists is a rejection of any national mission or interest, a rejection of any agenda to aid the transformation of poor societies fundamentally and a distancing from the legacy of modern development. In all three respects, volunteer tourism today contrasts with Peace Corps/VSO-type organisations in the past, and hence it is difficult to sustain the idea that the former shares any neocolonial characteristics with the latter.

It is likely, too, that Peace Corps volunteering means something rather different today compared to the 1950s and 1960s. One account from a very recent volunteer in Paraguay expresses guilt at affluence rather than the aspiration to generalise it, and a desire to bring back home a sense of what it means to be poor as a spur to ethical living.

> I tell people I joined the Peace Corps to understand what it means to be poor, but that's just part of the story. I joined the Peace Corps to figure out how to escape the guilt of having so much while other people have so little.
>
> (Katcoff, 2012)

It is unsurprising that volunteer tourism, and perhaps also the contemporary experience of the Peace Corps tradition, does not express a narrative of national interest. The lack of any clear narrative of national interest on the part of western states themselves in recent times is convincingly described by two writers on international relations, Zaki Laidi and David Chandler. Both of these authors consider international relations in the aftermath of the Cold War. Laidi emphasises how the Cold War underwrote the ideological framing of international relations (1998). It provided an 'other' against which each protagonist defined their mission and interests. Post-Cold War politics are characterised by a lack of clear, politically defined national identities. Chandler argues that the consequent disorientation and exhaustion of erstwhile political identities fuel the search for a moral mission in the international arena. This mission eschews national or economic interests and invokes abstract values (as in the rise of 'humanitarian intervention') as its *raison d'être* (2007).

If the new values-based foreign policy reflects a lack of any coherent political identity amongst western states, the ethics-heavy, politics-light public involvement in international development through volunteer tourism, Fairtrade and telethons reflects something similar for the individual. There are no coherent narratives, from Left, Right or nation to cohere the impulse to act upon the world through politics (Judt, 2005; Jacoby, 1999). Therefore to see volunteer tourists as postcolonial subjects, or anticolonial subjects for that matter, misunderstands the contemporary political subject. It is the absence of politics that shapes such lifestyle-oriented strategies for change.

Volunteer tourism as third space

In making the case for a progressive version of volunteer tourism, Wearing and Ponting (2009), and Wearing and Darcy (2011) draw on the postcolonial studies concept of 'third space' (Bhabha, 2004). For the concept's originator, political theorist Homi Bhabha, identity is formed through shifting and negotiable hybrid spaces and cultures. Third space is a metaphorical space in which people come together outside of the context of oppression, creating the possibility for a more authentic meeting of cultures. It is constituted by 'in-between spaces' that provide 'terrain for strategies of selfhood – singular or communal – that initiate new signs of identity and develop innovative sites of collaboration and contestation' (ibid.: 2). These in-between spaces are argued to have the potential to act as sites of resistance to dominant colonial and oppressive cultures and discourses: spaces where excluded voices can be heard, new identities explored and alternative communities formed.

In so far as Bhabha discusses travel, he is concerned with migration and the formation of diaspora communities in a postcolonial setting (ibid.: 12). However, third space is seen by a number of writers as a useful way to consider the cultural potential in alternative forms of tourism (Hollinshead, 1998; Wearing, Stevenson and Young, 2010; Amoamo, 2011). In particular, Stephen Wearing has argued that the encounters between volunteers and those they seek to assist can facilitate a mutually enriching and truly enlightening cultural exchange. As in Bhabha's conceptualisation, here third space is a metaphorical space within which neocolonial and neoliberal assumptions can be challenged and new social and political ideas forged. For Wearing, volunteer tourism projects are held to be a literal and physical expression of the concept.

Wearing's third space does not apply to all volunteer tourism, much of which he regards as turning altruism into a commodity. It is only possible where the volunteering is decommodified, organised on a not for profit basis (Wearing, 2001). Such decommodified tourism is viewed as offering a sustainable alternative to mass tourism, as the former exists outside the 'dominant market-driven framework of commodified tourism, and where profit objectives are secondary to a more altruistic desire to travel to assist communities' (Wearing, 2001: 12). In these circumstances progressive impulses towards altruism and solidarity can, he argues, lead to authentic cultural exchanges, untainted by a pernicious neoliberalism. Third space is presented as a counter to the market and mass consumption, the latter complicit in oppression and inequality.

Wearing and Ponting (2009) consider non-governmental organisations working with local communities as the best vehicle for delivering non-commercial or 'decommodified' volunteer and ecotourism projects. They cite Holidays With Purpose in islands off North West Sumatra as an example of best practice of this decommodified tourism product. Elsewhere the Santa Elena Rainforest Project (Wearing and Larsen, 1996) and Youth Challenge International in Costa Rica (Wearing, 2001) are noted as other examples. These projects are said to run counter to the 'commodified, normalizing and marketized nature of globalized Western tourism' (ibid.: 257). In this sense it is argued that volunteer tourism has the potential to act as 'ideal' ecotourism, addressing many of the shortfalls and criticisms levelled at mainstream and commercial ecotourism projects, particularly accusations of 'greenwashing' (Honey, 2002: 370; Buckley, 2003: xiv; Weaver and Lawton, 2007: 1174). Lyons and Wearing (2008: 7) argue that ecotourism has been unable to 'resist commodification by the international tourism market' and consider whether volunteer tourism can avoid the same fate.

Youth Challenge International: 'Our approach'

'YCI believes that young Canadians and Americans have a meaningful contribution to make to international development and global youth development. Over the years we have seen our youth volunteers become the leaders of non-profits and key contributors to society.

We have also seen local youth in developing countries become inspiring leaders and citizens in their own countries. And we have seen the local NGOs we partner with become effective and sustainable organizations. This is the heart of what we do.

How do we do it? By putting young Canadians and Americans together with local youth on hands-on projects that address real needs, identified by local partners. The benefits are powerful – team dynamics, cross-cultural understanding, youth energy and the spirit of volunteerism all combine to create a potent force for change.

But it's not a vacation – volunteers live under the most basic conditions in remote locations with little in the way of amenities. And the work schedules can be demanding, challenging youth to tap into hidden personal resources to achieve results.

Nor does it end with their return to their home countries. YCI is only the beginning of a lifetime of involvement in the critical issues that face youth in Canada, the United States and around the world.'

(Youth Challenge International, undated)

Unlike with regular tourism, or commercially oriented volunteer tourism, the third space tourist is deemed to be an individual who 'moves beyond the "gazer" to become an interactive contributor to the site' (Wearing and Neil, 2000: 392). They are considered less as passive tourists and more as active volunteers, working alongside their host community in pursuit of wellbeing goals. This argument holds that outside of the distorting influence of the market, the volunteers can learn about the realities of their hosts' lives, and actively learn from their culture. Hence the process moves beyond simple 'host' and 'guest' to a fluid two-way process of interaction through which both host and guest can benefit (Wearing, Stevenson and Young, 2010; Wearing and Darcy, 2011). In the case of the North American-based Youth Challenge International this process can be enhanced through 'edutainment' and sport:

> From drum circles, hip hop and dance in Tanzania, to role playing and theatre programming in Guyana, YCI continues to develop exciting new models for youth engagement through edutainment programming.
> Sport has proven an effective means of youth engagement for YCI; promoting inclusion amongst youth and helping to address discrimination

and marginalization for reasons of gender, religion, ability, ethnicity and disability, as well as providing an avenue for leadership, life skills and advocacy training through teamwork and collaboration.

(Youth Challenge International, undated a)

This is the argument for volunteer tourism as an ethical innovation with cultural potential.

Third space tourism is also held to have political potential. For Wearing and Darcy (2011: 21) through such tourism 'counter-hegemonic modes of interaction are possible' leading to a questioning of neoliberal assumptions and neocolonial influence. Elsewhere it is held to have the potential to challenge the dominant 'neoliberal paradigms of tourism' (Higgins-Desbiolles and Mundine, 2008: 182).

The advocacy of cultural agency and political enlightenment through volunteer tourism is refreshing in the face of the cynicism of some critics who see only naivety, calculation and personal gain as its drivers (Mustonen, 2005; Simpson, 2005; Söderman and Snead, 2008; Heath, 2007; Baillie Smith and Laurie, 2011). The impulse to look for new avenues to act on the world and improve people's lives is laudable.

Yet it also suffers from the wider limitations of postcolonialism as a starting point in this quest. The focus is on the intercultural encounter between peoples defined by their respective cultures. This encounter of difference is seen as both the problem (mass tourism) and also part of a solution (volunteer tourism). That the debate is framed in this way obscures the fact that both arguments – the critique of mass tourism consumption and behaviour and the search for remedies through alternative tourism consumption and behaviour – feed off the personalisation of development politics. Both feed into an emphasis on personal behaviour and experience in development, and a de facto shift away from social and political explanations of underdevelopment and global inequalities.

Third space tourism challenges market relations – 'commodification' – by creating an 'alternative economic space' (Leyshon *et al.*, 2003). Yet in challenging the market in the name of fairness this approach ends up rejecting development itself – the baby is thrown out with the bathwater. The small-scale, localised development that this stance involves expresses a profound disillusionment not just with the market, but with development on any large-scale basis. The latter is frowned upon as an 'economistic pro-development' outlook (Wearing and Grabowski, 2011: 158). In short, third space tourism amounts to very little development at all.

The third space tourism approach does concede that the benefits accruing to the local community are frequently limited. Yet it also suggests that the contribution to development cannot be measured simply in terms of the projects themselves but through the 'journey of self-discovery and self-understanding through the experience of life style alternatives' (Wearing *et al.*, 2008: 70). Wearing highlights the long-term impacts the experience of volunteering can have in developing people who will, in the course of their careers and lives, act morally in favour of those less well off. Thus the experience of volunteering becomes 'an ongoing process which extends far beyond the actual tourist visit' (2001: 3).

The central problem with third space tourism, however, is not its limited development remit. Its flaw is that it assumes a diminished concept of the political subject. National sovereignty, elected assemblies and democracy itself are at best ignored or at worst disparaged in favour of the more nebulous and extremely localised concept of cultural encounters in third spaces. Agency is presented as local and cultural, not national and political.

In third space, people in the global South are not political subjects acting in their own interests, but are seen as 'reflexive educators and interpreters' (Wearing and Ponting, 2009: 263); facilitating mutual understanding between cultures (Conran, 2011: 1466) or gaining confidence and self-esteem (McIntosh and Zahra, 2008). Neocolonial and neoliberal assumptions may be disrupted in third space (Wearing and Darcy, 2011: 22) but they are replaced with an image of the global South in need of therapeutic interventions and wellbeing. This shift in the view of peoples in the developing world – from subject of independence and national self-determination to facilitator in a global identity politics – is striking.

Third space tourism is regarded as having potential to forge a progressive politics (Wearing and Ponting, 2009: 257), a politics from the margins (Wearing and Darcy, 2011) or potentially the beginnings of a more radical approach to challenging global inequalities (Mostafanezhad, 2013). This approach abandons formal politics and the polity, and turns instead towards the cultural subject acting in third space. Its ambition for development or for reviving a wide debate on development possibilities can only ever be very limited as a result.

The limits of postcolonialism

Over the last thirty years postcolonialism has become a key intellectual perspective on the relationship between the West and the global South. Central to much postcolonial writing is a radical cultural relativism, pitted against the universalising tendencies of capitalism, the market and the West (Loomba, 2005). Yet looking at volunteer tourism through the lens of postcolonialism is problematic. The cultural relativism and poststructuralism central to much critical postcolonial thought are the very limiting assumptions underpinning the outlook of the volunteer tourist.

The assumption of the differences between societies – historical and cultural – as their defining characteristics, has been criticised as a one sided cultural relativism. Vivek Chibber, author of *Postcolonial Theory and the Spectre of Capital* (2013) argues that the cultural relativism of postcolonial thought actually amounts to a cultural essentialism. Not only are differences emphasised rather than what people have in common as human beings, but these differences are presented as the defining characteristic of societies. Hence knowledge that emanates from the West is presented as 'western' in more than a geographical sense, and development, too, is often prefixed by 'western' or 'Eurocentric' (Lushaba 2009; McMichael, 2000).

Generation NGO

Far from imposing western ideas onto the communities in which they work (something mainstream development is held to be culpable of), most contributors to Generation NGO (Apale and Stam, 2011), a volume of heartfelt reflections of young Canadian volunteers, want to return home with lessons for their lives and their societies.

One contributor, a volunteer in Madagascar, comments on seeing a subsistence community plant, harvest, prepare and eat their own food and comments: 'A part of me dreads returning to North America where, in comparison, everything seems rushed, wasteful and isolated from its source' (ibid.: 123). Another felt like 'an unwitting missionary of Northern beliefs and values' (ibid.: 36), but concludes that: 'Africa does not need me there, but perhaps it can use me here (in Canada) to share some of the things it has taught me' (ibid.: 45).

Echoing this rejection of 'western' development, a volunteer organising sports in a Rwandan refugee camp comments on being struck by 'a very vivid sense of my own ugliness … I feel like an eyesore, as if you were to happen upon a McDonalds on the middle of the rainforest' (ibid.: 147). Another contributor's view on helping beggars back home is transformed by her experience of beggars in Kenya.

This disillusionment with their own 'western' or 'northern' societies is at times linked to a disillusionment with humanity itself. For one contributor: 'Time moves on, few things really change, and injustice – this interminable characteristic of being human – weaves its way through life, endlessly assaulting its favourite victims' (ibid.: 99). Injustice, like the poor, is always with us … and always will be in this downbeat view.

One contributor articulates the shift to the expression of social aspirations through a personal narrative clearly. Motivated by a desire to expose the 'hidden costs' of western lifestyles, she sets off for Burma. Through her experience, 'social change' becomes 'entrenched ... as a lifestyle', a 'deeply personal battle, fought from within and without' (ibid.: 85). This volunteer does conclude with a downbeat assessment of what her lifestyle politics can achieve, but further concludes that this failure is due to a heartless world, not to the limits of her own narcissistic take on development.

(Apale and Stam, 2011)

Cultural differences are important, but for Chibber they exist in the context of an overarching humanism. His argument is twofold. First, all human societies share common aspirations to pursue a better life and to a degree of autonomy. Second, development, the knowledge on which it is based, and indeed the idea of progress itself are not 'western' or 'Eurocentric'. Rather they are categories borne out of general human experience. Such an assertion itself often attracts the accusation of being Eurocentric, but it is important to remember that for most of the modern era this humanism has been influential in anticolonial politics (ibid.).

Kenan Malik's classic book *The Meaning of Race* (1996) provides an explanation of how this cultural relativism came to hold sway. He argues that nineteenth-century biological racism, the ideology that legitimised imperialism and colonialism, was challenged over the course of the twentieth century by proponents of the category of culture. Culture, though, was understood through the prism of relativism – *cultures* plural rather than a humanist conception of culture as a universal. Malik argues that this cultural relativism was pioneered in the field of anthropology in the early decades of the twentieth century and, notwithstanding the continued influence of racial thinking, became important in social thought generally. Although the challenge to biological racism was progressive, the material differences between societies were legitimised through a more neutral language of culture, or to be precise, cultures. Cultures began to replace race as a marker of and rationalisation of difference. This was especially so after the experience of the Second World War, the Holocaust and anticolonial struggles which made biological racism untenable (Malik, 1996).

Malik usefully summarises his thesis in terms of a 'ladder' of assumed civilisational superiority and inferiority (with the colonisers assumed to be on higher and the colonised on lower rungs) being now placed upon its side in the name of the equal validity of, and respect for, different cultures. In this schema notions of natural inferiority and superiority became less tenable, which is of course in and of itself progressive. Yet with no ladder to climb – no way of transcending one's culturally defined place in the world – a given culture comes to define the individual.

Malik rejects cultural relativism, arguing that modern multicultural sensibilities produce culture as a cage limiting people's agency, or, as he describes it, a rung on a ladder turned on its side. One cannot transcend cultural difference in such a view, as we are defined by it, and there is nowhere else to go. Clearly this relativism has a profound impact on how one might conceive of development. It is also a sentiment common to the accounts of culturally aware volunteer tourists.

Cultural relativism has become influential in development thinking, in part through the influence of anthropology in this field in the 1970s (Milton, 1996). Categories derived from anthropology – staged authenticity, acculturation and the demonstration effect – have also become a staple in academic accounts of tourism's impact on host societies (Sharpley, 1999), and take as their epistemological starting point the relationship between two different cultures outside of any humanistic framework that would consider universal characteristics of culture (Butcher, 2003).

That volunteer tourists assume an air of cultural superiority is sometimes asserted, linking it to past colonialism (McGehee, 2012: 11). In fact there is a general myth in much writing on the sociology of tourism to the global South that asserts tourists go to 'view inferior natives whom they have no desire to emulate' (Azarya, 2004: 956).

Yet most accounts from volunteer tourists suggest something of a reversal of this assumption, portraying instead a strongly flawed western society with much to learn from communities in the developing world. Research indicates that the tourist is often self-critical of his or her own culture, rather deferential to the ways of life of their host and keen to bring truths gleaned from the experience back home (see for example contributions to Apale and Stam, 2011). Volunteer tourists see themselves and are often seen as attempting to challenge the lack of cultural sensitivity in mainstream tourism and mass consumption generally by exhibiting a sensitivity to the society visited.

Vrasti (2012) argues that volunteer tourists replace the material and historical conditions of inequality with multicultural sensibilities. It is precisely the benign culturally relativist appearance of volunteer tourism that makes its assumptions about other societies, including those relating to their lack of agency and their need for assistance, powerful in today's context. A radical deference to the culture of the hosts is a feature of many volunteer tourist accounts and much advocacy. The host's culture is regarded as in some respects more progressive than the developed societies from which the volunteers come. Yet the sympathetic and at times reverential assertions about the societies visited serve to reify differences in cultural terms, and provide a radical-sounding rationalisation of poverty (ibid.).

What the above analysis suggests is not a damaging residual cultural influence from colonialism shaping volunteer tourism, but that the assumptions of postcolonial analysis themselves, shared with much analysis of volunteer tourism, stand in the way of addressing development.

Postcolonialism also draws heavily on poststructuralist theories (Loomba, 2005; see Minca and Oakes, 2011 regarding tourism). These theories locate power at the level of the intercultural and linguistic, and reject 'grand narrative' attempts at understanding society. For example, Minca and Oakes regard tourism as 'real' in that it is 'a constitutive force in the social world' and in the sense that it is involves 'actual practices that defy simple categorisations or disembodied abstractions' (Minca and Oakes, 2011: 1). Their stated aim is to 'put to rest the lingering structuralism that continues its remarkable staying power in tourism theory' (ibid.: 3).

This reflects a neo-Foucauldian view of power, dispersed within societies, exercised through all sorts of social practices, but apparently originating in the human condition itself. Many authors have looked at tourism (Urry, 1996; Hollinshead, 1999; Jordan and Aitchison, 2008; Minca and Oakes, 2011) and volunteer tourism (Cheong and Miller, 2000; Wearing, 2001; Lyons and Wearing, 2008; Palacios, 2010; Wearing, Wearing, and McDonald, 2010) through this neo-Foucauldian prism. Many of the discussions of postcolonialism in relation to tourism look at culture in terms of the interpersonal, typically focusing on the 'host–tourist' encounter. This ends up with something akin to a lifestyle postcolonialism – forms of consumption and behaviour rather than culture in any broader sense are regarded as the expression of the colonial legacy, and also as the means to counter it.

This approach collapses power politics into the private and personal. The implication is that the humble tourist can be implicated in colonialism, or in challenging its legacy, a claim that would have been seen as marginal or even odd a generation ago. This marks a retreat from politics into culture, where culture is understood in terms of interpersonal encounters.

As a result, '[t]here is a disturbing tendency for poststructural discussions to see poverty in terms of the social construction of a deficient world rather than the material reality of absolute deprivation' (Peet and Hartwick, 2009: 285). Certainly, volunteer tourism seems to emphasise a sensitivity to cultural differences much more than a need for material development and growth.

Criticisms of volunteer tourism as implicated in a modern colonialism or a postcolonial legacy are no more valid than the pretensions of some volunteer tourists themselves to be living out a critique of neocolonial mass tourism. It is important to consider volunteer tourism from a humanist frame of reference that, as Malik and Chibber argue, upholds culture as a universal, human attribute. This enables development to be approached from the perspective of shared aspiration and common desires for development, rather than through a rejection of this as necessarily 'western' or 'Eurocentric'.

Neoliberal subjects?

Alongside the charge that volunteer tourism is informed by the legacy of colonialism is the associated view that it reflects the growth of neoliberalism as the pre-eminent influence upon political agency (Conran, 2011; Vrasti, 2012). Proponents of this view argue that our responses to the market's limits take the form of new ethical markets such as ethical tourism, reinforcing the hegemony of the market and its attendant values.

Certainly, the growth of the sector and the involvement of more mainstream tour operators suggests to some that volunteer tourism is simply business first and ethics a poor second. A number of studies suggest that the main beneficiaries are private companies seeking young professional employees with overseas experience (Simpson, 2005; Baillie Smith and Laurie, 2011; Jones, 2011; Lyons *et al.*, 2012).

It is certainly the case that many western companies and organisations welcome the experience gained though international volunteering (Vrasti, 2012), but the extent to which this represents the reinforcing of a neoliberal form of development practice is open to question (Vodopivec and Jaffe, 2011: 112).

There are other, more subtle connections drawn between volunteer tourism and neoliberalism. Attempts to act on perceived injustice, and even simple altruism, appear to be mediated through marketable opportunities to individuals based upon their ability to derive moral utility. The social question of development is marketised and we are encouraged to see ourselves as consumers in a marketplace of ethical development initiatives, be they volunteer tourism, Red or Fairtrade (Vrasti, 2012). Here issues of structural inequality are replaced by questions of individual morality (Mostafanezhad, 2014).

Where both the mainstream and the alternative look to the market, the mantra that 'there is no alternative' can only be reinforced. This argument is well made by Mostafanezhad (ibid.), who argues that the response to the market's limits take the form of new ethical niches, which reinforce the market and those same attendant limits. In short, the market provides ever more ethical products to meet the demands of moral consumers and contributes to the expansion of neoliberal policies and practices: 'Neoliberal times' seem to shape what is possible.

Vrasti considers the private acts of consumption and conduct to be significant in maintaining a neoliberal status quo. Yet whilst arguing that volunteer tourism is compromised, Mostafanezhad, Vrasti, Wearing and other market-critical writers look to more politically aware types of the same niche to facilitate critical reflection and political enlightenment. Mostafanezad (2014) looks to volunteer tourism to question the aestheticisation of poverty (ibid.), whilst Vrasti (2012) sees some potential for equitable encounters resulting in a greater understanding and awareness of global issues. Wearing, McDonald and Ponting look to a decommodified tourism – trips that operate outside the parameters and assumptions of the global market through non-governmental organisations and with the community centrally involved (2005). For these authors, in different ways, the goal is to inject the right politics into the encounter in order to counter neoliberal orthodoxy.

The emphasis on neoliberal ideology may be overstating the case. As discussed elsewhere, the collapse of faith in alternatives has left the market pre-eminent by default in contemporary consciousness. It is hardly surprising that consumption rather than questioning the basis of society is the focus for people's social aspirations. Daniel Miller argues that: 'most people have a minimal relationship to production and distribution such that consumption provides the only arena left to us through which we might potentially forge a relationship with the world' (1995: 17). Yet whilst the market reigns by default, there is little endorsement of it as a positive moral basis for organising society. Fukuyama's *The End of History and the Last Man*, whilst viewing the market as unchallenged, also admits that it has only limited cultural support (1992). Hartwich notes that 'these days hardly anyone self identifies as a neoliberal' (2009: 4) and Furedi also notes that neoliberal has been regarded as a negative since the 1990s (2014). Geographers in particular would be hard pressed to find endorsements of the 'neoliberal project' in print or at the annual conferences for the subject, and certainly there is no mention of the market as a positive in analyses of volunteer tourism.

In fact Furedi argues that in historical terms liberalism has not acted as a positive endorsement of capitalist society since 1914 (2014). Capitalism's dynamism was exposed by its failure to systematically develop wealth and the two World Wars that dominated the first half of the twentieth century (Hobsbawm, 1995). The end of the Cold War has left the market lacking even the negative moral justification it enjoyed when compared to the bureaucratically planned alternative.

There is often an implied and sometimes explicit criticism of consumer sovereignty and rational economic man in discussions of volunteer tourism's merits. Both are at the centre of any ideological endorsement of the market. Many volunteers are roundly critical of the result of consumer sovereignty via their distaste for an overly materialist consumer society. Many seek authentic experience and enlightenment through the societies they visit, not economic development based on growth and technology.

Vrasti claims that the voluntary simplicity approach associated with volunteer tourism helps to rationalise neoliberal markets (2012). But whilst voluntary simplicity creates its own markets, to regard it as a part of a disciplining of the populace for the global market is questionable. Voluntary simplicity implies a rejection of important tenets of classical and neoclassical economics: the maximisation of utility through consumption and rational economic decision making. The notion of a rational, self-interested 'economic man' as described by Adam Smith and John Stuart Mill, central to liberalism, is antithetical to the impulse fuelling volunteer tourism.

The results of the market are also held to be circumspect. For example, volunteer tourism is typically presented as a counter to mass tourism, the latter viewed by many as a damaging result of the unfettered tourism market and a mass consumerism unconcerned with ethics. Volunteer tourism tends to share the assumptions of postdevelopment thinking (see Chapter 3). It focuses on linking conservation and community wellbeing goals through small-scale projects rather than economic development through infrastructural development and international trade (Butcher and Smith, 2010).

The advocacy of smallness of scale and localism implicit in volunteer tourism does not challenge the market, but is anything but a ringing endorsement of it. The emphases on organic agriculture, sustaining livelihoods and supporting local cultures in many projects also all carry a critique of the results of the free market. Rather than an exemplar of neoliberalism they reflect the decline of macro political agendas based on economic growth and social transformation of the global South, such agendas considered unsustainable or unrealistic.

Wearing presents volunteer tourism as a way of challenging the pre-eminence of the market in human affairs through effectively stepping outside of it and creating alternative ways to interact with others. This view echoes the advocacy of 'alternative economic spaces' (see Leyshon *et al.*, 2011) or 'doing consumption differently' (Barnett *et al.*, 2011) in human geography that claim to facilitate trade on an equal and fair footing by sidestepping the global market, the latter characterised as unjust. Fairtrade is a prominent example that is associated with such alternative economic spaces (ibid.).

As we argue further in Chapter 4, the problem here is that such initiatives are less oppositional to capitalism and the market per se, but more to large-scale production, mass consumption and material progress. In turning away from the perceived excesses of neoliberalisam and cultural levelling of global markets, they also turn away from the immense potential in modern science, mass production, economies of scale and international trade to liberate people from poverty (Butcher, 2012). The ecodevelopment that this stance involves expresses a profound disillusionment not just with the market, but with development itself. In practice it offers very little development at all. History has demonstrated that meaningful development and poverty alleviation are premised upon large-scale, systematic and transformative economic development, something that alternative economic spaces simply cannot and do not aspire to.

The diminished subject

Neocolonialism and neoliberalism offer insights into the significance of volunteer tourism as a social and political practice. Postcolonialism shows us that practices such as volunteer tourism can be important in shaping assumptions about the developing world, and these assumptions – notably relating to the agency of the societies concerned – can be profound. The discussion of neoliberalism reveals that a focus on markets as the economic and also moral focus of life limits political vision. However, neither is adequate in framing volunteer tourism. It is not best understood in relation to the legacy of colonialism, nor as an endorsement or reaction to neoliberalism.

The desire to act upon the world through volunteer tourism is better understood as agency in antipolitical times, cut adrift from power and class or any notion of collective politics. As such it is less part of a neoliberal subject, or linked to colonialism, and better described as a *diminished* subjectivity. It reflects less an adherence to or strengthening of belief in the market, and more a retreat from any political outlook at all, less a relationship with western or any other interests and more their replacement by abstract values that eschew interest.

Why a 'diminished subject'? The end of the Cold War and capitalism's inability to resolve its contradictions left a dual crisis at the level of political identity. The collapse of communism pulled the rug from under parties and movements of the Left. Not that such parties were necessarily sympathetic to the Stalinist system, but their alternative of nationalisation seemed untenable in the light of economic recession and the collapse of a system based on a bureaucratically planned economy. Many on the Left looked elsewhere, to new social movements, feminism or communitarianism for alternatives (Offe, 1987; Melucci, 1988). The growth of the politics of consumption and lifestyle as an avenue for the impulse to act upon the world is the corollary of the decline in belief in political change. Whilst this process was described as far back as 1960 by Daniel Bell as *The End of Ideology* (1960), it was brought sharply into relief by the end of the Cold War.

Market triumphalism following victory in the Cold War was shallow, short lived and pyrrhic (Furedi, 2014; Jacoby, 1999). Politically, the West had defined itself against its other, the East. With no East, whither the West? There was not and has not been a celebration of market capitalism. The cultural associations of the capitalist market include 'fat cats', greedy bankers, irresponsible sub-prime mortgage lenders and tax-dodging multinationals. There is simply no positive moral or political narrative extolling the market in the West.

The collapse of the ideas that constituted politics brought into relief by the end of the Cold War left a legacy. Political agency has retreated from the public realm as alternatives have been closed off. Political institutions and parties, or the shells that exist, are increasingly dominated by managerialism and a politics of personal qualities. The political subject has been squeezed back into the private realm, most notably lifestyle and consumption (see Chapters 4 and 5). Private qualities and the (often self-conscious) development of the 'self' become more of a focus for social and political agency.

Parallel to the decline and fall of the parameters that had informed political identities has been the growth of critiques of development itself. Development was linked to the political projects of Left, Right and nation, political worldviews that appear exhausted. Therefore it is unsurprising that disillusionment and disorientation regarding politics are reflected in disillusionment with development. This disillusionment has manifested itself in the growth of development's many prefixes – postdevelopment, alternative development, green development, antidevelopment, community development.

These ideas focus on vulnerability – cultural, economic and environmental – in the face of development. They focus on real issues – environmental damage, social injustice – but without a future orientation rooted in positive political and economic choices they tend towards a presentism, and see change as disruptive of the present, of 'ways of life' or 'local culture'. Their valid critique that western countries have shaped patterns of development elsewhere swiftly moves into a critique that sees *development itself* as an external imposition, as 'western' (Escobar, 1995).

Without a political framework capable of presenting viable alternatives to the market (itself viewed as operating irrespective of politics anyway) the form development takes is elided with development itself. The desperate conditions of life of millions of workers and peasants do not lead to demands for better technology and greater levels of development, but instead to calls for lower levels of development and the linking of development more closely to localised natural limits in the name of sustainable development. The desire to share the world's scientific discoveries and wealth for the good of all, associated with internationalism of the past, is deemed naive or dangerous, and is largely absent from these discussions.

This vulnerability applies to those in the West, deemed burdened by consumerism and disillusioned with urbanism, as much as it does to poor populations in the developing world. This is not an assumption of colonial superiority. In fact as western societies experience a disillusionment with their own culture, often societies in the global South are presented as places western tourists can learn lessons from with regard to community, nature and sustainability (Campbell, 1997). This cultural rejection of what has been incredibly progressive about development, and the absence of the simple humanist aspiration to see the benefits of economic growth generalised, is expressed in the diminished subject.

From national political to local cultural citizenship

Perhaps the clearest manifestation of a diminished subjectivity is the reduced importance placed on democratic institutions at national or regional level in the debates about volunteer tourism oriented towards politics and development. Agency is presented as local and cultural, both on the part of the tourist and the host. National institutions of politics rarely feature, other than as external impositions upon local agency.

This marks a retreat on three counts: spatially, from national to local; in terms of contesting power, from state to inter-group; and, conceptually, from politics to culture. These three facets of volunteer tourism have been explored throughout the book.

International relations expert David Chandler identified a similar shift in the understanding of international politics (2009). He argues that there is a breakdown of political identity fixed within nation states – effectively identity is 'deterritorialised'. New, ethical or humanitarian political identities exist outside of the nation state, geographically and politically. Yet the state remains the principal institution of political power. The rush to declare political issues 'global' sidesteps the national nature of political contestation and democratic accountability. This is replaced with global civil society, comprising international non-governmental organisations and the global market, neither of which is subject to a democratic imperative (ibid.).

Further, global citizenship emphasises the 'global/local' nexus: problems are deemed global in nature yet solvable through local initiatives. This assumption is commonplace in the affirmation of volunteer tourism as a progressive practice in schools, universities and in culture generally. The political subject becomes morally engaged with *global* issues, which they seek to address at the *local* level (which for volunteer tourists would be local communities in the global South).

Volunteer tourism is an exemplar of this culturally and interpersonally focused, locally oriented subject. As volunteer tourism, Fairtrade, telethons and set piece humanitarian events are prominent in the public face of development, this is also a *political* subject of sorts. It is a diminished subject: diminished in its capacity to address pressing political and social problems, and to promote a democratic and agonistic public forum through which to achieve this.

Going Green

'Going Green in Bulacan. Help on a simple organic farm. The farmhouse is built in a rural area. Many children and youth live near the farm. Besides manual work you can help take care of the mango trees, the fish pond and do other simple farm work. Play basketball with the youth and help the local children with their homework.

Healing in Nakar. Through the NGO Nakar's Women's Organisation, you can help women in this community by giving courses on hygiene, value formation or English while having fun interacting with the locals. The town of Nakar is known for its herbal gardens and knowledge in producing herbal medicine. Help in their herbal garden and allow the women to share their knowledge with you as a way of building their confidence in communicating.

A tree to lay under in Diadi. NGO Global Green Systems needs help planting trees to protect the environment. Locals of the small town Diadi benefit from interacting with visitors and discussing subjects like environmental awareness and garbage disposal and are willing to share stories with you about their way of life.

Dive in @ Apo Island. Apo Island is a small fishing community which over time developed a reputation as a top Philippine dive destination. Not long

> *ago, a high school was built to provide education on the island itself rather than students having to traverse open ocean to reach the mainland. Students on the island are frequently exposed to international visitors but never gained the confidence to interact with them. Volunteer your time with these kids through simple activities like playing games, assisting them with homework and giving these students individual attention through private conversations in order to boost individual and collective levels of self confidence.'*
> (excerpt from publicity, WorldActivity Philippines, undated a)

Vulnerability and the child

An assumption of vulnerability and a consequent therapeutic approach to developing societies has been noted by Pupavac in relation to humanitarian intervention (2001). She points out that there has been a shift towards viewing poverty in the developing world through the prism of therapy rather than politics. In conflicts, a 'psycho-social' approach has encroached upon a political approach. Psychological interventions to deal with 'trauma' are far more commonplace, whereas up until recently hunger and its alleviation would have been the sole focus of assistance (ibid.: 368). The therapeutic model seeks to intervene in people's lives rather than in development, and she argues that this tends to assume a diminished sense of autonomy for developing world societies. In effect, it presents societies as in need of therapeutic interventions, rather than greater opportunities. Pupavac also points out that this therapeutic approach is not a legacy of colonialism, but has more contemporary roots in post-Cold War crisis of political identity (ibid.).

Pupavac's analysis, whilst focusing on humanitarian intervention, is apposite. Volunteer tourism suggests an intimate and therapeutic intervention into poorer people's lives. Care, self-esteem, love and mutual cultural growth are consistently strong themes.

The therapeutic character of volunteer tourism is perhaps most evident in relation to its emphasis on children. The 'universal child' of developing nations – without politics, a victim, innocent – is strongly in evidence (Manzo, 2008: 642). Playing sport, hugs, smiles and simply spending time with children are commonly cited as ways to help and make a difference. Working in school is a common activity for volunteers, yet there is normally no expectation that volunteers will be trained or have expertise in this. The value is often seen as being in relating to the children, building confidence and bringing joy to their lives.

The focus on the third world child in matters of humanitarianism is, though, long established. Kate Manzo has shown that the focus on the poor child can act as a metaphor promoting the notion of a helpless victim (ibid.). 'A hungry child has no politics' – the rallying cry for US aid to Ethiopia in the 1984 famine – promotes sympathy for passive suffering, but not for the active struggle of societies to develop, nor for political struggles. Clearly there are parallels here with the colonial outlook, and volunteer tourists have been criticised for a sort of missionary outlook.

Children and volunteers

Chris, a 17-year-old South African volunteer in Thailand:

'Like traveling you are just kind of watching it like window shopping in a way. But by volunteering ... you get to, like I am doing, go to the schools, see the children, see the villages, see the rural life and also meet the people and get involved with the people ... you actually get to participate in the children's lives ... You get to know them when they are just being themselves. And that's the real experience, that's the real nice part.'

(cited in Conran, 2011: 1460)

Adam, a 28-year- old German volunteer in Thailand:

'The kids were the most memorable, because they're very honest and, what is the word ... authentic. You know if they like you or not and that's great to see every morning how 10 or 20 kids are running, come running to you and hug you and one is hanging on your leg, the other one on your arm, and yeah it's great to see that'.

(cited in Mostafanezhad 2013: 157)

Sannie, a 21-year-old Danish volunteer in Thailand:

'I think first of all for me I think it's just the whole theory of you are there to do something and do you do something meaningful. For example, right now I am taking care of the children at the orphanage... I feel that I have to, okay, like—okay, there are good reasons to get up in the morning. I feel like getting up in the morning a little bit more.'

(cited in Mostafanezhad, 2013: 160)

Modern humanitarian appeals in the media often focus upon more positive images of local life and children in particular (Chouliaraki, 2013). This is certainly the case with volunteer tourism – supporting local culture and the happy, playing child is the focus, rather than the image of the starving child. The most common image in volunteer tourism publicity is the volunteer with children or youth, smiling, playing or embracing.

Yet the positive, joyful representations of the local communities in volunteer tourism are problematic (ibid.). Private, shared joy with children does nothing to alleviate material hardship. Neither does it grant a wisdom regarding the state of the world and how to change it – 'global citizenship' through empathetic experience is illusory (see Chapter 6). The portrayal may be of the tourist and their host united in a community of virtue through joy and smiles, yet within that community, the agency of each is defined differently – gift giver, and glad recipient (ibid.).

A popular focus of volunteer tourism is the child orphan. The asymmetry between volunteer tourist and orphan is stark. The hardship endured by families and their children is intense, and the desire to relieve is likely to be entirely genuine and heartfelt. Yet the lifestyle political engagement with poverty entailed by volunteer tourism to orphanages has had some quite disturbing consequences. Money accompanies volunteer tourists, and where there is little money this has led to children being placed in orphanages to benefit from volunteer tourism (see Chapter 4).

The focus on the child reflects a diminished political and social agency. The simple impulse to care is at its strongest. Yet the intensity of the private impulse to help the child, and the intimacy involved in doing so, reinforce a therapeutic emphasis that replaces a search for political answers with care, intimacy and a search for shared joy.

Modern primitives?

Aiden Campbell's study of cultural relations between the West and Africa develops a number of points that highlight the diminished sense of agency that foregrounds many of the features of and attitudes associated with volunteer tourism. Campbell sets out the view that as western confidence in its achievements has ebbed, African society has become a positive rather than a negative model. It is the 'over civilised' who are now held responsible for barbarism. As a result, in some important respects, developing world societies are less an arena through which to impose western thinking, but more one to deal with its deficits (Campbell, 1997).

This is certainly reflected in the views of some volunteer tourists and advocates. Motivated by a rejection of development at home, and the consumer culture associated with it, volunteers want to help, but not to transform the context of the lives of the people they help. Such a transformation may be deemed to contradict 'sustainable' relationships between people and wildlife, or diminish the cultural depth that is assumed to define the societies visited.

Chabal has argued that Africa,

> embodies the mysterious and the exotic. Mysterious not just in the sense that we do not understand its reality well but also in that its reality is not really amenable to our understanding. Exotic in that it fulfils in us the most enduring need in us to find in some (suitably distant) 'other' that quality of inexplicability which is both frightening in its apparent irrationality and reassuring in that it highlights our own rationality.
>
> (1996: 41)

Chabal identifies an important feature of western assumptions of the global South – that the two cultures are deemed fundamentally different.

Yet Chabal's insight is only half true today in the context of volunteer tourism. Other societies may well be seen as beyond our full comprehension and a contrast to western rationalism. However, rationality is not celebrated and western volunteer tourists are not reassured by the rationality of their modern western lives. Instead, rationality is seen as cold, lacking a spiritual dimension. The tourists are more likely to elevate local knowledge above their own, on the basis that it is 'sustainable', more human and less sullied by consumerism (which they fear they could be complicit in promoting). At the heart of this is a disillusionment with modernity characteristic of our times – its science, its rationality and its materialism (Taverne, 2006).

A part of this deference to indigenous ways of life is the tendency to decry the legacy of modern science and laud the merits of indigenous knowledge in less developed societies (Campbell, 1997). This has an important and negative impact on how development is envisaged. For Campbell, by 'interpreting African dire necessity as a product of "indigenous knowledge" rather than a product of grinding poverty, the concept of indigenism can be served up to gullible westerners as a "sustainable" system that they should be proud to live by' (ibid.).

Notwithstanding the vagueness and confusion surrounding the term 'sustainable development', it is notable that many volunteer tourism projects that prioritise local or indigenous knowledge claim to constitute attempts to forge more earth-friendly, sustainable ways of living. Also there is a desire to bring back home what has been learnt to inform more sustainable ways in the tourists' countries. This is a humility born of a disillusionment with western development and a search for meaning in societies less associated with mass consumption.

Some western volunteer tourists, and many of the advocates of this ethical niche, seem to have disowned the benefits of modern developed societies, associating these with a colonial legacy in the global South and a pernicious neoliberalism at home.

Conclusion

Volunteer tourism is in a sense over-analysed. It is held to be an expression of postcolonial arrogance by some, and a counter to this by others. Some see it as rampant neoliberalism, and others as a pointer to more authentic economic and social encounters.

The emphasis on the actions of private individuals on their holidays is, however, a sign of a diminished subject. Holidays can only become 'political' when politics is empty of content. Private emotions, purchases, relationships and charitable impulses can only be discussed as shaping the public realm of politics because the public sphere is empty.

Therefore it is the shaping of what is conceived of as 'politics' that is key. Volunteer tourism reflects a diminished politics and a diminished subject, one that can only act by projecting private feelings and impulses, unmediated, onto political issues (see Chapter 4). This is not a legacy of colonialism. In fact, many of the limiting assumptions regarding development are articulated precisely through a rhetorical anticolonialism that sees development as synonymous with western arrogance and thus rejects it on that basis. Neither is neoliberalism the principal problem with the focus of volunteer tourism. Volunteer tourism carries a critique of the market and has attracted market-critical academics as its standard bearers. Neither critique does anything to revive development as transformation and liberating. Both endorse a development-wary outlook, associating it with colonialism and the evils of the market.

References

Amoamo, M. (2011) Tourism and hybridity: re-visiting Bhabha's third space, *Annals of Tourism Research*, 38 (4), 1254–73.

Apale, A. and Stam, V. (eds) (2011), *Generation NGO*, Between the Lines Books, Toronto.

Azarya, V. (2004) Globalization and international tourism in developing countries: marginality as a commercial commodity, *Current Sociology*, 52 (6), 949–67.

Baillie Smith, M. and Laurie, N. (2011) International volunteering and development: global citizenship and neo-liberal professionalisation today, *Transactions of the Institute of British Geographers*, 36, 545–59.

Barnett, C., Clarke, N., Cloke, P. and Malpass, A. (2011) *Globalising Responsibility: the Political Rationalities of Ethical Consumption*, Wiley-Blackwell, London.

Bell, D. (1960) *The End of Ideology: On the Exhaustion of Political Ideas in the Fifties*, Free Press, New York.

Bhabha, H.K. (2004) *The Location of Culture*, Routledge, Abingdon.

Buckley, R. (2003) *Case Studies in Ecotourism*, CABI, Wallingford.

Butcher, J. (2003) *The Moralization of Tourism*, Routledge, London.

Butcher, J. (2012) Putting the personal into development. *Spiked Review of Books*, May. Available at http://www.spiked-online.com/review_of_books/article/12487 (accessed 17 October 2014).

Butcher, J. and Smith, P. (2010) 'Making a difference': volunteer tourism and development, *Tourism Recreation Research*, 35 (1), 27–36.

Campbell, A. (1997) *Western Primitivism: African Ethnicity, a Study in Cultural Relations*, Cassell, London.

Chabal, P. (1996) The African crisis: context and interpretation, in *Postcolonial Identities in Africa*, (eds) R. Werbner and T. Ranger, Zed Books, London, pp.29–54.

Chandler, D. (2007) Hollow hegemony: theorising the shift from interest-based to value-based international policy-making, *Millennium, Journal of International Studies*, 35 (3), 703–23.

Chandler, D. (2009) *Hollow Hegemony: Rethinking Global Politics, Power and Resistance*, Pluto Press, London.

Cheong, S. and Miller, M. (2000) Power and tourism: a Foucaldian observation, *Annals of Tourism Research*, 27, 371–90.

Chibber, V. (2013) *Postcolonial Theory and the Spectre of Capital*, Verso, London.

Chouliaraki, L. (2013) *The Ironic Spectator: Solidarity in the Age of Post Humanitarianism*, Polity, London.

Cobbs-Hoffman, E. (1998) *All You Need Is Love: the Peace Corps and the Spirit of the 1960s*, Harvard University Press, Cambridge, MA.

Cohen, E. (1972) Towards a sociology of international tourism, *Social Research*, 39, 179–201.

Conran, M. (2011) They really love me! Intimacy in volunteer tourism, *Annals of Tourism Research*, 38 (4), 1454–73.

Escobar, A. (1995) *Encountering Development – The Making and Unmaking of the Third World*, Princeton University Press, Chichester.

Flusty, S. (2011) Rime of the frequent flyer or what the elephant has got in his trunk, in *Real Tourism: Practice, Care, and Politics in Contemporary Travel Culture*, (eds) C. Minca and T. Oakes, Routledge, London.

Fukuyama, F. (1992) *The End of History and the Last Man*, Penguin, Harmondsworth.

Furedi, F. (1994) *The New Ideology of Imperialism: Renewing the Moral Imperative*, Pluto, London.

Furedi, F. (2013) *Authority: a Sociological History*, Cambridge University Press, Cambridge.

Furedi, F. (2014) *The First World War: Still No End in Sight*, Bloomsbury, London.

Hall, CM. and Tucker, H. (2004) *Tourism and Postcolonialism: Contested Discourses, Identities and Representations*, Routledge, London.

Hall, S., Massey, D. and Rustin, M. (2013) *After Neoliberalism: The Kilburn Manifesto*. Soundings. Available at http://www.lwbooks.co.uk/journals/soundings/manifesto.html (accessed 17 October 2014).

Hartwich, O. (2009) *Neoliberalism, the Genesis of the Political Swearword*. Centre for Independent Studies. Available at www.cis.org.aus/publications/ (accessed 20 September 2014).

Heartfield, J. (2002) *The 'Death of the Subject' Explained*, Perpetuity Press, London.

Heath, S. (2007) Widening the gap: pre-university gap years and the 'economy of experience', *British Journal of Sociology of Education*, 28 (1), 89–103.

Hickman, L. (2007) *The Final Call: In Search of the True Cost of Our Holidays*, Eden Project, London.

Higgins-Desboilles, F. and Russell-Mundine, G. (2008) Absences in the volunteer tourism phenomenon: the right to travel, solidarity tours and transformation beyond the one-way, in *Journeys of Discovery in Volunteer Tourism: International Case Study Perspectives*, (eds) K.D. Lyons and S. Wearing, CABI Publishing, London, pp.182–94.

Hobsbawm, E. (1995) *Age of the Extremes: the Short History of the Twentieth Century 1914–1991*, Abacus, London.

Hobson, J.A. (2011) *Imperialism: a Study*, Spokesman Books, London. Original 1902.

Hollinshead, K. (1998) Tourism, hybridity and ambiguity: the relevance of Bhabha's third space cultures. *Journal of Leisure Research*, 30 (1), 121–56.

Hollinshead, K. (1999) Surveillance of the worlds of tourism: Foucault and the eye-of-power. *Tourism Management*, 20 (1), 7–23.

Honey, M. (2002) Conclusions, in *Ecotourism and Certification*, (ed.) M. Honey, Island Press, Washington DC, pp.357–71.

Jacoby, R. (1999) *The End of Utopia: Politics and Culture in an Age of Apathy*, Basic Books, New York.

Jones, A. (2011) Theorising international youth volunteering: training for global (corporate) work?, *Transactions of the Institute of British Geographers* 36, 530–44.

Jordan, F. and Aitchison, C. (2008) Tourism and the sexualisation of the gaze: solo female tourists' experiences of gendered power, surveillance and embodiment, *Leisure Studies*, 27 (3), 329–49.

Judt, T. (2005) *Postwar: a History of Europe Since 1945*, Heinemann, London.

Katcoff, E. (11 January 2012) Peace Corps guilt, *Huffington Post*. Available at http://www.huffingtonpost.com/esther-katcoff/peace-corps-guilt_b_2059161.html (accessed 17 October 2014).

Krippendorf, J. (1987) *The Holidaymakers: Understanding the Impact of Leisure and Travel*, Butterworth-Heinemann, London.

Laidi, Z. (1998) *A World Without Meaning: the Crisis of Meaning in International Politics*, Routledge, Abingdon.

Lenin, V.I. (1996) *Imperialism: the Highest Stage of Capitalism*, Pluto Press, London. Original 1916.

Leyshon, A. Lee, R., and Williams, C. (eds) (2003) *Alternative Economic Spaces*, Sage, London.

Leyshon, A., Lee, R. and Williams, C. (eds) (2011) *Alternative Economic Spaces*, Sage, London.

Loomba. A. (2005) *Colonialism/Postcolonialism*, Routledge, London.

Lozanski, K. (2011) Independent travel: colonialism, liberalism and the self, *Critical Sociology*, 37 (4), 465–82.

Lushaba, L. (2009) *Development as Modernity, Modernity as Development*, CODESRIA, Dakar. Available at http://www.codesria.org/spip.php?article1316 (accessed 17 January 2004).

Lyons, K.D. and Wearing, S. (2008) Volunteer tourism as alternative tourism: journeys beyond otherness, in *Journeys of Discovery in Volunteer Tourism: International Case Study Perspectives*, (eds) K.D. Lyons and S. Wearing, CABI, London, pp.3–12.

Lyons, K., Hanley, J., Wearing, S. and Neil, J. (2012) Gap year volunteer tourism: myths of global citizenship?, *Annals of Tourism Research*, 39 (1), 361–78.

Malik, K. (1996) *The Meaning of Race*. Palgrave Macmillan, London.

Manzo, K. (2008) Imaging humanitarianism: NGO identity and the iconography of childhood, *Antipode*, 40 (4), 632–57.

McGehee, N. (2002) Alternative tourism and social movements, *Annals of Tourism Research*, 29, 124–43.

McGehee, N.G. (2012) Oppression, emancipation, and volunteer tourism: research propositions, *Annals of Tourism Research*, 39 (1), 84–107.

McIntosh, A. and Zahra, A. (2008) Journeys for experience: the experiences of volunteer tourists in an indigenous community in a developed nation – a case study of New Zealand, in *Journeys of Discovery in Volunteer Tourism: International Case Study Perspectives*, (eds) K.D. Lyons and S. Wearing, CABI, London, pp.166–81.

McMichael, P. (2000) *Development and Social Change: a Global Perspective*, Pine Forge Press, Thousand Oaks, CA.

Melucci, A. (1988) Social movements and the democratization of everyday life, in *Civil Society and the State: New European Perspectives*, (ed.) J. Keane, Verso, London.

Miller, D. (1995) Consumption as the vanguard of history: a polemic by way of an introduction, in acknowledging consumption: a review of new studies, (ed.) D. Miller, Routledge, London, pp.1–57.

Milton. K. (1996) *Environmentalism and Cultural Theory*, Routledge, London.

Minca, C. and Oakes T. (2011) Real tourism, in *Real Tourism: Practice, Care, and Politics in Contemporary Travel Culture*, (eds) C. Minca and T. Oakes, Routledge, Abingdon.

Mostafanezhad, M. (2013) The politics of aesthetics in volunteer tourism, *Annals of Tourism Research*, 43, 150–69.

Mostafanezhad, M. (2014) *Volunteer Tourism: Popular Humanitarianism in Neoliberal Times*, Ashgate, Farnham.

Mustonen, P. (2005) Volunteer tourism: postmodern pilgrimage? *Journal of Tourism and Cultural Change*, 30 (3), 160–77.

Nash, D. (1989) Tourism and colonialism, in *Hosts and Guests: The Anthropology of Tourism* (eds) D. Nash and V. Smith, University of Pennsylvania Press, Philadelphia, pp. 37–52.

Nkrumah, K. (1965) *Neocolonialism: the Last Stage of Imperialism*, Nelson, London.

Offe, C. (1987) Challenging the boundaries of institutional politics, in *Changing the Boundaries of the Political*, (ed.) C. Maier, Cambridge University Press, Cambridge.

Page, S.J., Brunt, P., Busby, G. and Connell, J. (2001) *Tourism: a Modern Synthesis*, Thomson Learning, London.

Palacios, C. (2010) Volunteer tourism, development, and education in a postcolonial world: conceiving global connections beyond aid, *Journal of Sustainable Tourism*, 18 (7), 861–78.

Pearce, P.L. and Coghlan, A. (2008) The dynamics behind volunteer tourism, in *Journeys of Discovery in Volunteer Tourism: International Case Study Perspectives*, (eds) K.D. Lyons and S. Wearing, CABI, London, pp. 130–143.

Peet, R. and Hartwick, E. (2009) *Theories of Development: Contentions, Arguments, Alternatives, second edition*, Guilford Press, New York.

Pupavac, V. (2001) Therapeutic governance: psycho-social intervention and trauma risk management, *Disasters*, 25, 358–72.

Sharpley, R. (1999*) Tourism, Tourists and Society*, Elm Publications, Huntington.

Simpson, K. (2005) Dropping out or signing up? The professionalisation of youth travel, *Antipode*, 37 (3), 447–69.

Sin, H.L. (2010) Who are we responsible to? Locals' tales of volunteer tourism, *Geoforum*, 41 (6), 983–92.

Söderman, N. and Snead, S. (2008) Opening the gap: the motivation of gap year travellers to volunteer in Latin America, in *Journeys of Discovery in Volunteer Tourism: International Case Study Perspectives*, (eds) K.D. Lyons and S. Wearing, CABI, London, pp.118–29.

Taverne, D. (2006) *The March of Unreason: Science, Democracy, and the New Fundamentalism*, Oxford University Press, Oxford.

Turner, L. and Ash, J. (1975) *The Golden Hordes: International Tourism and the Pleasure Periphery*, Constable, London.

Urry, J. (1996) *The Tourist Gaze*, Sage, London.

Vodopivec, B. and Jaffe, R. (2011) Save the world in a week: volunteer tourism, development and difference, *European Journal of Development Research*, 23 (1), 111–28.

Vrasti, W. (2012) *Volunteer Tourism in the Global South: Giving Back in Neoliberal Times*, Routledge, Abingdon.

Wearing, S. (2001) *Volunteer Tourism: Experiences that Make a Difference*, CABI Publishing, Wallingford.

Wearing, S. and Darcy, S. (2011) Inclusion of the 'othered' in tourism, *Cosmopolitan Civil Societies Journal*, 3 (2), 18–34.

Wearing, S. and Grabowski, S. (2011) International volunteer tourism: one mechanism for development, *Migracoes*, 9 October 2011, 145–65.

Wearing, S. and Larsen, L. (1996) Assessing and managing the sociocultural impacts of ecotourism: revisiting the Santa Elena rainforest project, *Environmentalist*, 16 (2), 117–33.

Wearing, S. and Neil, J. (2000) Refiguring self and identity through volunteer tourism, *Society and Leisure*, 23 (2), 389–419.

Wearing, S. and Ponting, J. (2009). Breaking down the system: how volunteer tourism contributes to new ways of viewing commodified tourism, in *The Sage Handbook of Tourism Studies*, (eds) T. Jamal and M. Robinson, Sage, London, pp.254–69.

Wearing, S. and Wearing, M. (1999) Decommodifying ecotourism: rethinking global–local interactions with host communities, *Society and Leisure*, 22 (1), 39–70.

Wearing, S., Deville, A. and Lyons, K. (2008) The volunteer's journey through leisure into the self, in *Journeys of Discovery in Volunteer Tourism: International Case Study Perspectives*, (Eds) K.D. Lyons, S. Wearing, CABI, London, pp. 65–71.

Wearing, S., McDonald, M. and Ponting, J. (2005) Building a decommodified research paradigm in tourism: the contribution of NGOs, *Journal of Sustainable Tourism*, 13 (5), 424–39.

Wearing, S. L., Wearing, M. and McDonald, M. (2010) Understanding local power and interactional processes in sustainable tourism: exploring village–tour operator relations on the Kokoda Track, Papua New Guinea, *Journal of Sustainable Tourism*, 18 (1), 61–76.

Wearing, S., Stevenson, D. and Young, T. (2010) *Tourist Cultures: Identity, Place and the Traveller*, Sage, London.

Weaver, D. and Lawton, L. (2007) Twenty years on: the state of contemporary ecotourism research, *Tourism Management*, 28 (5), 1168–79.

WorldActivity Philippines (undated) Testimonials. Available at: http://www.worldactivity. ph/ (accessed 17 October 2014).

WorldActivity Philippines (undated a), Going green. Available at www.worldactivity.ph/ node/140 (accessed 17 October 2014).

Youth Challenge International (undated) Our approach. Available at http://www.yci.org/ html/who/approach.asp (accessed 17 September 2014).

Youth Challenge International (undated a) YCI's key methodologies for youth engagement. Accessed at http://www.yci.org/html/what/Key_Methodologies.asp (accessed 17 September 2014).

Zimmerman, J. (2001) *Innocents Abroad: American Teachers in the American Century*, Harvard University Press, London.

Zizek, S. (1999) *The Ticklish Subject: the Absent Centre of Political Ontology*, Verso, London.

8 Conclusion

In the spirit of the book, we are not looking to say whether volunteer tourism is good or bad, or how to make it more ethical. Rather we set out to comment on what the advent of the worthy gap year project and volunteer tourism as a significant rite of passage of aspirant, socially conscious people tells us about the politics of our day.

By way of conclusion, we suggest a few avenues for thinking through volunteer tourism as an expression of a diminished political subjectivity, whilst at the same time recognising the importance of volunteering, celebrating travel and affirming humanitarianism. These are not finished views, but perspectives for future thinking and research in the area of volunteer tourism, and ethical consumption in general.

Development

The claims made to be acting in the sphere of development through volunteer tourism are spurious. The small differences made to societies can never even meet the alternative possibilities had the money paid by the tourists simply been given to host communities to use as they see fit. However, the association with development remains (Wearing and McDonald, 2002; Simpson, 2004). This is less due to inflated claims from volunteer tourism tour operators and their clientele and more to the retreat of significant and influential stands of alternative development thinking from transformative development. Where development has been redefined as wellbeing on a local scale, where grand development projects are linked to exhausted grand narratives and where modernity is viewed as destructive rather than liberating, small personal initiatives can be talked up as 'development', 'wellbeing' or 'making a difference' (Scheyvens 2002: 108; Simpson 2004; Raymond 2008).

Parts of what has been labelled the third world in the past have experienced growth rates in excess of those in Europe and North America in the last decade. This economic growth – for all its limitations and faults – has reduced poverty and enhanced the life chances of millions. Lifestyle political interventions in development through volunteer holidays have not contributed to that significantly, and its critical advocacy is very often tied to a 'small is beautiful' postdevelopment philosophy that eulogises about small changes yet criticises large-scale development. Such lifestyle politics, in so far as it is political, has adopted a conservative approach to social change, one that seeks to shield poor societies from modernity rather than demand its benefits be generalised.

It has been argued that the progressive potential in volunteer tourism lies in its capacity to transform the volunteer into an ethical, global citizen (Howes, 2008; Lyons and Wearing, 2011). Justifying humanitarian acts with reference to their impact on the individual's ethical identity is simply not good enough – it amounts to a development discourse without any actual, material development. In fact, the postdevelopment sentiments of some authors who look to volunteer tourism as a progressive antidote to mass tourism, not only fail to offer development, but also to present development in any way transformative of an existing way of life as complicit in a pernicious 'neoliberalism' or 'western' in origin (Escobar, 1995). Large-scale development is rarely, if ever, in the debates around ethical tourism and ethical trade, given the prefix 'ethical'.

Localism in development is given an ethical twist through neopopulism – the notion that on a local and small-scale level people are involved in their own development, rather than dependent on or subject to big government and big business. Whilst this neopopulism has a strong appeal in antipolitical times, it fails to envisage the political subject beyond the local level. Volunteer tourism projects led by non-governmental organisations seek to facilitate local agency and intercultural learning. Sovereign government as an expression of or with the potential to express democracy rarely makes an appearance.

Therefore it is important to challenge the limited vision for development through considering the potential for liberation from want via modern technology and development. Also, the casual deference to localism, common in the advocacy of volunteer tourism, should be challenged.

Travel

Yet pointing out that development is neglected in volunteer tourism is not an argument against travelling or following one's heart in responding to the issues of concern. It is an argument against seeing this as an ethical lifestyle, as an especially moral intervention into the world, and as part of a lived critique of the perils of mass tourism and modern society. Travel can be an adventure and an experiment. It can be inspiring and, no doubt, from time to time life changing. There is truth in the accounts of 'life-changing experiences' and 'unforgettable encounters'.

It is also true that the accounts of volunteer tourists' experiences often exhibit an independence of spirit that means these experiences are more open ended than the non-governmental organisations and volunteer tour companies may have envisaged. Volunteers sometimes find themselves at odds with projects, or consider their time away rather differently from the over-the-top marketing of volunteer holidays (Vrasti, 2012).

It would be positive to divorce volunteer tourism from development pretentions (Palacios, 2010), but equally it would be positive to challenge its assumed moral status in generating ethically minded consumers and global citizens. Global citizenship carries its own assumptions – its emphasis on a global civil society of non-governmental organisations and ethical consumers. If stripped of its pretensions to the ethical transformation of societies tourism could be more open ended, experimental and exploratory in a true sense. Personal experience is a key to the development of moral autonomy. Linking travel experience to particular ethical agendas could serve to limit its moral potential, almost the opposite of what is proposed in the marketing of volunteer tourism.

Humanitarianism

Whilst criticising claims made for volunteer tourism, it is also important to uphold and celebrate the simple humanitarianism which motivates volunteers.

The traditional notion of humanitarianism is associated with kindness, benevolence and sympathy, these qualities extended universally and impartially to all. In the Christian tradition the Good Samaritan is an icon of humanitarianism. He crosses the road in order to help another, without regard for anything other than the condition of the injured party. Today simple private humanitarianism, acts that take place all the time, seems at times to be overshadowed by the prominence of set piece humanitarian acts linked to more public and often expensive displays of altruism. The latter are affirmed in contemporary culture through certification, school and university credits, CVs and their assumed role in achieving global citizenship (Baillie Smith and Laurie, 2011; Jones, 2011; Lyons *et al.*, 2012).

Many critics of volunteer tourism are concerned that humanitarianism, or altruism, are being turned into commodities, and consumed on the basis of moral utility for the humanitarian. Neoliberalism, referring to the increasing colonisation of all aspects of life by the market, is commonly blamed (Vrasti, 2012; Mostafanezhad, 2014). There is truth in this. There is certainly a dynamic whereby new 'ethical' products vie for a share of the market for an ethical social capital consisting of life-changing altruistic experiences.

However, a deeper point is that the private humanitarian impulse has readily become a part of a self-conscious process of personal identity formation played out in the public sphere. Emotion, affect and sentiment – private and intimate feelings and reactions to what we see around us – become part of a conspicuous lifestyle political identity. Affect and emotion are not only prominent in the way we may react to poverty and oppression, but are also the frame of reference through which we are encouraged to then make sense of and act upon them.

This is a product of the times we live in. The rise of a politics of personal experience reflects the collapse of the public sphere, emptied of the political philosophies and ideas through which people made sense of themselves in the world and attempted to act upon it. Private virtues – being 'good', caring, becoming aware and being responsible – are the almost pre-political impulses that now animate the public face of development. These private virtues are exhibited, often conspicuously, through lifestyle and consumption. Volunteer tourism is a case in point.

In this book we have emphasised the emptying of the public sphere and the exhaustion of political ideology as context for volunteer tourism. We have argued that this process is a long-standing phenomenon, but one that has become a defining feature of recent decades. The elevation of private activities (shopping, holidays) and private virtues (care, responsibility) into the public sphere means that narratives of self-development, disclosure of personal feelings and emotional responses to the world around us are prominent in the public face of development. This is a trend in which tourism, as a conspicuous aspect of lifestyle, features strongly. Accounts from volunteers often focus on emotional response and affect (Sin, 2010; Crossley, 2012; Mostafanezhad, 2013). The tour is frequently accompanied by a blog, often expressing existential angst and very private reflections on personal encounters.

The simple humanitarian or altruistic impulse felt by many at the sight of suffering becomes, or replaces, politics. It fills the space vacated by the exhaustion of political ideologies and choices. This is *the lifestyle politics of development* – the desperate image prompting the charitable donation on a Friday evening telethon, the purchase of the Fairtrade coffee in the hope that a small farmer and his family may see more of the price paid, the ethical holiday that we hope can offer succour to a poor community and especially the children (innocent, vulnerable and apart from politics).

Chouliaraki in *The Ironic Spectator* paints a similar picture and sets out a consequent 'posthumanitarianism' (2013). For Chouliaraki, humanitarianism as a human impulse in the past prompted a questioning that could lead to religious or revolutionary inclinations on the part of the individual. Pity prompted by witnessing suffering could lead to the individual recognising a common humanity through transcendental religious belief, or to them seeking to change the very society they see as at the root of that suffering through fundamental social change. However, for the latter to occur requires the potential for other forms of society to exist, and the capacity for people, collectively, to challenge society as it exists. It requires what Arendt terms an 'agonistic' public sphere (Arendt, 1958 ; Mouffe, 2005).

Chouliaraki argues that, especially since the Cold War's end, political narratives are conspicuous by their absence, and as a result political choices appear untenable. In such circumstances humanitarianism, unmediated by a political framing, occupies the public sphere (2013). Moreover, without a public sphere through which to create a 'world in common' humanitarianism can only be expressed as a 'self-oriented', rather than an 'other oriented', morality (ibid.). Without politics, personal experience and the cultivation of the 'self' trumps critical reflection upon the plight of others. It really is all about the tourist.

Championing simple humanitarianism means freeing it from notions of lifestyle politics. A politics expressed in terms of emotional reactions and sympathy, in search of empathy with those less fortunate, represents an attenuated political sphere. Hannah Arendt argued for an understanding of the public sphere as separate from, but linked to, the private sphere (1958). The former reflected the widening of human freedom beyond their private feeling, interests and action, and the creation of a common world in which people could act in relation to society as a whole. Engagement with this common world requires dialogue with others and discussion of differing perspectives on issues rather than simply private reflection (ibid.).

Arendt's vision of the individual, able to live both a private and a public life, is very different to that implied by volunteer tourism. The former implies a subject able to experience the world but to reflect and frame that experience politically and philosophically: to reflect in private but to act in common with others *in public*. The latter seeks experience and derives their actions to effect the world more directly through those experiences, through lifestyle. The former involves political contestation and negotiation, whilst the latter involves existential dilemmas.

Citizenship

Volunteer tourism has a strong affinity with global citizenship, which in turn has become a very influential point of reference in popular culture (Standish, 2012; Bianchi and Stephenson, 2014). Where this is not explicit, it is often implicit. The aspiration to make citizens more globally aware, responsible and caring is rarely contested, and in many ways is laudable.

However, the particular context of the promotion of global citizenship today is the emptying of citizenship domestically. Institutions of politics and democracy are replaced by a global civil society comprising the market and pressure groups as the focus for people's aspirations to act on their world (Chandler, 2009). Ethical consumption via the market is conspicuous humanitarianism for the well off. This is rationalised in contemporary culture through the notion of using one's privilege creatively. Through non-governmental organisations it is tied to pressure groups, a wholly legitimate part of the political scene, but unaccountable and outside of the key relationship for citizenship, that between state and individual.

There is a need for a renaissance of citizenship on a civic republican basis rather than a global citizenship basis. Civic republican citizenship prioritises the principal relationship between the state and the individual citizen. It is within this that citizenship can potentially act politically through democratic structures. It is here that they can create, or recreate, a public sphere of open dialogue with the potential to inform politics.

Civic republican citizenship has a number of advantages over global citizenship in relation to current debates about volunteers. It prompts us in our desire to help and make a difference to people in other societies to respect them as sovereign societies and polities, and to respect people as political subjects within those societies. It pushes to the fore that the struggles that they face are not our struggles for moral meaning, but their realities. It emphasises the role of sovereign states and a public sphere that relates to these. Civic republican citizenship also prompts us to examine our own public sphere and our domestic political scene. That is not a call for moral isolationism, in fact the opposite. It is through institutions that wield political power that citizens can express and force onto the agenda their perspective on global as well as domestic affairs.

Knowledge of the world is important, but there is no evidence that it has grown as young people have become more mobile or global citizenship has become the norm in western educational institutions. Volunteer tourism, and the attendant claims to global citizenship, prioritise particular ways of looking at the world as universally good, 'ethical' aims. A more open-ended approach to learning through travel (or indeed through books) is worthy.

Solidarity

Alongside humanitarianism is a desire for solidarity in a world that is globally connected but feels morally disaggregated. Smith and Yanacopulos see possibilities in new presentations of development:

> The production of different public faces of development by a wide range of civil society and other development actors, offers the possibility of prompting shifts in the relationships that currently shape relations between north and south, such as affording opportunities beyond the traditional giver and receiver, enabling the south to better represent itself, and the framing of relationships centred on forms of solidarity.
>
> (2004: 661)

'Solidarity tours' and 'Eco Solidarity Tours' are recent additions to the plethora of ethical brands that attempt this. Graburn argues that:

> If we are to study the nature of solidarity and identity in modern society, we cannot neglect tourism, which is one of the major forces shaping modern societies and bringing (and changing) meaning in the lives of the people of today's world.
>
> (Graburn, 1980: 64)

Certainly, accounts from volunteer tourists suggest a commendable desire for some sort of solidarity with people living lives very different from their own.

The growth of 'solidarity' via consumption marks the decline of real solidarity. Consumption and lifestyle solidarity is fleeting, lacking in commitment, working around the rhythms of one's own life.

Today there is, as philosopher Richard Rorty points out, a tendency to reject moral attachment premised on religion or political interest in what he regards as a postmodern world (1989). Without a political basis for solidarity with our peers in the global South or without bonds of brotherhood/sisterhood through religious belief, what is the basis for a common bond across societies? Only private, personal responses remain.

Volunteer tourism presents care, concern or a sense of responsibility as the basis for solidarity. These responses – immediate, emotional and unmediated by critical distance or perspective – fill up a public debate devoid of politics. There is no shortage of official, public backing for this form of post-humanitarian solidarity. The United Nation's sponsorship of celebrity humanitarians such as Angelina Jolie, now a prominent commentator on third world poverty, is illustrative of care (especially for suffering children) and shared emotion as the bond between us (Mostafanezhad, 2013).

The moral bond that survives the exhaustion of ideology is the base recognition that we all suffer. For Rorty, a focus on pain, hardship and suffering as shaping how we act inevitably means that images and accounts of pain and suffering come to dominate the humanitarian imagination, unmediated by analysis of political interest or common religious obligation (Rorty, 1989). So the question that underpins moral life is 'are you in pain?', 'are you in need?'

In the case of volunteer tourism the focus is much more on emotional need rather than physical pain. Many of the images associated with volunteer tourism marketing show shared happiness in the midst of hardship, or a shared burden of work under difficult circumstances. Chouliaraki points out that this more upbeat imagery of the global South has become more prevalent than the images of abject suffering and starvation associated with the Ethiopian famine of 1984 prompting Bob Geldof's Live Aid initiative (2013). Even so, Rorty's argument that solidarity is no longer performed as any sort of transcendental or political obligation towards the 'mass of mankind', only as care for suffering individuals, holds true (Rorty, 1989: 175).

Not so long ago it would have been assumed that solidarity meant something collective and based on a common goal or a common enemy. But the new 'solidarity' of posthumanitarianism turns out to be pretty empty. It flourishes in the form of stories of suffering, by way of a 'sentimental education', through which we are encouraged to cultivate the 'virtue' of 'being kind to others as the only social bond that is needed' (Rorty 1989: 93). This is reflected in the lifestyle politics of development – be a good person, shop ethically, show that you care.

This analysis is not a slight on the motives or actions of ordinary people motivated to be volunteer tourists. However, it suggests that solidarity on the basis proposed through volunteer tourism and other examples of the lifestyle politics of development is limited. Being kind, thoughtful and caring – private virtues that everyone warms to – indicate nothing at all about where one stands on policy, development or much else at the level of the organisation of society. There is no sense of a common struggle rooted in a commonality of interest, and in fact there is a disavowal of interest in favour of affect.

Rorty also argues that the politics of conviction have diminished as political philosophies of Left, Right and nation (as well as religious philosophies of common brotherhood) have lost their purchase on contemporary consciousness, and that the solidarity we are left with is a solidarity of self-doubt. Rorty describes a seemingly paradoxical moral subjectivity dominating the humanitarian imagination in terms of 'private irony' and 'liberal hope'. Whilst public hope can be sustained by our altruistic response to the question 'are you in pain?' it is private irony that informs such responses in so far as our solidarity relies not on our conviction of a common humanity but on sentimental stories of suffering that touch our feelings (Rorty, 1989).

Volunteer tourism bases itself on liberal hope in this fashion, and hope is always preferable to giving up. Idealism, though, needs broader horizons than hope alone can offer.

Politics

The problem with volunteer tourism is not a naivety on the part of volunteers. This accusation often replaces the desire to travel to do good with a detached and cynical worldliness and ultimately a sense that nothing can be done (as noted by Vrasti, 2012). The problem, at root, is not to be found in how volunteers interact, how much they learn, how respectful they are and how able they are at digging trenches, building wooden huts or teaching English classes. The problem lies in the abject politics of development.

There is a tradition in political and popular thought that focuses on the role of mass consumption in breeding passivity regard to politics. The Frankfurt School argued in the post-Second World War years that the masses lost sight of their common political interest and were bought off by mass consumption (Adorno and Horkheimer, 1997). Today, political interest is replaced by personal morality in this formulation. Not least in relation to mass tourism, mass consumption is viewed as self-interested indulgence, promoting thoughtlessness with regard to the environment and cultural diversity (Poon, 1993; Croall, 1995; Singh, 2004).

Alternative forms of consumption, of which volunteer tourism is one, are presented as a partial antidote to this – a means, albeit limited, for people to challenge the mainstream and to help others through consumption patterns deemed to be ethical.

Yet mass consumption makes no claims to be acting in relation to global issues. Mass tourism is never associated with the prefix ethical. Despite its role in economic development and in the extension of mobility (the 'democratisation of travel'), it is the unethical other to the ethical tourist's self. Mass tourism makes no claims to be political – it is not a part of the public face of development.

Ethical tourism, with volunteer tourism prominent, is strongly associated with acting on the world, with progressive economic and cultural development and even political outcomes. Hence it is ethical tourism niches such as volunteer tourism that promote the realm of consumption and everyday life as the place to 'make a difference' in the world. If as many sociologists claim consumption breeds passivity, then consumption *that claims to be politics* should be answerable to that charge.

Care, love and generosity are intrinsic to our humanity. Equally it is important to recognise that these private virtues do not facilitate reflection and judgement, and do not provide the basis for people to come together in pursuit of a common world. The aim to make volunteer tourism more ethical, more aware or even more political is the wrong one for people interested in reviving a public sphere and political debate worthy of the issues of the day. Rather, political debate on development – open and free from moralising about how people should consume and how they should behave – is better served by deproblematising leisure travel and looking elsewhere for answers.

References

Adorno, T.W. and Horkheimer, M. (1997) *Dialectic of Enlightenment*, Verso, London.

Arendt, H. (1958) *The Human Condition*, University of Chicago Press, Chicago.

Baillie Smith, M. and Laurie, N. (2011) International volunteering and development: global citizenship and neo-liberal professionalisation today, *Transactions of the Institute of British Geographers*, 36, 545–59.

Bianchi, R. and Stephenson, M. (2014) *Tourism and Citizenship: Rights, Freedoms and Responsibilities in the Global Order*, Routledge, London.

Chandler, D. (2009) *Hollow Hegemony: Rethinking Global Politics, Power and Resistance*, Pluto Press, London.

Chouliaraki, L. (2013) *The Ironic Spectator: Solidarity in the Age of Post Humanitarianism*, Polity, London.

Croall, J. (1995) *Preserve or Destroy? Tourism and the Environment*, Calouste Gulbenkian Foundation, London.

Crossley, E. (2012) Poor but happy: volunteer tourists' encounters with poverty, *Tourism Geographies*, 14 (2) 235–53.

Escobar, A. (1995) *Encountering Development – The Making and Unmaking of the Third World*, Princeton University Press, Chichester.

Graburn, N. (1980) Teaching the anthropology of tourism, *International Social Science Journal*, 32, 56–68.

Howes, A.J. (2008) Learning in the contact zone: revisiting neglected aspects of development through an analysis of volunteer placements in Indonesia, *Compare*, 38 (1), 23–38.

Jones, A. (2011) Theorising international youth volunteering: training for global (corporate) work?, *Transactions of the Institute of British Geographers* 36, 530–44.

Lyons, K. and Wearing, S. (2011) Gap year travel alternatives: Gen-Y, volunteer tourism and global citizenship, in *Tourism and Demography*, (eds) K.A. Smith, I. Yeoman, C. Hsu and S. Watson, Goodfellow Publishers, London, pp.101–16.

Lyons, K., Hanley, J., Wearing, S. and Neil, J. (2012) Gap year volunteer tourism: myths of global citizenship?, *Annals of Tourism Research*, 39 (1), 361–78.

Mostafanezhad, M. (2013) Getting in touch with your inner Angelina: celebrity humanitarianism and the cultural politics of gendered generosity in volunteer tourism, *Third World Quarterly*, 34, 3.

Mostafanezhad, M. (2014) *Volunteer Tourism: Popular Humanitarianism in Neoliberal Times*, Ashgate, Farnham.

Mouffe, C. (2005) *On the Political*, Routledge, London.

Palacios, C. (2010) Volunteer tourism, development, and education in a postcolonial world: conceiving global connections beyond aid, *Journal of Sustainable Tourism*, 18 (7), 861–78.

Poon, A. (1993) *Tourism, Technology and Competitive Strategy*, CABI Publishing, Wallingford.

Raymond, E. (2008) Make a difference! The role of sending organizations in volunteer tourism, in *Journeys of Discovery in Volunteer Tourism: International Case Study Perspectives*, (eds) K.D. Lyons and S. Wearing, CABI, London.

Rorty, R. (1989) *Contingency, Irony and Solidarity*, Cambridge University Press, Cambridge.

Scheyvens, R. (2002) *Tourism for Development: Empowering Communities*, Prentice Hall, Harlow.

Simpson, K. (2004) 'Doing development': the gap year, volunteer-tourists and a popular practice of development, *Journal of International Development*, 16 (5), 681–92.

Sin, H.L. (2010) Who are we responsible to? Locals' tales of volunteer tourism, *Geoforum*, 41 (6), 983–92.

Singh, T.V. (2004) *New Horizons in Tourism: Strange Experiences and Stranger Practices*, CABI, Wallingford.

Smith, M. and Yanacopulos, H. (2004) The public faces of development: an introduction, *Journal of International Development, Special Issue: The Public Faces of Development*, 16 (5), 657–64.

Standish, A. (2012) *The False Promise of Global Learning: Why Education Needs Boundaries*, Continuum, London.

Vrasti, W. (2012) *Volunteer Tourism in the Global South: Giving Back in Neoliberal Times*, Routledge, Abingdon.

Wearing, S. and McDonald, M. (2002) The development of community-based tourism: re-thinking the relationship between tour operators and development agents as intermediaries in rural and isolated area communities, *Journal of Sustainable Tourism*, 1 (3), 191–206.

Index

Adams, M. 24
affect 135, 139
African Conservation Experiences 4
agency 67, 104–5, 113–14, 121–2, 126,
    134; *local* and *cultural* 113–14, 122,
    134; *political* 105, 121, 126
'alternative development' 10, 40, 50, 133
'alternative economic spaces' 120
'alternative politics' 82
'alternative tourism' 81, 84, 86, 113
altruism 26, 29, 109, 111, 135–6
American values 21, 27–8, 109
anthropology 116
Apo Island 123–4
Arendt, Hannah 6, 58, 60–1, 93–4, 136–7
Aristotle 58–9
Ash, J. 80, 106
Australia 19, 23–4
authentic and *inauthentic* travel 77
Azarya, V. 116

Baptista, J.A. 84
Barnett, C. 5, 64, 82
Bauman, Z. 69, 84
Bell, Daniel 28, 78, 121
Bhabha, Homi 110–11
Biddle, P. 43
Bookchin, Murray 79
Boorstin, Daniel 77
bourgeois culture 78–9
Brazil 4
Brown, Chris 100
bureaucratic institutions 69
Bush, George 54
business ethics 100
Butcher, J. (co-author) 96

Cambodia 67, 70
Cameron, David 91

Campbell, Aiden 126–7
Canada 19, 23–4
Cape Town Declaration on tourism (2002)
    56
capitalism 19, 28, 40, 57, 69, 80, 94,
    107–8, 119, 121
Cassidy, Jonathan 100
Chabal, P. 126
Chambers, Robert 12–13, 45–9
Chandler, David 110, 123
Chang, Ha-Joon 45
Chibber, Vivek 114–15, 118
Chouliaraki, L. 29, 56, 62, 66–7, 136, 139
citizenship: civic republican 137; crisis of
    94–5; *critical* 98; national 14, 94, 99,
    101; origin of the concept of 89;
    outsourcing of 99–100; *see also* global
    citizenship
civil society 40; global 90, 101, 123, 134–7
Clemmons, David 2
Club Med 78, 85–6
Cobbs-Hoffman, E. 21, 23–4, 38
codes of conduct for tourists 57
coffee houses 59, 62
Coghlan, A. 100, 108
Cohen, Ben 54
Cohen, Erik 77, 81, 106
Cold War 21, 25–7, 37, 40, 57, 62, 80,
    109–10, 121
colonialism and neocolonialism 14, 19, 27,
    30, 94, 104–10, 114, 117–18, 121,
    127–8
commercialisation of tourism 76
commodification and *decommodification* of
    tourism 111, 119
communism 40; collapse of 121
community-based development 40
community-oriented tourism 75
community service 3, 91

Printed in the USA/Agawam, MA
October 28, 2015

625386.105